OP 8/19

Have Many others
in the Series

RECREATION
LEISURE IN AMERICAN SOCIETY

ISSN 1554-4389

RECREATION
LEISURE IN AMERICAN SOCIETY

Frank Uhle

INFORMATION PLUS® REFERENCE SERIES
Formerly published by Information Plus, Wylie, Texas

Detroit • New York • San Francisco • San Diego • New Haven, Conn. • Waterville, Maine • London • Munich

Recreation: Leisure in American Society

Frank Uhle

Paula Kepos, Series Editor

Project Editor
John McCoy

Permissions
Margaret Abendroth, Edna Hedblad, Emma Hull

Composition and Electronic Prepress
Evi Seoud

Manufacturing
Drew Kalasky

LIBRARY OF CONGRESS CATALOGING-IN-PUBLICATION DATA

ISBN 0-7876-5103-6 (set)
ISBN 0-7876-9080-5
ISSN 1554-4389

Printed in the United States of America
10 9 8 7 6 5 4 3 2 1

TABLE OF CONTENTS

PREFACE

Recreation: Leisure in American Society is part of the *Information Plus Reference Series*. The purpose of each volume of the series is to present the latest facts on a topic of pressing concern in modern American life. These topics include today's most controversial and most studied social issues: abortion, capital punishment, care for the elderly, crime, the environment, health care, immigration, minorities, national security, social welfare, women, youth, and many more. Although written especially for the high school and undergraduate student, this series is an excellent resource for anyone in need of factual information on current affairs.

By presenting the facts, it is Thomson Gale's intention to provide its readers with everything they need to reach an informed opinion on current issues. To that end, there is a particular emphasis in this series on the presentation of scientific studies, surveys, and statistics. These data are generally presented in the form of tables, charts, and other graphics placed within the text of each book. Every graphic is directly referred to and carefully explained in the text. The source of each graphic is presented within the graphic itself. The data used in these graphics are drawn from the most reputable and reliable sources, in particular from the various branches of the U.S. government and from major independent polling organizations. Every effort has been made to secure the most recent information available. The reader should bear in mind that many major studies take years to conduct, and that additional years often pass before the data from these studies are made available to the public. Therefore, in many cases the most recent information available in 2005 dated from 2002 or 2003. Older statistics are sometimes presented as well, if they are of particular interest and no more-recent information exists.

Although statistics are a major focus of the *Information Plus Reference Series* they are by no means its only content. Each book also presents the widely held positions and important ideas that shape how the book's subject is discussed in the United States. These positions are explained in detail and, where possible, in the words of their proponents. Some of the other material to be found in these books includes: historical background; descriptions of major events related to the subject; relevant laws and court cases; and examples of how these issues play out in American life. Some books also feature primary documents, or have pro and con debate sections giving the words and opinions of prominent Americans on both sides of a controversial topic. All material is presented in an even-handed and unbiased manner; the reader will never be encouraged to accept one view of an issue over another.

HOW TO USE THIS BOOK

People have favorite activities that they enjoy doing during their free time—however much, or little, free time they have available. Most Americans enjoy watching television, reading, and spending time with friends and family, but beyond that their interests run in many directions. Some like to see movies in the theater or at home, others prefer gambling. Many Americans enjoy sports, but while some like to play basketball, others just like to watch, or prefer "extreme" sports such as mountain biking or bungee jumping. A huge entertainment industry has developed in the United States to meet these varied needs. This book presents the latest information on Americans' leisure activities and compares it with years past to highlight trends in how Americans use their free time. For example, watching movies at home is an increasingly popular way for Americans to spend an evening. Also, the number of weekend trips that Americans take has increased dramatically.

Recreation: Leisure in American Society consists of eight chapters and three appendices. Each of the chapters is devoted to a particular aspect of recreation in the United States. For a summary of the information covered in each chapter, please see the synopses provided in the Table of Contents at the front of the book. Chapters generally begin with an overview of the basic facts and background information on the chapter's topic, then proceed to examine subtopics of particular interest. For example, Chapter 5: Football, Baseball, Basketball, and Other Popular Sports begins with an overview of the most popular spectator and participatory sports in the United States. Differences between male and female sports enthusiasts are highlighted. The chapter then proceeds into more detailed examinations of some of the most popular participatory sports, including basketball, soccer, and bowling. Readers can find their way through a chapter by looking for the section and subsection headings, which are clearly set off from the text. Or, they can refer to the book's extensive index, if they already know what they are looking for.

Statistical Information

The tables and figures featured throughout *Recreation: Leisure in American Society* will be of particular use to the reader in learning about this topic. These tables and figures represent an extensive collection of the most recent and valuable statistics on recreation, as well as related issues—for example, graphics in the book cover how much Americans spend on different types of leisure activities; the number of Americans who gamble; the differences in the favorite leisure activities of Americans based on sex and income; and the impact of computers on recreation. Thomson Gale believes that making this information available to the reader is the most important way in which we fulfill the goal of this book: to help readers understand the issues and controversies surrounding recreation in the United States and reach their own conclusions.

Each table or figure has a unique identifier appearing above it, for ease of identification and reference. Titles for the tables and figures explain their purpose. At the end of each table or figure, the original source of the data is provided.

In order to help readers understand these often complicated statistics, all tables and figures are explained in the text. References in the text direct the reader to the relevant statistics. Furthermore, the contents of all tables and figures are fully indexed. Please see the opening section of the index at the back of this volume for a description of how to find tables and figures within it.

Appendices

In addition to the main body text and images, *Recreation: Leisure in American Society* has three appendices.

The first is the Important Names and Addresses directory. Here the reader will find contact information for a number of government and private organizations that can provide further information on aspects of recreation. The second appendix is the Resources section, which can also assist the reader in conducting his or her own research. In this section, the author and editors of *Recreation: Leisure in American Society* describe some of the sources that were most useful during the compilation of this book. The final appendix is the index.

ADVISORY BOARD CONTRIBUTIONS

The staff of Information Plus would like to extend their heartfelt appreciation to the Information Plus Advisory Board. This dedicated group of media professionals provides feedback on the series on an ongoing basis. Their comments allow the editorial staff who work on the project to continually make the series better and more user-friendly. Our top priorities are to produce the highest-quality and most useful books possible, and the Advisory Board's contributions to this process are invaluable.

The members of the Information Plus Advisory Board are:

- Kathleen R. Bonn, Librarian, Newbury Park High School, Newbury Park, California

- Madelyn Garner, Librarian, San Jacinto College—North Campus, Houston, Texas

- Anne Oxenrider, Media Specialist, Dundee High School, Dundee, Michigan

- Charles R. Rodgers, Director of Libraries, Pasco-Hernando Community College, Dade City, Florida

- James N. Zitzelsberger, Library Media Department Chairman, Oshkosh West High School, Oshkosh, Wisconsin

COMMENTS AND SUGGESTIONS

The editors of the *Information Plus Reference Series* welcome your feedback on *Recreation: Leisure in American Society*. Please direct all correspondence to:

Editors
Information Plus Reference Series
27500 Drake Rd.
Farmington Hills, MI 48331-3535

CHAPTER 1
HOW AMERICANS SPEND THEIR TIME

DEFINING LEISURE AND RECREATION

The word "leisure" comes from the Latin word *licere,* which means "to be allowed." A common American view considers leisure as something allowed after one's work is done: time that is free after required activities. Recreation, however, is a different matter. The *Oxford American Dictionary* defines recreation as "a process or means of refreshing or entertaining oneself after work by some pleasurable activity." Its Latin and French roots, which mean "restore to health" or "create anew," suggest rejuvenation of strength or spirit. While leisure activities are pastimes, recreational activities are intended to restore physical or mental health.

HOW MUCH FREE TIME?

Americans enjoy some of the highest standards of living in the world. Although the United States trails other countries in such significant measures of health and well-being as infant mortality and life expectancy, the world generally respects—even envies—the quality of life enjoyed by most Americans.

Americans do work hard. Although the number of hours of nonwork time available to Americans has not changed significantly since the 1970s, public opinion surveys consistently report that Americans believe they have less free time today than in the past. Workers who participated in the *Shell Poll,* a study conducted by Shell Oil Company in 2000, indicated that if given a choice between an extra day off from work or an extra day's wages every two weeks, they preferred more time off by a margin of 58% to 40%. For workers aged thirty-five to sixty-four, 67% indicated that they would rather have more time off.

Working parents report the least free time. According to the *Shell Poll,* only 48% of mothers believe they have enough personal leisure time. This reflects a dramatic decline from a Gallup survey conducted in 1963, when 70% of mothers were happy with their free time. Almost three-quarters of working mothers reported to Shell that on Sunday nights, after doing household chores and running errands on weekends, they do not feel rested and ready for a new work week.

In the free time Americans do have, they are sleeping less. According to *Sleep in America,* a survey published in 2002 by the nonprofit National Sleep Foundation, 68% of poll respondents admitted getting less than eight hours' sleep on weeknights. Nearly a quarter of those surveyed believed they were not getting the minimum amount needed to avoid feelings of drowsiness during the day.

A PERSONAL CHOICE

People who perform certain activities all day at a job often pursue dramatically different activities during their time off. For example, someone who sits behind a desk at work may choose a physically active pastime, such as recreational walking. Similarly, a person with a job that requires demanding physical labor may choose a more sedentary activity, such as playing computer games, reading, or painting. A person who lives in a flat region may go to the mountains to seek excitement, while someone living in the mountains might seek a sandy ocean beach on which to relax.

Other people may enjoy one field so much that they perform that activity not only professionally but also as a form of recreation. For workers who derive little satisfaction from their occupation, recreation can become even more important to personal happiness.

HOW DO AMERICANS LIKE TO SPEND THEIR LEISURE TIME?

A survey conducted in October 2003 by Humphrey Taylor of the Harris organization asked Americans to name their two or three favorite ways to spend leisure time. The top response was reading, chosen by 24% of those polled, with watching television and spending time with family or children each following closely, both being cited by 17% of those asked. Other popular activities included fishing (9%), going to movies (7%), socializing with friends or neighbors (7%), playing team sports (6%), exercise activities such as weights and aerobics (6%), and gardening (6%). To a lesser extent the respondents also mentioned using a computer, participating in church activities, dining out, and watching sports (5% each); and walking, listening to music, shopping, traveling, hunting, and making crafts (4% each), among other choices.

Over the eight-year span this poll was conducted, the popularity of most of these activities remained relatively constant, although watching television and reading showed slight declines over that time, with perhaps the most significant change being the decline in activities that involved exercise, which fell from 38% in 1995 to 29% in 2003.

Although Americans named these as their favorite recreational activities, the way they actually spent their leisure time was not necessarily the same, according to a 2001 survey conducted by the Leisure Trends Group. While this poll found reading to be the most-cited activity, when asked how they had spent their leisure time the previous day, twice as many survey respondents reported watching television as reading. Americans may also not always have a choice of how to spend their free time. For example, housecleaning ranked eighth in the survey of how Americans spent leisure time but did not rank at all among the top ten favorite leisure-time activities.

Teenagers

The 2003 *Gallup Youth Survey* found that teens' favorite ways to spend an evening included hanging out with friends or family (34%); watching television, movies, or sports (19%); playing video games (8%); or playing sports/exercising (7%). Only 3% each said they liked to read or talk on the phone, and using the Internet or a computer, sleeping, shopping, listening to music, and eating were each mentioned by just 1%.

There were significant differences in responses between boys and girls—only 26% of boys liked to hang out with friends or family, while this activity was preferred by 43% of girls. On the other hand, 15% of boys mentioned playing video games, while no girls cited this activity. Five percent of girls liked to read, while only 1% of boys did, and 5% of girls liked to talk on the phone, while less than 1% of boys did. More than twice as many boys (10%) as girls (4%) said they liked to play sports or exercise.

READING

Reading is one of the favorite leisure activities of Americans. A 2002 Gallup poll found that the over-

whelming majority (83.5%) of Americans said they had read all or part of at least one book in the year preceding the survey. The average number of books read per year was sixteen among those who had read one book or more.

Choosing Books to Read

According to a 2002 Gallup poll, Americans had a wide range of reading interests. Thirty percent of those polled said they were "very likely" to choose biographies or books about history, with thriller or suspense novels appealing to 24% of those who were asked. Books about religion or theology followed close behind, at 24%, while self-improvement books (23%), mystery novels (21%), current fiction (20%) and books about current events (16%) were also popular. When asked what motivated them to read, 32% said they did so for entertainment, while 47% said they primarily read to learn.

Reading interests differed depending on age, although there was some overlap in the subjects that drew the most readers. In *Do Reading Tastes Age?* (2003), Gallup researchers Jennifer Robison and Steve Crabtree found that a higher percentage of those aged eighteen to twenty-nine said that they were "very likely" or "somewhat likely" to read horror novels (44%) than those age sixty-five and older (7%); the same relationship held up for science fiction novels, with 40% of young adults citing these compared to 23% of seniors. Americans between thirty and forty-nine had the most interest in business management and leadership books (48%) and personal finance books (44%) of any age group, perhaps due to their need to enhance careers or pay for the costs of raising children and sending them to college. Biographies and books about history (the most popular category overall), mystery novels, thriller or suspense novels, classic literature, current events books, books on religion and theology, and current literary fiction held relatively steady among age groups, with the last-named category most popular with adults aged fifty to sixty-four (59%) and least popular with young adults and seniors (44% each). (See Table 1.1.)

SOCIALIZING

Second in popularity as a leisure-time activity, according to the Harris poll conducted by Taylor in 2003, was the time-honored tradition of socializing with family or children. When the 17% who named this activity were added to the 7% who cited socializing with friends or neighbors, the total who chose socializing was 24%, the same amount as the number one choice of reading.

TELEVISION VIEWING

Americans also spend a considerable amount of their leisure time in front of the television, according to Harris Interactive. Where once all television viewers had only a handful of broadcast networks to choose from, by 2003

TABLE 1.1

Public opinion on book selection, by age, 2003

WHEN CHOOSING BOOKS TO READ, HOW LIKELY ARE YOU TO SELECT A BOOK FROM EACH OF THE FOLLOWING CATEGORIES?

(Base: Those who read at least one book in past year)
Percent saying "somewhat likely" or "very likely"

Type of book	18–29	30–49	50–64	65+
Biographies or books about history	72%	72%	74%	76%
Business management and leadership books	38%	48%	39%	23%
Classic literature	46%	50%	45%	43%
Current events books	49%	53%	57%	53%
Current literary fiction	44%	54%	59%	44%
Horror novels	44%	21%	17%	7%
Mystery novels	48%	56%	58%	53%
Personal finance books	29%	44%	31%	27%
Religion and theology	47%	60%	52%	58%
Self improvement books	60%	60%	60%	49%
Thriller or suspense novels	58%	54%	53%	48%
Science fiction novels	40%	36%	29%	23%
Romance novels	36%	24%	22%	27%

SOURCE: Jennifer Robison and Steve Crabtree, "Book Selection by Age," in *Do Reading Tastes Age?"* http://www.gallup.com/content/default.aspx?ci=7732&pg=1 (accessed September 10, 2004). Copyright © 2003 by The Gallup Organization. Reproduced by permission of The Gallup Organization.

there were 283 different cable and satellite channels available, according to *Screen Digest*. A 2003 study done by Nielsen Media Research found that 73.9 million American households with televisions subscribed to at least a basic package of cable channels, while another 19.4 million had satellite systems. Combined, the two made up close to 90% of all viewing households.

The types of programs Americans watch has evolved over time as well. Hour-long dramas and half-hour comedies once dominated the prime time schedules of the three major networks (NBC, CBS, and ABC), but the success of *Survivor* and other so-called reality shows has changed the landscape of television. Some observers suggest that, like any fad, such programs will fade into the background after their novelty value has worn thin, while others believe that they will remain a permanent part of the major networks' programming.

Many television viewers enjoy watching rented digital videodisc (DVD) or videocassette copies of movies at home. A 2001 Gallup poll found that 83% of all respondents stated that they had watched a movie at home in the month preceding the poll. Among young adults aged eighteen to twenty-nine, this figure was 96%. Older adults tended to watch the fewest movies at home.

COMPUTERS IN DAILY HOME USE

Personal computing is an important leisure activity for many Americans. Accessing the Internet, using educational or entertainment software, playing music, and com-

municating with friends or family are all typical activities of home computer users.

Internet Use

Americans' use of the Internet has grown dramatically since the mid-1990s. In 1995 the Pew Research Center for The People & The Press found that just 14% of American adults were "online users," a number that had increased to 46% of adults by March 2000, or eighty-six million people. By mid-2004 the Pew Internet & American Life Project found that nearly 63% of American adults (128 million) had gone online.

Internet access in public schools has increased dramatically since the mid-1990s, giving school children more opportunity to go online. According to the National Center for Education Statistics, in *Internet Access in U.S. Public Schools and Classrooms: 1994-2002* (2003), by 2001 99% of American public schools had gained access to the Internet, up from just 35% in 1994. The report further noted that 92% of public schools offered Internet connections in instructional rooms in 2002, up from 3% in 1994.

Americans without Internet access in their homes or at school could also go online at local public libraries. According to researchers John Carlo Bertot and Charles R. McClure in *Public Libraries and the Internet 2002: Internet Connectivity and Networked Services* (December 2002), by 2002 95% of all public libraries provided public access to the Internet, and 100% of urban public libraries did.

The Pew Internet & American Life Project (Pew/Internet) found that in 2004 the Internet audience was not only growing but also increasingly resembled the population as a whole. Whereas white males were once by far the most common users of the Internet, women, African-Americans, and Hispanics were using it more and more. A Pew/Internet tracking survey conducted in May and June 2004 found that almost 66% of American males and 61% of American females went online, along with 59% of English-speaking Hispanics and 43% of African-Americans. (See Table 1.2.)

The Pew Internet & American Life survey further revealed that by mid-2004, 32% of persons with less than a high school education and 52% of high school graduates were online, compared to 88% of college graduates. The costs of buying a computer and paying Internet access fees were barriers to some Americans, however. Just 44% of persons with household incomes below $30,000 used the Internet versus 69% of those with incomes from $30,000 to $50,000, 81% with incomes ranging from $50,000 to $75,000, and 89% of those in the highest income bracket. Location also affected connectivity, and rural Americans lagged behind, with only 56% going online compared to 62% of urban dwellers and 68% of those in the suburbs. (See Table 1.2.)

TABLE 1.2

Demographics of Internet users, 2004

	Go online
Women	61%
Men	66
Age	
18–29	78%
30–49	74
50–64	60
65+	25
Race/ethnicity	
White, non-Hispanic	67%
Black, non-Hispanic	43
Hispanic	59
Community type	
Urban	62%
Suburban	68
Rural	56
Household income	
Less than $30,000/yr	44%
$30,000–$50,000	69
$50,000–$75,000	81
More than $75,000	89
Educational attainment	
Less than high school	32%
High school	52
Some college	75
College +	88

SOURCE: "Demographics of Internet Users," in *Pew Internet & American Life Project May–June 2004 Tracking Survey*, Pew Internet & American Life Project, http://www.pewinternet.org/trends/DemographicsofInternetUsers.htm (accessed July 7, 2004)

Pew/Internet found significant differences among age groups in Internet use in 2004. While 78% of those eighteen to twenty-nine were online, and 74% of Americans aged thirty to forty-nine were using the Internet, the number dropped to 60% of those fifty to sixty-four and just 25% of those aged sixty-five and over. (See Table 1.2.)

In *Counting on the Internet,* a 2002 Pew/Internet report, researchers concluded that the popularity and reliability of the Internet as a source of information had raised Americans' expectations about the scope and availability of information online. Three-quarters of Internet users reported positive experiences in finding information about health care, government agencies, news, and shopping. Many users cited the Internet as the first place they turned to for news and information.

According to Pew/Internet surveys conducted from 2001 to 2004, nearly all persons with Internet access were sending e-mail (93%), while 84% used online search engines to find information, 84% looked for maps or driving directions, and more than three-quarters of users researched products before they bought them or went online in pursuit of information about their hobbies. Other common uses included looking for weather forecasts (75%), seeking travel information (73%), getting news (72%), looking for health or medical information (66%),

or simply surfing the Web for fun (67%). Many also found the Web useful for shopping and other transactions, with 65% of Internet users buying a product online, 55% making travel reservations, 34% doing online banking, and 23% participating in an online auction. (See Table 1.3.)

In June 2004 Pew/Internet researchers estimated that 53% of American adults with Internet access, or sixty-eight million, went online on an average day. Typical daily Internet activities included sending e-mail (45%), using a search engine to find information (30%), getting news (27%), looking for information on a hobby or interest (21%), checking the weather (20%), and performing job-related research (19%). Only 2% said they downloaded music files, or went to a Web site to meet other people, while just 1% of those surveyed said their typical daily Internet activities included gambling or visiting adult Web sites. Nearly one-quarter went online for recreation—that is, to surf the Web with no specific purpose in mind. (See Table 1.4.)

ACCESSING MUSIC ONLINE. Internet users can go online to hear music from "streaming" Internet radio stations and other Web sites, or download music files—either legally (by paying a fee to a service such as iTunes) or illegally (via a peer-to-peer network or from a newsgroup or Web site). Concerned about the impact on music recording sales, which dropped from $14.6 billion to $11.9 billion per year between 1999 and 2003 (see Table 4.9 in Chapter 4), the Recording Industry Association of America (RIAA) began filing lawsuits against a number of file-sharing services such as Napster, and, beginning in the fall of 2003, against individual users.

A survey conducted in November and December 2003 by Pew/Internet found that music downloads declined dramatically after the RIAA began suing specific individuals. While a survey conducted in March through May 2003 found that 29% of Internet users (thirty-five million) regularly downloaded music files, by year's end this had declined to just 14% (eighteen million). In February and March 2004, however, Pew/Internet found that the percentage of downloaders had rebounded to 18% (twenty-three million). (See Table 1.5.) Many were now using such paid services as Apple's iTunes, Musicmatch.com, or the relaunched, fee-charging Napster.

As Internet connection speeds and computer data storage capacity continued to increase, data-intensive video downloads were becoming popular as well, with 15% of Internet users reporting to Pew/Internet researchers in February and March of 2004 that they had downloaded videos from the Web. (See Table 1.5.) While some downloads, like movie trailers and commercials, were from legitimate Web sites, others were not. The Motion Picture Association of America issued a number of warnings in 2004 that copyright infringement lawsuits

TABLE 1.3

Internet activities, 2001–04

	Percent of those with Internet access	Most recent survey date
Send e-mail	93	May-June 2004
Use a search engine to find information	84	May-June 2004
Search for a map or driving directions	84	Feb-04
Do an Internet search to answer a specific question	80	Nov-Dec 2003
Research a product or service before buying it	78	Feb-04
Look for info on a hobby or interest	76	March-May 2003
Check the weather	75	Jun-03
Get travel info	73	May-June 2004
Get news	72	May-June 2004
Surf the Web for fun	67	March-May 2003
Look for health/medical info	66	Dec-02
Look for info from a government website	66	Aug-03
Buy a product	65	Feb-04
Research for school or training	60	May-June 2004
Buy or make a reservation for travel	55	May-June 2004
Go to a website that provides info or support for a specific medical condition or personal situation	54	Dec-02
Look up phone number or address	54	Feb-04
Watch a video clip or listen to an audio clip	52	March-May 2003
Do any type of research for your job	51	Feb-04
Look for political news/info	49	May-June 2004
Get financial info	44	March-May 2003
Check sports scores or info	43	Feb-04
Look for info about a job	42	May-June 2004
Download other files such as games, videos, or pictures	42	Jun-03
Send an instant message	42	May-June 2004
Play a game	39	March-May 2003
Listen to music online at a website	34	May-June 2004
Look for info about a place to live	34	May-June 2004
Bank online	34	Jun-03
Look for religious/spiritual info	29	March-May 2003
Search for info about someone you know or might meet	28	Sep-02
Chat in a chat room or in an online discussion	25	June-July 2002
Research your family's history or genealogy	24	March-May 2003
Look for weight loss or general fitness info	24	Jan-02
Participate in an online auction	23	Feb-04
Look for info about a mental health issue	23	June-July 2002
Share files from own computer w/ others	23	Feb-04
Use Internet to get photos developed/display photos	21	August-October 2001
Download music files to your computer	20	May-June 2004
Create content for the Internet	19	Oct-02
Look for info on something sensitive or embarrassing	18	June-July 2002
Read someone else's web log or "blog"	17	Feb-04
Log onto the Internet using a wireless device	17	Feb-04
Take part in an online group	16	Oct-02
Download video files to your computer	15	Feb-04
Visit an adult website	15	May-June 2004
Buy or sell stocks, bonds, or mutual funds	12	Feb-04
Buy groceries online	12	March-May 2003
Take a class online for college credit	10	Jun-03
Go to a dating website or other sites where you can meet other people online	9	May-June 2004
Take any other class online	8	Jun-03
Look for info about domestic violence	8	Dec-02
Make a phone call online	7	Jun-03
Make a donation to a charity online	7	Dec-02
Create a web log or "blog"	5	Feb-04
Check e-mail on a hand-held computer	5	August-October 2001
Play lottery or gamble online	4	March-May 2003

SOURCE: "Internet Activities," in *Pew Internet & American Life Project Tracking Surveys (March 2000–Present)*, Pew Internet & American Life Project, http://www.pewinternet.org/trends/Internet_Activities_4.23.04.htm (accessed July 7, 2004)

would be brought against those sharing movies via peer-to-peer networks.

Teens and College Students on the Internet

The Pew Internet & American Life Project estimated in 2003 that 78% of Americans aged twelve to seventeen were online. Of these, 92% used e-mail, 84% surfed the Web for fun, 74% used instant messaging, and 71% had used the Internet as the major source for their most recent major school project.

According to the 2002 Pew/Internet report *The Internet Goes to College,* college students were among the heaviest users of the Internet. This finding was not surprising since about one-fifth of the surveyed college students had begun using computers as young children. All

TABLE 1.4

Daily Internet activities, 2001–04

	Percent of those with Internet access	Most recent survey date
Go online	53	May–June 2004
Send e-mail	45	May–June 2004
Use a search engine to find information	30	May–June 2004
Get news	27	May–June 2004
Surf the Web for fun	23	March–May 2003
Look for info on a hobby or interest	21	March–May 2003
Do an Internet search to answer a specific question	21	Nov–Dec 2003
Check the weather	20	Jun-03
Do an Internet search to answer a specific question	19	Sep-02
Do any type of research for your job	19	February 2004
Research a product or service before buying it	15	Feb-04
Look for political news/info	13	May–June 2004
Send an instant message	12	May–June 2004
Get financial info	12	March–May 2003
Check sports scores and info	11	Feb-04
Watch a video clip or listen to an audio clip	11	March–May 2003
Research for school or training	11	May–June 2004
Look for info from a government website	9	Jun-03
Play a game	9	March–May 2003
Bank online	9	Jun-03
Get travel info	8	May–June 2004
Look up phone number or address	7	Feb-04
Search for a map or driving directions	7	Feb-04
Log onto the Internet using a wireless device	6	Feb-04
Look for health/medical info	6	Dec-02
Take part in an online group	6	Oct-02
Listen to music online at a website	6	May–June 2004
Download other files such as games, videos, or pictures	6	Jun-03
Create content for the Internet	4	Oct-02
Look for religious/spiritual info	4	March–May 2003
Chat in a chat room or in an online discussion	4	June–July 2002
Look for info about a job	4	May–June 2004
Go to a website that provides info or support for a specific medical condition or personal situation	4	Dec-02
Look for info about a place to live	3	May–June 2004
Buy or make a reservation for travel	3	May–June 2004
Participate in an online auction	3	Feb-04
Read someone else's web log or "blog"	3	Feb-04
Buy a product	3	Feb-04
Search for info about someone you know or might meet	3	Sep-02
Look for weight loss or general fitness info	3	Jan-02
Share files from own computer w/ others	2	February 2004
Download video files to your computer	2	Feb-04
Download music files to your computer	2	May–June 2004
Go to a dating website or other sites where you can meet other people online	2	May–June 2004
Visit an adult website	1	May–June 2004
Buy groceries online	1	March–May 2003
Create a web log or "blog"	1	Feb-04
Buy or sell stocks, bonds, or mutual funds	1	Feb-04
Look for info about a mental health issue	1	June–July 2002
Play lottery or gamble online	1	March–May 2003
Use Internet to get photos developed/display photos	1	August–October 2001
Check e-mail on a hand-held computer	1	August–October 2001
Research your family's history or genealogy	1	March–May 2003
Take a class online for college credit	*	Jun-03
Take any other class online	*	Jun-03
Make a phone call online	*	Jun-03
Make a donation to a charity online	*	Dec-02
Look for info about domestic violence	*	Dec-02
Look for info on something sensitive or embarrassing	*	June–July 2002

*Percentage of Internet users who do these activities on a typical day is less than 1%

SOURCE: "Daily Internet Activities," in *Pew Internet & American Life Project Tracking Surveys (March 2000–Present)*, Pew Internet & American Life Project, http://www.pewinternet.org/trends/Daily_Activities_4.23.04.htm (accessed July 7, 2004)

college students who responded to the survey had used computers by age 16, and most were Internet users.

A study published in 2004 in the *Journal of College and University Student Housing* found that of 253 freshmen and sophomores living in residence halls at Ball State University, 94% had access to a computer in their living quarters, and 75% reported using computer technology more than five hours per week. Seventy percent of the students reported using a computer daily or several times per week to complete assignments or papers, and 59% report-

TABLE 1.5

Internet music and video downloads, 2004

(In percent)

I'M GOING TO READ YOU [A] SHORT LIST OF ACTIVITIES. PLEASE TELL ME IF YOU EVER DO ANY OF THE FOLLOWING WHEN YOU GO ONLINE. DO YOU EVER.../DID YOU HAPPEN TO DO THIS YESTERDAY, OR NOT?

	Total have ever done this	Did yesterday	Have not done this	Don't know/ refused
Download music files onto your computer so you can play them at any time you want				
Feb/March 2004	18	1	82	*
Nov 2003	14	1	85	*
June 2003	30	3	70	*
April/May 2003	30	4	70	*
March 12–19, 2003	28	5	72	*
Oct 2002	32	5	68	*
Sept 12–19, 2001	26	3	73	*
Aug 2001	26	3	73	*
Feb 2001	29	6	71	*
Fall 2000	24	4	76	*
July/August 2000	22	3	78	*
Share files from own computer, such as music, video or picture files,or computer games with others online				
Feb/March 2004	23	2	77	*
Nov 2003	20	4	79	*
June 2003	28	5	72	*
Sept 12–19, 2001	28	4	72	1
August 2001	25	4	75	*
Download video files onto your computer so you can play them at any time you want				
Feb/March 2004	15	2	85	*
Nov 2003	13	2	86	*

SOURCE: Peter Rainie, Mary Madden, Dan Hess, and Graham Mudd, "February 2004 Pew Internet Tracking Survey Excerpt," in *Pew Internet Project and Comscore Media Metrix Data Memo*, Pew Internet & American Life Project, April 2004, http://www.pewinternet.org/pdfs/PIP_Filesharing_April_04.pdf (accessed July 22, 2004)

ed using one to surf the Internet. E-mail or instant messaging was used daily by 78%, with another 17% using such communications programs several times per week.

Computer Use among Older Adults

According to Pew/Internet, persons over age sixty-five were dispelling myths about their reluctance to embrace new technology, as they surfed the Web in record numbers. In 2000 an estimated 12% of older Americans were online, but this number had grown to 20% by 2002 and to 25% in the spring of 2004.

Computers have been readily integrated into the lives of older adults in many settings, ranging from nursing homes to senior recreation centers. For older adults who are homebound as a result of illness or disability, Internet access can offer opportunities to socialize, contact friends and family, and purchase food, medications, and other necessities without leaving their homes.

SPORTS AND FITNESS ACTIVITIES ARE IMPORTANT TO MANY AMERICANS

Like tastes in food, fashion, and music, American exercise habits have undergone significant shifts. Participation in

sports and other fitness activities is important to many Americans. In *Sports Participation Topline Report* (2004), the Sporting Goods Manufacturers Association (SGMA) described facts about Americans who were frequent or occasional sports participants, along with Americans' preoccupation with fitness and trends in fitness activity (see Table 1.6):

• Participation in team sports generally decreased between 1998 and 2003.

• More people were participating in camping, hiking, and mountaineering, while hunting and fishing declined in popularity.

• Recreational activities that were considered enjoyable continued to attract enthusiasts—there were an estimated 96.4 million recreational swimmers, 88.8 million recreational walkers, and 53.7 million recreational bicyclists.

• Interest in weight-reducing and muscle-toning fitness exercises remained high—participation in the Pilates method of flexibility and strength training grew by 444.5% in three years, while use of elliptical motion trainers (which combine elements of ski machines and stair climbers) grew by 247.3% in five years.

• Extreme sports was an area of strong growth—from 1987 to 2003 participation in mountain biking jumped by 359%, while snowboarding grew by 269.5% from 1990 to 2003.

The SGMA report also concluded that Americans preferred noncompetitive sports and fitness activities that were less intense. Of the top twenty most popular sports, basketball was the only team sport named. It claimed 35.4 million participants, twice as many as football's eighteen million, soccer's 17.7 million, and softball's sixteen million.

America's Most Popular Sports

The SGMA's list of the top thirty most popular sports in America based on the number of participants for 2003 was topped by bowling, with fifty-five million. It was followed by treadmill exercise (45.6 million), freshwater fishing (43.8 million), stretching (42.1 million), tent camping (41.9 million), and billiards (40.7 million). Twelve of the top thirty were fitness-related activities. (See Table 1.7.)

Gender and Age Influence Sports and Fitness Choices

Athletically inclined American men seemed to prefer individual rather than team sports. Fourteen out of the top fifteen most popular sports for male participants were solo activities. The most popular sports activity for men in 2003 was freshwater fishing, with 9.2 million participating in it at least fifteen days during the year. Men also found fitness activities appealing, with 8.5 million of them lifting barbells a hundred or more days a year, and 7.9 million lifting dumbbells. Stretching (7.6 million),

TABLE 1.6

Sports participation trends, reported by SGMA International, selected years 1987–2003

	1987 Benchmark	1993	1998	2001	2002	2003	1 year % change (2002–2003)	16 year % change (1987–2003)
Fitness activities								
Aerobics (high impact)	13,961	10,356	7,460	6,401	5,423	5,875	+8.3	−57.9
Aerobics (low impact)	11,888	13,418	12,774	10,026	9,286	8,813	−5.1	−25.9
Aerobics (step)	n.a.	11,502	10,784	8,542	8,336	8,457	+1.5	−26.5[2]
Aerobics (net)	21,225	24,839	21,017	16,948	16,046	16,451	+2.5	−22.5
Other exercise to music	n.a.	n.a.	13,846	13,076	13,540	14,159	+4.6	+2.3[4]
Aquatic exercise	n.a.	n.a.	6,685	7,103	6,995	7,141	+2.1	+6.8[4]
Calisthenics	n.a.	n.a.	30,982	29,392	26,862	28,007	+4.3	−9.6[4]
Cardio kickboxing	n.a.	n.a.	n.a.	6,665	5,940	5,489	−7.6	−27.8[5]
Fitness bicycling	n.a.	n.a.	13,556	10,761	11,153	12,048	+8.0	−11.1[4]
Fitness walking	27,164	36,325	36,395	36,445	37,981	37,945	−0.1	+39.7
Running/Jogging	37,136	34,057	34,962	34,857	35,866	36,152	+0.8	−2.6
Fitness swimming	16,912	17,485	15,258	15,300	14,542	15,899	+9.3	−6.0
Pilates training	n.a.	n.a.	n.a.	2,437	4,671	9,469	+102.7	+444.5[6]
Stretching	n.a.	n.a.	35,114	38,120	38,367	42,096	+9.7	+19.9[4]
Yoga/Tai Chi	n.a.	n.a.	5,708	9,741	11,106	13,371	+20.4	+134.3[4]
Equipment exercise								
Barbells	n.a.	n.a.	21,263	23,030	24,812	25,645	+3.4	+20.6[4]
Dumbells	n.a.	n.a.	23,414	26,773	28,933	30,549	+5.6	+30.5[4]
Hand weights	n.a.	n.a.	23,325	27,086	28,453	29,720	+4.5	+27.4[4]
Free weights (net)	22,553	28,564	41,266	45,407	48,261	51,567	+6.9	+128.6
Weight/resistance machines	15,261	19,446	22,519	25,942	27,848	29,996	+7.7	+96.6
Home gym exercise	3,905	6,258	7,577	8,497	8,924	9,260	+3.8	+137.1
Abdominal machine/device	n.a.	n.a.	16,534	18,692	17,370	17,364	0	+5.0[6]
Rowing machine exercise	14,481	11,263	7,485	7,089	7,092	6,484	−8.6	−55.2
Stationary cycling (upright bike)	n.a.	n.a.	20,744	17,483	17,403	17,488	+0.5	−15.7[4]
Stationary cycling (spinning)	n.a.	n.a.	6,776	6,418	6,135	6,462	+5.3	−4.6[4]
Stationary cycling (recumbent bike)	n.a.	n.a.	6,773	8,654	10,217	10,683	+4.6	+57.7[4]
Stationary cycling (net)	30,765	35,975	30,791	28,720	29,083	30,952	+6.4	+0.6
Treadmill exercise	4,396	19,685	37,073	41,638	43,431	45,572	+4.9	+936.7
Stair-climbing machine exercise	2,121	22,494	18,609	15,117	14,251	14,321	+0.5	+575.2
Aerobic rider	n.a.	n.a.	5,868	3,918	3,654	2,955	−19.1	−49.6[4]
Elliptical motion trainer	n.a.	n.a.	3,863	8,255	10,695	13,415	+25.4	+247.3[4]
Cross-country ski machine exercise	n.a.	9,792	6,870	4,924	5,074	4,744	−6.5	−25.8[1]
Team sports								
Baseball	15,098	15,586	12,318	11,405	10,402	10,885	+4.6	−27.1
Basketball	35,737	42,138	42,417	38,663	36,584	35,439	−3.1	−0.8
Cheerleading	n.a.	3,257	3,266	3,844	3,596	3,574	−0.6	+17.6
Ice hockey	2,393	3,204	2,915	2,344	2,612	2,789	+6.8	+16.5
Field hockey	n.a.	n.a.	1,375	1,249	1,096	n.a.	n.a.	n.a.
Football (touch)	20,292	21,241	17,382	16,675	14,903	14,119	−5.3	−30.4
Football (tackle)	n.a.	n.a.	n.a.	5,400	5,783	5,751	−0.6	+16.6[5]
Football (net)	n.a.	n.a.	n.a.	19,199	18,703	17,958	−4.0	−4.1[5]
Lacrosse	n.a.	n.a.	926	1,099	921	1,132	+22.9	+22.2[4]
Rugby	n.a.	n.a.	546	573	n.a.	n.a.	n.a.	n.a.
Soccer (indoor)	n.a.	n.a.	n.a.	n.a.	n.a.	4,563	n.a.	n.a.
Soccer (outdoor)	n.a.	n.a.	n.a.	n.a.	n.a.	16,133	n.a.	n.a.
Soccer (net)	15,388	16,365	18,176	19,042	17,641	17,679	+0.2	+14.9
Softball (regular)	n.a.	n.a.	19,407	17,679	14,372	14,410	+0.3	−25.7[4]
Softball (fast-pitch)	n.a.	n.a.	3,702	4,117	3,658	3,487	−4.7	−5.8[4]
Softball (net)	n.a.	n.a.	21,352	20,123	16,587	16,020	−3.4	−25.0[4]
Volleyball (hard surface)	n.a.	n.a.	n.a.	12,802	11,748	11,008	−6.3	−14.0[7]
Volleyball (grass)	n.a.	n.a.	n.a.	10,330	8,621	7,953	−7.7	−23.0[7]
Volleyball (beach)	n.a.	13,509	10,572	7,791	7,516	7,454	−0.8	−35.5[1]
Volleyball (net)	35,984	37,757	26,637	24,123	21,488	20,286	−5.6	−43.6
Racquet sports								
Badminton	14,793	11,908	9,936	7,684	6,765	5,937	−12.2	−59.9
Racquetball	10,395	7,412	5,853	5,296	4,840	4,875	+0.7	−53.1
Squash	n.a.	n.a.	289	n.a.	302	473	+56.6	n.a.
Tennis	21,147	19,346	16,937	15,098	16,353	17,325	+5.9	−18.1
Personal contact sports								
Boxing	n.a.	n.a.	n.a.	932	908	945	+4.1	+4.5[5]
Martial arts	n.a.	n.a.	5,368	5,999	5,996	6,883	+14.8	+28.2[4]
Wrestling	n.a.	n.a.	n.a.	2,360	2,026	1,820	−10.2	−28.5[5]

calisthenics (6.7 million), and fitness walking (6.6 million) followed closely behind. The highest-ranked team sport, basketball, was played by 5.6 million men at least once a week. (See Table 1.8.)

Women also chose individual fitness activities over team sports. In 2003 the most popular choices of female fitness enthusiasts included stretching (10.7 million participants), fitness walking (9.8 million), treadmill exercise

TABLE 1.6

Sports participation trends, reported by SGMA International, selected years 1987–2003 [CONTINUED]

	1987 Benchmark	1993	1998	2001	2002	2003	1 year % change (2002–2003)	16 year % change (1987–2003)
Indoor sports								
Billiards/Pool	35,297	40,254	39,654	39,263	39,527	40,726	+3.0	**+15.4**
Bowling	47,823	49,022	50,593	55,452	53,160	55,035	+3.5	**+15.1**
Darts	n.a.	n.a.	21,792	19,460	19,703	19,486	−1.1	**−10.6**[4]
Table tennis	n.a.	17,689	14,999	13,239	12,796	13,511	+5.6	**−32.7**[1]
Wheel sports								
Roller hockey	n.a.	2,323	3,876	2,733	2,875	2,718	−5.5	**+17.0**[2]
Roller skating (2x2 wheels)	n.a.	24,223	14,752	11,443	10,968	11,746	+7.1	**−56.7**[1]
Roller skating (inline wheels)	n.a.	13,689	32,010	26,022	21,572	19,233	**−10.8**	**+309.6**[1]
Scooter riding (non-motorized)	n.a.	n.a.	n.a.	15,796	13,858	11,493	**−17.1**	**−17.2**[6]
Skateboarding	10,888	5,388	7,190	12,459	12,997	11,090	**−14.7**	**+1.9**
Other sports/activities								
Bicycling (BMX)	n.a.	n.a.	n.a.	3,668	3,885	3,365	−13.4	**−9.8**[5]
Bicycling (recreational)	n.a.	n.a.	54,575	52,948	53,524	53,710	+0.3	**−1.6**[4]
Golf	26,261	28,610	29,961	29,382	27,812	27,314	−1.8	**+4.0**[4]
Gymnastics	n.a.	n.a.	6,224	5,557	5,149	5,189	+0.8	**−16.6**[4]
Swimming (recreational)	n.a.	n.a.	94,371	93,571	92,667	96,429	**+4.1**	**+2.2**[4]
Walking (recreational)	n.a.	n.a.	80,864	84,182	84,986	88,799	**+4.5**	**−9.8**[4]
Outdoors activities								
Camping (tent)	35,232	34,772	42,677	43,472	40,316	41,891	**+3.9**	**+18.9**
Camping (recreational vehicle)	22,655	22,187	18,188	19,117	18,747	19,022	**+1.5**	**−16.0**
Camping (net)	50,386	49,858	50,650	52,929	49,808	51,007	**+2.4**	**+1.2**
Hiking (day)	n.a.	n.a.	38,629	36,915	36,778	39,096	**+6.3**	**+1.2**[4]
Hiking (overnight)	n.a.	n.a.	6,821	6,007	5,839	6,213	**+6.4**	**−8.9**[4]
Hiking (net)	n.a.	n.a.	40,117	37,999	37,888	40,409	**+6.7**	**+0.7**[4]
Horseback riding	n.a.	n.a.	16,522	16,648	14,641	16,009	**+9.3**	**−3.1**[4]
Mountain biking	1,512	7,408	8,611	6,189	6,719	6,940	**+3.3**	**+359.0**
Mountain/Rock climbing	n.a.	n.a.	2,004	1,819	2,089	2,169	**+3.8**	**+8.2**[4]
Artificial wall climbing	n.a.	n.a.	4,696	7,377	7,185	8,634	**+20.2**	**+83.9**[4]
Trail running	n.a.	n.a.	5,249	5,773	5,625	6,109	**+8.6**	**+16.4**[4]
Shooting sports								
Archery	8,558	8,648	7,109	6,442	6,650	7,111	**+6.9**	**−16.9**
Hunting (shotgun/rifle)	25,241	23,189	16,684	16,672	16,471	15,232	**−7.5**	**−39.7**
Hunting (bow)	n.a.	n.a.	4,719	4,435	4,752	4,155	−12.6	**+12.0**[4]
Paintball	n.a.	n.a.	5,923	7,678	8,679	9,835	**+13.3**	**+66.0**[4]
Shooting (sport clays)	n.a.	3,100	2,734	3,324	3,017	3,867	**+28.2**	**+31.9**[1]
Shooting (trap/skeet)	5,073	n.a.	3,800	3,904	3,696	4,496	**+21.6**	**+11.4**
Target shooting (rifle)	n.a.	n.a.	14,042	13,979	14,336	15,176	**+5.9**	**+8.1**[4]
Target shooting (handgun)[8]	n.a.	n.a.	12,110	11,402	11,064	13,836	**+25.1**	**+14.3**[4]
Target shooting (net)[8]	18,947	23,498	18,330	17,838	17,558	19,788	**+12.7**	**+4.4**
Fishing								
Fishing (fly)	11,359	6,598	7,269	5,999	6,034	6,033	0	**−46.9**
Fishing (freshwater-other)	50,500	50,198	45,807	43,547	42,605	43,819	+2.8	**−13.2**
Fishing (saltwater)	19,646	18,490	15,671	13,871	14,874	15,221	+2.3	**−22.5**
Fishing (net)	58,402	55,442	55,488	53,137	51,426	52,970	+3.0	**−9.3**
Winter sports								
Ice skating	n.a.	n.a.	18,710	16,753	14,530	17,049	**+17.3**	**−8.9**[4]
Skiing (cross-country)	8,344	6,489	4,728	4,123	4,080	4,171	**+2.2**	**−50.0**
Skiing (downhill)	17,676	17,567	14,836	13,202	14,249	13,633	−4.3	**−22.9**
Snowboarding	n.a.	2,567	5,461	6,797	7,691	7,818	**+1.7**	**+269.5**[1]
Snowmobiling	n.a.	n.a.	6,492	6,451	4,515	5,509	**+22.0**	**−15.1**[4]
Snowshoeing	n.a.	n.a.	1,721	2,042	2,006	2,479	**+23.6**	**+44.0**[4]

(6.2 million), lifting hand weights (4.6 million), and running or jogging (4.2 million). The preferred activity of men, fishing, ranked eleventh for women, with 3.1 million participants. (See Table 1.9.)

Popular Sports for Children and Seniors

America's love of sports and fitness was not bounded by age. The SGMA studied recreational activities that were "frequent" among youths aged six to seventeen during 2003. Active American children and teens enjoyed both team and individual sports, with their top choices being basketball (4.1 million participants), fishing (3.5 million), inline skat-

ing (3.5 million), and running/jogging (3.1 million). Stretching, calisthenics, baseball, outdoor soccer, skateboarding, and touch football rounded out the top ten most popular pursuits of younger Americans. (See Table 1.10.)

Many of America's older adults (those over age fifty-five) have embraced exercise as a strategy for enhancing health and wellness, and the 2003 SGMA survey found that seniors were frequent participants in recreational and fitness activities. Thirteen of the fifteen most popular sports and activities were fitness or outdoor pursuits, led by fitness walking (6.3 million participants), stretching (four million), treadmill exercise (3.1 million), golf (three

TABLE 1.6

Sports participation trends, reported by SGMA International, selected years 1987–2003 [CONTINUED]

	1987 Benchmark	1993	1998	2001	2002	2003	1 year % change (2002–2003)	16 year % change (1987–2003)
Water sports								
Boardsailing/Windsurfing	1,145	835	1,075	537	496	779	+57.1	−32.0
Canoeing	n.a.	n.a.	13,615	12,044	10,933	11,632	+6.4	−14.6⁴
Kayaking	n.a.	n.a.	3,501	4,727	5,562	6,324	+13.7	+80.6⁴
Rafting	n.a.	n.a.	5,570	4,580	4,431	4,553	+2.8	−18.3⁴
Jet skiing	n.a.	n.a.	11,203	10,593	9,806	10,648	+8.6	−5.0⁴
Sailing	6,368	3,918	5,902	5,230	5,161	5,232	+1.4	−17.8
Scuba diving	2,433	2,306	3,448	2,744	3,328	3,215	−3.4	+32.1
Snorkeling	n.a.	n.a.	10,575	9,788	9,865	10,179	+3.2	−3.7⁴
Surfing	1,459	n.a.	1,395	1,601	1,879	2,087	+11.1	+43.0
Wakeboarding	n.a.	n.a.	2,253	3,097	3,142	3,356	+6.8	+49.0⁴
Water skiing	19,902	16,626	10,161	8,301	8,204	8,425	+2.7	−57.7
Water sports								

¹Thirteen-year change
²Ten-year change
³Six-year change
⁴Five-year change
⁵Four-year change
⁶Three-year change
⁷Two-year change
⁸2003 figure is elevated due to change in category definition from "Pistol" to "Handgun."

SOURCE: "SGMA Sports Participation Trends," in "Sports Participation Topline Report," *Superstudy of Sports Participation,* SGMA International, 2004, http://www.sgma.com/reports/2004/report1081955240-11847.html (accessed September 9, 2004)

TABLE 1.7

Most popular sports and activities, 2003

Sport/activity	Number of participants aged 6 and above (in millions)
1. Bowling	55
2. Treadmill exercise	45.6
3. Fishing (freshwater - other)	43.8
4. Stretching	42.1
5. Tent camping	41.9
6. Billiards/pool	40.7
7. Day hiking	39.1
8. Fitness walking	37.9
9. Running/jogging	36.2
10. Basketball	35.4
11. Dumbbells	30.5
12. Weight/resistance machines	30
13. Hand weights	29.7
14. Calisthenics	28
15. Golf	27.3
16. Barbells	25.6
17. Darts	19.5
18. Inline skating	19.2
19. RV camping	19
20. Stationary cycling (upright bike)	17.5
21. Abdominal machine/device	17.4
22. Tennis	17.3
23. Ice skating	17
24. Soccer (outdoor)	16.1
25. Horseback riding	16
26. Fitness swimming	15.9
27. Hunting (rifle)	15.2
27. Saltwater fishing	15.2
27. Target shooting (rifle)	15.2
30. Softball (regular)	14.4

SOURCE: "America's Favorite Sports and Activites in 2003," in *Superstudy of Sports Participation,* SGMA International, April 9, 2004, http://www.sgma.com/press/2004/press1081869229-23051.html (accessed September 9, 2004)

million), and fishing (2.6 million). Other popular choices in the seniors' top ten included recreational vehicle camping, free weight training, bowling, weight and resistance machines, and day hiking. (See Table 1.11.)

PETS—COMPANIONSHIP, PLEASURE, AND WELL-BEING

Pets often provide more than recreation for their owners—they may become companions and family members, and most pet owners report that their pets bring pleasure to their lives. Many pet owners, wanting to extend their pets' lives and improve their health, are willing to spend large amounts on veterinary care; some purchase health insurance for their pets. Some even send their pampered pets to day camps and spas and make arrangements for the care of their pets in the event of their own illness or death.

The numbers of dog and cat owners are almost equal. According to the American Pet Products Manufacturers Association's *2003–2004 National Pet Owners Survey,* there were about sixty-five million owned dogs in the United States and 77.7 million owned cats. Nearly four out of ten households (40.6 million) owned at least one dog, and a third (35.4 million) owned at least one cat. Seven out of ten dogs that were owned and eight out of ten owned cats were spayed or neutered.

Eighteen percent of owned dogs, and 16% of owned cats, were adopted from animal shelters. Sixty-five percent of owners had just one dog, while half of cat-owners had one cat and the remaining half owned two or more. The

TABLE 1.8

Most popular sports for men (age 6 and older) based on "frequent" participation, 2003

Activity	Year 2003
1 Fishing (freshwater/other) - 15+ days/year	9,169,000
2 Free weights: Barbells - 100+ days/year	8,484,000
3 Free weights: Dumbbells - 100+ days/year	7,878,000
4 Stretching - 100+ days/year	7,569,000
5 Calisthenics - 100+ days/year	6,748,000
6 Fitness walking - 100+ days/year	6,626,000
7 Billiards/pool - 25+ days/year	6,381,000
8 Running/jogging - 100+ days/year	6,209,000
9 Weight/resistance machines - 100+ days/year	5,812,000
10 Basketball - 52+ days/year (25+ in 2002)	5,640,000
11 Golf - 25+ days/year	5,552,000
12 Treadmill exercise - 100+ days/year	5,375,000
13 Hunting (shotgun/rifle) - 15+ days/year	4,327,000
14 Day hiking - 15+ days/year	4,260,000
15 Bowling - 25+ days/year	3,783,000

SOURCE: "Most Popular Sports for Men in the USA Based on 'Frequent' Participation (Age 6 and Older)," in "Solo Sports Appeal to U.S. Men," *Superstudy of Sports Participation,* SGMA International, May 28, 2004, http://www.sgma.com/press/2004/press1085581679-16624.html (accessed September 9, 2004)

TABLE 1.9

Most popular sports for women (age 6 and older) based on "frequent" participation, 2003

Activity	Year 2003
1 Stretching (100+ days/year)	10,710,000
2 Fitness walking (100+ days/year)	9,788,000
3 Treadmill exercise (100+ days/year)	6,160,000
4 Free weights: Hand weights (100+ days/year)	4,587,000
5 Running/jogging (100+ days/year)	4,247,000
6 Weight/resistance machines (100+ days/year)	4,073,000
7 Calisthenics (100+ days/year)	3,921,000
8 Day hiking (15+ days/year)	3,749,000
9 Bowling (25+ days/year)	3,552,000
10 Recreational vehicle camping (15+ days/year)	3,373,000
11 Fishing (freshwater/other) (15+ days/year)	3,103,000
12 Free weights: Dumbbells (100+ days/year)	3,011,000
13 Billiards/pool (25+ days/year)	2,973,000
14 Other exercise to music (100+ days/year)	2,942,000
15 Abdominal machine/device (100+ days/year)	2,208,000

SOURCE: "Most Popular Sports for Women Based on 'Frequent' Participation (Age 6 and Older)," in "U.S. Women Set Their Sights on the Gym," *Superstudy of Sports Participation,* SGMA International, May 24, 2004, http://www.sgma.com/press/2004/press1085420837-20560.html (accessed September 9, 2004)"

average number of dogs per owner was 1.6, compared to an average of 2.2 cats per owner. On average, dog owners spent more than twice what cat owners did on veterinary expenses during the twelve months preceding the survey—dog owners spent $263 while cat owners averaged $113. During 2003 the American Pet Products Manufacturers Association reported that Americans spent a total of $32.4 billion on pet food, toys, and care. For 2004, this figure was projected to rise 5.9%, to $34.3 billion, double the amount of ten years earlier. Of this, $14.3 billion would be spent on food, $8.3 billion on veterinary care, and $7.9 billion on supplies and nonprescription medicine.

Pets Contribute to Health and Wellness

Research conducted during the late 1990s found that pet ownership was related to better health. At first, it was believed that the effects were simply increased well-being—the obvious delight of hospital and nursing home patients petting puppies, watching kittens play, or viewing fish in an aquarium clearly demonstrated pets' abilities to calm frayed nerves and make people smile.

A study published in the *Journal of the American Geriatrics Society* (March 1999) reported that attachment to a companion animal was linked to maintaining or slightly improving the physical and psychological well-being of older adults. Following nearly a thousand older adults for one year, researcher Parminder Raina and her associates found that pet owners were more satisfied with their physical health, mental health, family relationships, living arrangements, finances, and friends.

The physiological mechanisms responsible for these health benefits were as yet unidentified; however, some researchers think that pets connect people to the natural world, enabling them to focus on others rather than simply themselves. Other investigators have observed that dog owners walk more than persons without dogs do and credit pet owners' improved health to exercise. Nearly everyone agrees that the nonjudgmental affection pets offer boosts health and wellness.

Other research has revealed some specific health benefits of human interaction with animals. Several researchers have observed that petting dogs and cats lowers blood pressure. Preliminary results of a study presented in 2004 by Rebecca Johnson, of the University of Missouri—Columbia Center for the Study of Animal Wellness, showed that after human subjects petted a dog, they experienced a massive release of beneficial hormones, including serotonin, beta endorphin, prolactin, dopamine, oxytocin, and beta phenylethalamine. A similar release was also observed in the dog.

HOBBIES

A hobby is an activity or pastime that is performed primarily for pleasure rather than for business. Hobbies were once the mainstay of leisure time. While this sort of activity still exists, industry observers believe it is less popular, seeming to have been surpassed by collecting, a profit-motivated activity.

Some of the most common hobbies are cross-stitching/embroidering, crocheting, quilting, knitting, cake decorating, model train collecting, wreath making, art/drawing, photography, gardening, studying genealogy, floral arranging, woodworking, and solving crossword puzzles. Children and teens often enjoy playing board games; drawing,

TABLE 1.10

Most popular sports for youth (ages 6–17) based on "frequent" participation, 2003

Activity	Year 2003
1 Basketball - 52+ days/year (25+ in 2002)	4,127,000
2 Fishing (freshwater/other) - 15+ days/year	3,472,000
3 Inline skating - 25+ days/year	3,467,000
4 Running/jogging - 100+ days/year	3,054,000
5 Stretching - 100+ days/year	3,052,000
6 Calisthenics - 100+ days/year	2,704,000
7 Baseball - 52+ days/year (25+ in 2002)	2,531,000
8 Outdoor soccer - 52+ days/year (25+ in 2002)*	2,435,000
9 Skateboarding - 52+ days/year	2,107,000
10 Touch football - 52+ days/year	1,998,000
11 Scooter riding -52+ days/year	1,954,000
12 Court volleyball - 25+ days/year	1,894,000
13 Tent camping - 15+ days/year	1,880,000
14 Billiards/pool - 25+ days/year	1,879,000
15 Tackle football - 52+ days/year	1,840,000

* 2003 Soccer participation has been broken into outdoor and indoor soccer categories.

SOURCE: "Most Popular Sports for U.S. Youth Based on 'Frequent' Participation (Ages 6–17)," in "America's Children Seek Action and Adventure," *Superstudy of Sports Participation,* SGMA International, June 2, 2004, http://www.sgma.com/press/2004/press1086353384-1753.html (accessed September 9, 2004)

TABLE 1.11

Most popular sports for seniors (age 55 and older) based on "frequent" participation, 2003

Activity	Year 2003
1 Fitness walking - 100+ days/year	6,277,000
2 Stretching - 100+ days/year	4,011,000
3 Treadmill exercise - 100+ days/year	3,059,000
4 Golf - 25+ days/year	2,966,000
5 Fishing (freshwater/other) - 15+ days/year	2,625,000
6 Recreational vehicle camping - 15+ days/year	2,189,000
7 Free weights: Hand weights - 100+ days/year	1,735,000
8 Bowling - 25+ days/year	1,647,000
9 Weight/resistance machines - 100+ days/year	1,493,000
10 Day hiking - 15+ days/year	1,414,000
11 Calisthenics - 100+ days/year	1,161,000
12 Fishing (saltwater) - 15+ days/year	1,147,000
13 Free weights: Dumbbells - 100+ days/year	1,040,000
14 Stationary cycling: Upright bike (regular) - 100+ days/year	1,031,000
15 Hunting (shotgun/rifle) - 15+ days/year	960,000

SOURCE: "Most Popular Sports for U.S. Seniors Based on 'Frequent' Participation (Age 55+ and Older)," in "America's Seniors Are Active: Indoors and Outdoors," *Superstudy of Sports Participation,* SGMA International, June 1, 2004, http://www.sgma.com/press/2004/press 1086103721-19570.html (accessed September 9, 2004)

painting and sculpting; playing musical instruments; and card collecting.

The Hobby Industry Association (HIA), an industry trade group, in the *2002 Nationwide Craft and Hobby Consumer Usage and Purchases Study,* found that 77% of surveyed households reported that at least one member engaged in a craft or hobby, a slight increase from 76% in 2001. Craft and hobby participants were often married, had children, were better educated, and had higher household incomes than noncrafters.

In 2002 the HIA reported that the U.S. craft and hobby industry accounted for $29 billion in sales, which was broken down into four categories: general crafts (43%), needlecrafts (29%), painting and finishing (18%), and floral crafts (10%). Crafters primarily created their projects for friends or household use. A majority made crafts to give as gifts (79%), or for themselves (69%), and for home decorating (61%), while many also made crafts for holiday decorating (43%). Only 15% made crafts to sell. So-called "heavy crafters," who accounted for 25% of total participants, spent an average of $1,552 on crafts and hobbies during 2002 and accounted for 77% of total dollar sales for the industry.

Collecting as Recreation

Collectors devote time, energy, and often considerable financial resources to amassing, compiling, and organizing their collections. Along with more common pursuits, such as stamp, coin, and sports card collecting, there are individuals and groups devoted to collecting everything imaginable, from antique automobiles, celebrity autographs, and memorabilia from events such as the 1939 World's Fair, to toys, action figures, and favors distributed with children's meals at fast-food restaurants.

Unity Marketing's *Collectibles Industry Report 2002* found that 40% of U.S. households were involved with collectibles and characterized the typical collector as someone who was "younger, smarter, more affluent and shop[ped] in a much wider range of retail venues than yesterday's collector." While collectors had traditionally been female, men were now emerging as collectors, attracted by online auction sites such as eBay.

VOLUNTEER WORK

Many Americans spend their leisure time in volunteer work helping others. The U.S. Bureau of Labor Statistics (BLS) survey *Volunteering in the United States 2003* found that 63.8 million people did volunteer work of some type between September 2002 and September 2003, up from 59.8 million a year earlier. During the same period the rate of Americans volunteering rose from 27.4% of those age sixteen or older to 28.8%. The median number of hours a volunteer gave during the year was fifty-two. (See Table 1.12.)

Who Volunteers?

The BLS survey found that women were more likely to volunteer, with 32.2% of females over sixteen giving their time compared with 25.1% of men. Americans between the ages of thirty-five and forty-four volunteered the most, at 34.7%, followed by forty-five- to fifty-four-year-olds at 32.7%. Those ages sixty-five and older were least likely to volunteer, at 23.7%, but senior citizens who

TABLE 1.12

Volunteers, by selected characteristics, September 2002 and 2003

(Numbers in thousands)

Characteristic	September 2002r			September 2003		
	Number	Percent of population	Median annual hours	Number	Percent of population	Median annual hours
Sex						
Total, both sexes	59,783	27.4	52	63,791	28.8	52
Men	24,706	23.6	52	26,805	25.1	52
Women	35,076	31.0	50	36,987	32.2	52
Age						
Total, 16 years and over	59,783	27.4	52	63,791	28.8	52
16 to 24 years	7,742	21.9	40	8,671	24.1	40
25 to 34 years	9,574	24.8	33	10,337	26.5	36
35 to 44 years	14,971	34.1	52	15,165	34.7	50
45 to 54 years	12, 477	31.3	52	13,302	32.7	52
55 to 64 years	7,331	27.5	60	8,170	29.2	60
65 years and over	7,687	22.7	96	8,146	23.7	88
Race and Hispanic or Latino ethnicity						
White[1]	52,591	29.2	52	55,572	30.6	52
Black or African American[1]	4,896	19.1	52	5,145	20.0	52
Asian[1]	[2]	[2]	[2]	1,735	18.7	40
Hispanic or Latino ethnicity	4,059	15.5	40	4,364	15.7	40
Educational attainment[3]						
Less than a high school diploma	2,806	10.1	48	2,793	9.9	48
High school graduate, no college[4]	12,542	21.2	49	12,882	21.7	48
Less than a bachelor's degree[5]	15, 066	32.8	52	15,966	34.1	52
College graduates	21,627	43.3	60	23,481	45.6	60
Employment status						
Civilian labor force	42,773	29.3	48	45,499	30.9	48
Employed	40,742	29.5	48	43,138	31.2	48
Full time[6]	32,210	28.3	46	33,599	29.6	48
Part time[7]	8,532	35.4	52	9,539	38.4	52
Unemployed	2,031	25.1	50	2,361	26.7	48
Not in the labor force	17,010	23.7	72	18,293	24.6	66

[1]Beginning in 2003, persons who selected this race group only; persons who selected more than one race group are not included. Prior to 2003, persons who reported more than one race group were in the group they identified as the main race.
[2]Data for Asians were not tabulated in 2002.
[3]Data refer to persons 25 years and over.
[4]Includes high school diploma or equivalent.
[5]Includes the categories, some college, no degree; and associate degree.
[6]Usually work 35 hours or more a week at all jobs.
[7]Usually work less than 35 hours a week at all jobs.
r=revised. Estimates for 2002 have been revised to reflect the use of Census 2000-based population controls.
Note: Estimates for the above race groups (white, black or African-American, and Asian) do not sum to totals because data are not presented for all races. In addition, persons whose ethnicity is identified as Hispanic or Latino maybe of any race and, therefore, are classified by ethnicity as well as by race.

SOURCE: "Table A. Volunteers by Selected Characteristics, September 2002 and 2003," in *Volunteering in the United States, 2003,* U.S. Department of Labor, Bureau of Labor Statistics, December 17, 2003, http://stats.bls.gov/news.release/archives/volun_12172003.pdf (accessed September 9, 2004)

did participate gave more of their time, putting in a median number of eighty-eight hours in 2003.

Among ethnic groups in 2003, volunteer work was performed by 30.6% of whites, 20% of African-Americans, 18.7% of Asians, and 15.7% of Hispanic Americans. Educational attainment was a significant predictor of volunteer status, with 45.6% of college graduates participating, as compared to 9.9% of those who did not graduate from high school. Job status was also important, with 31.2% of employees giving of their time contrasted with 26.7% of those unemployed. The largest percentage of volunteers came from those working part-time, at 38.4%.

The BLS found that the leading reason volunteers became involved in 2003 was that they had been asked (43.6%), while slightly more than two-fifths (40.7%) approached the organization themselves. These figures held relatively constant between men and women and among the various economic and ethnic groups, although Asians were more likely to approach an organization about joining (48.2%) and less likely to have joined because they were asked (38.7%). (See Table 1.13.) When volunteers stopped participating, the reasons they cited most were lack of time (44.7%), health or medical problems (14.7%), and family responsibilities or childcare problems (9.5%).

What Do Volunteers Do?

The BLS found that the most popular ways volunteers gave their time was working with religious groups

TABLE 1.13

Volunteers, by how they became involved with the volunteer organization and by selected characteristics, September 2003

		Percent distribution of how volunteers became involved with [1]			Was asked by:					Not reporting how became involved
Characteristics in September 2003	Total volunteers (thousands)	Total	Approached the organization	Total[2]	Boss or employer	Relative, friend, or co-worker	Someone in the organization/ school	Someone else	Other	
Sex										
Total, both sexes	63,791	100.0	40.7	43.6	1.2	14.4	26.8	1.0	13.4	2.3
Men	26,805	100.0	40.6	44.3	1.2	15.9	26.0	1.1	12.8	2.3
Women	36,987	100.0	40.9	43.0	1.1	13.3	27.4	1.0	13.8	2.3
Age										
Total, 16 years and over	63,791	100.0	40.7	43.6	1.2	14.4	26.8	1.0	13.4	2.3
16 to 24 years	8,671	100.0	41.8	41.8	1.0	16.6	22.5	1.5	13.8	2.7
16 to 19 years	4,758	100.0	41.7	41.4	.4	16.3	23.1	1.5	14.7	2.2
20 to 24 years	3,912	100.0	41.8	42.2	1.8	16.9	21.7	1.4	12.7	3.3
25 years and over	55,121	100.0	40.6	43.8	1.2	14.0	27.5	1.0	13.4	2.2
25 to 34 years	10,337	100.0	39.3	44.3	1.7	14.9	26.4	1.2	14.3	2.1
35 to 44 years	15,165	100.0	41.0	44.2	1.4	13.0	28.9	.8	12.6	2.1
45 to 54 years	13,302	100.0	40.6	43.6	1.2	13.7	27.7	.7	13.3	2.5
55 to 64 years	8,170	100.0	40.3	43.2	1.1	14.4	26.2	1.1	14.3	2.3
65 years and over	8,146	100.0	41.7	43.7	.2	14.8	27.4	1.2	12.6	2.1
Race and Hispanic or Latino ethnicity										
White	55,572	100.0	40.8	43.8	1.1	14.4	27.1	1.0	13.2	2.2
Black or African-American	5,145	100.0	39.2	41.7	2.0	13.5	25.3	1.0	15.6	3.5
Asian	1,735	100.0	48.2	38.7	1.3	12.1	23.3	2.0	11.1	2.0
Hispanic or Latino ethnicity	4,364	100.0	38.2	46.8	1.1	15.6	29.1	.9	12.6	2.4
Educational attainment[3]										
Less than a high school diploma	2,793	100.0	38.6	46.2	.4	15.5	29.4	.6	12.8	2.4
High school graduate, no college[4]	12,882	100.0	39.1	45.9	.9	15.4	28.6	.8	13.2	1.8
Less than a bachelor's degree[5]	15,966	100.0	40.9	42.7	1.3	13.7	26.3	1.2	14.2	2.2
College graduates	23,481	100.0	41.4	43.2	1.3	13.2	27.5	1.0	12.9	2.4
Marital status										
Single, never married	13,670	100.0	41.0	41.4	1.3	16.9	21.6	1.4	14.5	3.0
Married, spouse present	40,486	100.0	40.9	44.4	1.1	13.2	29.0	.9	12.7	2.0
Other marital status[6]	9,635	100.0	39.8	43.0	1.4	15.5	25.1	.9	15.1	2.1
Presence of own children under 18 years[7]										
Men										
No own children under 18 years old	16,969	100.0	40.7	43.6	1.2	16.7	24.3	1.1	13.6	2.2
With own children under 18 years old	9,836	100.0	40.4	45.6	1.2	14.4	28.9	1.0	11.6	2.3
Women:										
No own children under 18 years old	21,938	100.0	40.9	42.0	1.2	15.2	24.3	1.0	14.7	2.4
With own children under 18 years old	15,049	100.0	40.8	44.5	1.1	10.5	32.0	.9	12.6	2.1
Employment status										
Civilian labor force	45,499	100.0	40.0	44.2	1.5	14.6	26.9	.9	13.6	2.3
Employed	43,138	100.0	39.9	44.2	1.6	14.6	27.0	.9	13.6	2.3
Full time[8]	33,599	100.0	39.3	45.0	1.9	15.4	26.6	.8	13.3	2.4
Part time[9]	9,539	100.0	42.0	41.6	.6	11.5	28.2	1.2	14.5	1.9
Unemployed	2,361	100.0	40.4	43.7	1.0	15.6	25.4	1.4	13.7	2.2
Not in the labor force	18,293	100.0	42.7	41.9	.2	13.7	26.6	1.2	13.1	2.3

[1]Main organization is defined as the organization for which the volunteer worked the most hours during the year.
[2]Includes persons who did not specify who asked them to volunteer, not shown separately.
[3]Data refer to persons 25 years and over.
[4]Includes high school diploma or equivalent.
[5]Includes the categories, some college, no degree; and associate degree.
[6]Includes divorced, separated, and widowed persons.
[7]Own children include sons, daughters, stepchildren, and adopted children. Not included are nieces, nephews, grandchildren, and other related and unrelated children.
[8]Usually work 35 hours or more a week at all jobs.
[9]Usually work less than 35 hours a week at all jobs.
Note: Data on volunteers relate to persons who performed unpaid volunteer activities for an organization at any point from September 1, 2002, through the survey period in September 2003. Estimates for the above race groups (white, black or African-American, and Asian) do not sum to totals because data are not presented for all races. In addition, persons whose ethnicity is identified as Hispanic or Latino may be of any race and, therefore, are classified by ethnicity as well as by race.

SOURCE: "Table 6. Volunteers by How They Became Involved with Main Organization for Which Volunteer Activities Were Performed and Selected Characteristics, September 2003," in *Volunteering in the United States, 2003*, United States Department of Labor, Bureau of Labor Statistics, December 17, 2003, http://stats.bls.gov/news.release/archives/volun_12172003.pdf (accessed September 9, 2004)

TABLE 1.14

Volunteers, by type of volunteer organization and by selected characteristics, September 2003

Characteristics in September 2003	Total volunteers (thousands)	Percent distribution of volunteers by type of main organization[1]										
		Total	Civic, political, professional, or international	Educational or youth service	Environmental or animal care	Hospital or other health	Public safety	Religious	Social or community service	Sport, hobby, cultural, or arts	Other	Not determined
Sex												
Total, both sexes	63,791	100.00	6.4	27.4	1.7	8.2	1.2	34.6	11.8	4.1	3.1	1.5
Men	26,805	100.00	8.1	24.7	1.9	6.3	2.1	33.9	12.6	5.5	3.4	1.5
Women	36,987	100.00	5.2	29.3	1.5	9.6	.5	35.1	11.2	3.2	3.0	1.5
Age												
Total, 16 years and over	63,791	100.00	6.4	27.4	1.7	8.2	1.2	34.6	11.8	4.1	3.1	1.5
16 to 24 years	8,671	100.00	4.6	31.9	2.4	8.6	1.3	29.1	13.4	4.0	3.0	1.7
16 to 19 years	4,758	100.00	4.0	35.5	2.0	6.5	1.2	29.8	13.0	3.7	2.6	1.7
20 to 24 years	3,912	100.00	5.4	27.5	2.9	11.2	1.5	28.3	13.8	4.3	3.5	1.8
25 years and over	55,121	100.00	6.7	26.7	1.6	8.1	1.2	35.4	11.5	4.2	3.2	1.5
25 to 34 years	10,337	100.00	5.3	35.1	1.7	8.4	1.6	29.7	10.7	3.3	2.8	1.4
35 to 44 years	15,165	100.00	5.3	38.5	1.3	5.8	1.2	31.5	8.8	3.9	2.4	1.3
45 to 54 years	13,302	100.00	6.3	27.2	2.1	8.0	1.2	35.3	10.6	4.5	3.2	1.5
55 to 64 years	8,170	100.00	9.8	13.5	1.8	9.4	1.0	39.1	14.5	4.7	4.4	1.8
65 years and over	8,146	100.00	8.4	6.4	.8	10.9	.7	46.5	16.3	4.5	3.8	1.6
Race and Hispanic or Latino ethnicity												
White	55,572	100.00	6.5	27.3	1.7	8.4	1.3	33.7	11.9	4.3	3.3	1.5
Black or African-American	5,145	100.00	5.0	27.4	.4	5.9	.5	44.7	10.5	1.7	1.8	2.1
Asian	1,735	100.00	5.6	25.7	2.0	8.7	.4	38.0	10.5	5.2	3.5	.4
Hispanic or Latino ethnicity[4]	4,364	100.00	5.8	38.5	.7	5.5	.6	32.4	9.6	1.9	3.5	1.7
Educational attainment[2]												
Less than a high school diploma	2,793	100.00	6.0	22.2	1.0	5.1	1.3	45.7	12.0	2.1	3.0	1.6
High school graduate, no college[3]	12,882	100.00	6.0	25.7	1.2	7.8	1.6	39.1	11.7	3.0	2.7	1.2
Less than a bachelor's degree[4]	15,966	100.00	6.0	27.3	1.4	8.5	1.6	35.5	10.9	4.1	3.4	1.3
College graduates	23,481	100.00	7.6	27.3	2.0	8.4	.6	32.2	11.9	5.0	3.3	1.8
Marital status												
Single, never married	13,670	100.00	6.1	29.3	2.6	9.7	1.3	26.6	13.8	4.7	3.7	2.0
Married, spouse present	40,486	100.00	6.4	28.1	1.3	7.1	1.2	37.7	10.3	3.8	2.7	1.4
Other marital status[5]	9,635	100.00	6.9	21.7	2.0	10.5	.9	32.7	15.2	4.5	4.2	1.2
Presence of own children under 18 years[6]												
Men:												
No own children under 18 years old	16,969	100.00	9.6	18.2	2.3	7.4	2.0	34.3	15.0	5.3	4.2	1.7
With own children under 18 years old	9,836	100.00	5.6	36.1	1.1	4.2	2.3	33.2	8.4	5.8	2.1	1.3
Women:												
No own children under 18 years old	21,938	100.00	6.4	17.0	2.2	12.8	.6	37.5	14.5	4.0	3.4	1.7
With own children under 18 years old	15,049	100.00	3.4	47.2	.6	4.8	.4	31.6	6.5	2.0	2.3	1.2
Employment status												
Civilian labor force	45,499	100.00	6.5	29.1	1.8	8.1	1.4	33.1	11.2	4.4	3.0	1.5
Employed	43,138	100.00	6.6	28.8	1.8	8.1	1.4	33.2	11.2	4.4	3.0	1.5
Full time[7]	33,599	100.00	6.9	28.0	1.7	8.4	1.6	32.8	11.4	4.6	3.0	1.6
Part time[8]	9,539	100.00	5.4	31.7	1.9	7.2	.8	34.5	10.7	3.8	2.8	1.2
Unemployed	2,361	100.00	5.3	34.2	3.1	7.8	.5	31.2	10.6	3.4	3.0	.9
Not in the labor force	18,293	100.00	6.1	23.2	1.3	8.4	.7	38.2	13.3	3.5	3.6	1.7

[1]Main organization is defined as the organization for which the volunteer worked the most hours during the year.
[2]Data refer to persons 25 years and over.
[3]Includes high school diploma or equivalent.
[4]Includes the categories, some college, no degree; and associate degree.
[5]Includes divorced, separated, and widowed persons.
[6]Own children include sons, daughters, stepchildren, and adopted children. Not included are nieces, nephews, grandchildren, and other related and unrelated children.
[7]Usually work 35 hours or more a week at all jobs.
[8]Usually work less than 35 hours a week at all jobs.
Note: Data on volunteers relate to persons who performed unpaid volunteer activities for an organization at any point from September 1, 2002, through the survey period in September 2003. Estimates for the above race groups (white, black or African-American, and Asian) do not sum to totals because data are not presented for all races. In addition, persons whose ethnicity is identified as Hispanic or Latino may be of any race and, therefore, are classified by ethnicity as well as by race.

SOURCE: "Table 4. Volunteers by Type of Main Organization for Which Volunteer Activities Were Performed and Selected Characteristics, September 2003," in *Volunteering in the United States, 2003,* United States Department of Labor, Bureau of Labor Statistics, December 17, 2003, http://stats.bls.gov/news.release/archives/volun_12172003.pdf (accessed September 10, 2004)

(34.6%), educational or youth service organizations (27.4%), social or community service agencies (11.8%), and hospital or health organizations (8.2%). Fewer were

involved with civic, political, professional, or international groups (6.4%); sport, hobby, cultural, or arts organizations (4.1%); environmental or animal care groups (1.7%); and public safety agencies (1.2%). (See Table 1.14.)

The BLS survey found that the most frequent activities performed by volunteers included fund-raising, done at some time by 28.8% of the total; coaching, refereeing, tutoring or teaching (28.6%); collecting, preparing distributing, or serving food (24.9%); providing information, ushering, greeting, or ministering (22%); or engaging in general labor (21.8%). (See Table 1.15.)

TABLE 1.15

Volunteer activities, by selected characteristics, September 2003

Characteristics in September 2003	Total volunteers (thousands)	Coach, referee, tutor, or teacher	Provide information; be an usher, greeter, or minister	Collect, prepare, distribute, or serve food	Collect, make or distribute clothing, crafts, or goods, other than food	Fundraise or sell items to raise money	Provide counseling, medical care, fire/EMS or protective services	Supply transportation for people	Provide general office services	Provide professional or management assistance including serving on a board or committee	Engage in music performance, or other artistic activities	Engage in general labor	Other	Not reporting type of activities
Sex														
Total, both sexes	63,791	28.6	22.0	24.9	15.1	28.8	8.4	12.6	13.1	19.1	12.1	21.8	16.0	1.7
Men	26,805	30.9	22.5	19.2	10.1	25.6	9.6	13.3	9.8	21.6	10.4	26.9	15.1	1.9
Women	36,987	26.9	21.7	28.9	18.8	31.2	7.5	12.1	15.4	17.3	13.2	18.1	16.7	1.6
Age														
Total, 16 years and over	63,791	28.6	22.0	24.9	15.1	28.8	8.4	12.6	13.1	19.1	12.1	21.8	16.0	1.7
16 to 24 years	8,671	33.4	19.0	22.1	15.3	24.3	7.9	8.3	10.6	8.2	17.9	26.4	16.9	2.5
16 to 19 years	4,758	32.5	17.5	22.5	15.5	24.5	5.3	6.8	10.0	6.2	19.0	29.8	17.4	2.0
20 to 24 years	3,912	34.6	20.9	21.7	15.2	24.0	11.1	10.1	11.3	10.8	16.7	22.2	16.4	3.2
25 years and over	55,121	27.8	22.5	25.3	15.1	29.6	8.5	13.3	13.4	20.8	11.1	21.0	15.9	1.6
25 to 34 years	10,337	34.1	20.3	23.0	14.4	29.3	9.2	11.8	11.6	14.1	13.2	21.9	15.4	1.8
35 to 44 years	15,165	35.5	19.4	24.7	14.9	32.4	7.3	15.2	12.8	19.2	11.7	21.9	15.2	1.6
45 to 54 years	13,302	28.0	24.1	24.7	14.4	32.5	9.5	14.2	13.6	23.0	11.0	22.2	15.4	1.8
55 to 64 years	8,170	20.6	25.4	26.6	15.2	27.4	9.8	12.4	15.3	28.2	9.3	21.3	16.7	1.5
65 years and over	8,146	12.5	25.7	28.9	17.5	22.0	6.9	11.1	15.0	21.5	9.6	16.3	17.8	1.2
Race and Hispanic or Latino ethnicity														
White	55,572	28.5	21.7	24.7	15.2	29.5	8.1	12.6	12.9	19.8	11.7	22.2	16.2	1.6
Black or African-American	5,145	30.8	27.5	26.7	16.0	23.8	11.0	14.1	14.6	14.8	15.0	17.6	12.5	3.3
Asian	1,735	24.8	17.3	22.4	10.5	23.6	8.1	8.9	13.2	13.7	10.5	17.7	21.3	1.1
Hispanic or Latino ethnicity	4,364	28.3	16.7	25.4	14.1	25.3	5.8	10.7	10.6	8.4	9.5	18.6	17.4	2.2
Educational attainment[2]														
Less than a high school diploma	2,793	16.6	16.6	29.1	12.9	22.0	3.8	10.2	7.1	6.5	8.7	23.6	19.1	1.9
High school graduate, no college[3]	12,882	23.0	20.4	29.4	15.4	28.6	7.0	13.2	12.1	14.4	9.4	21.6	16.2	1.3
Less than a bachelor's degree[4]	15,966	27.8	22.9	26.1	16.5	29.9	8.8	14.9	14.1	18.5	11.8	23.1	17.0	1.6
College graduates	23,481	31.8	24.1	22.0	14.3	30.8	9.6	12.6	14.5	27.7	11.9	19.0	14.6	1.8
Marital status														
Single, never married	13,670	29.5	19.4	21.2	13.6	24.9	8.6	8.4	11.8	11.4	15.3	23.6	16.9	2.5
Married, spouse present	40,486	30.0	22.9	25.4	15.4	30.8	8.6	14.2	13.4	22.5	11.3	22.0	15.0	1.5
Other marital status[5]	9,635	21.3	22.3	27.6	16.1	26.3	7.4	11.7	13.6	15.9	10.7	18.4	19.0	1.4

Percent distribution of volunteer activities for main organization[1]

TABLE 1.15

Volunteer activities, by selected characteristics, September 2003 [CONTINUED]

Percent distribution of volunteer activities for main organization[1]

Characteristics in September 2003	Total volunteers (thousands)	Coach, referee, tutor, or teacher	Provide information; be an usher, greeter, or minister	Collect, prepare, distribute, or serve food	Collect, make or distribute clothing, crafts, or goods, other than food	Fundraise or sell items to raise money	Provide counseling, medical care, fire/ EMS or protective services	Supply transpor-tation for people	Provide general office services	Provide professional or management assistance including serving on a board or committee	Engage in music perform-ance, or other artistic activities	Engage in general labor	Other	Not reporting type of activities
Presence of own children under 18 years[6]														
Men:														
No own children under 18 years old	16,969	24.0	23.2	19.6	10.4	24.3	9.6	11.4	10.3	21.7	10.8	27.1	16.7	2.0
With own children under 18 years old	9,836	42.9	21.4	18.5	9.7	28.0	9.6	16.7	9.0	21.6	9.8	26.4	12.3	1.7
Women:														
No own children under 18 years old	21,938	22.0	23.7	28.2	18.0	27.1	8.5	9.6	15.5	17.8	12.9	17.8	16.7	1.7
With own children under 18 years old	15,049	34.1	18.8	30.1	19.8	37.2	6.1	15.7	15.2	16.6	13.8	18.5	16.8	1.5
Employment status														
Civilian labor force	45,499	31.0	22.4	23.7	14.2	30.3	9.1	13.2	12.4	20.3	12.1	22.5	15.3	1.6
Employed	43,138	31.0	22.5	23.5	14.1	30.7	9.2	13.4	12.3	20.7	12.0	22.5	15.2	1.7
Full time[7]	33,599	30.6	22.6	22.8	13.4	31.2	9.4	13.3	11.7	21.9	11.1	22.7	14.9	1.7
Part time[8]	9,539	32.3	22.5	25.8	16.6	29.0	8.6	13.6	14.7	16.8	15.2	21.9	16.2	1.5
Unemployed	2,361	31.4	20.5	26.2	15.1	23.1	7.0	10.6	13.3	12.6	13.8	22.9	16.9	1.4
Not in the labor force	18,293	22.5	21.0	27.8	17.6	25.2	6.7	11.0	14.7	16.2	12.0	19.8	17.9	1.9

[1]Main organization is defined as the organization for which the volunteer worked the most hours during the year.
[2]Data refer to persons 25 years and over.
[3]Includes high school diploma or equivalent.
[4]Includes the categories, some college, no degree; and associate degree.
[5]Includes divorced, separated, and widowed persons.
[6]Own children include sons, daughters, stepchildren, and adopted children. Not included are nieces, nephews, grandchildren, and other related and unrelated children.
[7]Usually work 35 hours or more a week at all jobs.
[8]Usually work less than 35 hours a week at all jobs.
Note: Data on volunteers relate to persons who performed unpaid volunteer activities for an organization at any point from September 1, 2002, through the survey period in September 2003. Estimates for the above race groups (white, black or African-American, and Asian) do not sum to totals because data are not presented for all races. In addition, persons whose ethnicity is identified as Hispanic or Latino may be of any race and, therefore, are classified by ethnicity as well as by race. Detail will sum to greater than 100 percent because respondents could choose more than one activity.

SOURCE: "Table 5. Volunteer Activities for Main Organization for Which Activities Were Performed and Selected Characteristics, September 2003," in *Volunteering in the United States, 2003*, United States Department of Labor, Bureau of Labor Statistics, December 17, 2003, http://stats.bls.gov/news.release/ archives/volun_12172003.pdf (accessed September 10, 2004)

CHAPTER 2
THE COST OF HAVING FUN

CONSUMER EXPENDITURES FOR RECREATION

Americans are always finding new ways to spend their free time and money. In good economic times, people generally have more discretionary income to spend on leisure and recreation. The U.S. Bureau of Labor Statistics reported in *Consumer Expenditures in 2002* that in 2002 Americans spent an average of $2,079 on entertainment, slightly more than the $1,953 that was spent in 2001. (See Table 2.1.) The study further noted that persons aged thirty-five to forty-four spent the most on entertainment ($2,685), and those over seventy-five spent the least ($896).

Research by the Bureau of Economic Analysis (BEA), a division of the U.S. Department of Commerce, showed that consumers steadily increased their total spending on entertainment from 1998 through 2002. According to the BEA's *National Income and Product Accounts Tables,* in 2002 Americans spent a total of $628.3 billion on recreation, up from $604 billion in 2001. Almost one-fifth of those dollars ($119.1 billion) was spent on video and audio goods. Toys and sports supplies accounted for $59 billion. According to the BEA, Americans spent $34.6 billion in 2002 to see such spectator amusements as performing arts, movies, and spectator sports, up from $26.2 million five years earlier. (See Table 2.2.)

Although total expenditures for various forms of entertainment increased from 1998 to 2002, most goods and services experienced incremental or gradual growth. Examples of goods and activities that sustained modest increases were books and maps, gardening supplies (flowers, seeds, and potted pants), admissions to spectator amusements, and clubs and fraternal organizations. (See Table 2.2.)

CONSUMER ELECTRONICS

The explosion of digital technology has changed the consumer electronics industry, making possible a wide array of new products and blurring the difference between information management and entertainment equipment. According to the Consumer Electronics Association (CEA), an industry advocacy group comprising more than 1,700 member companies, the wholesale value of electronics products sold to Americans was an estimated $96.4 billion in 2003, an increase of 2.3% over the 2002 figure, $94.2 billion. Sales growth was expected to continue, with a projected 5% rise in 2004 to $101 billion. (See Table 2.3.)

Spending on Computers Levels Off

After a period of dramatic increases in spending on computer products, this category was showing signs of leveling off. In 1998, $37 billion was spent on computers, peripherals, and software; two years later Americans spent $43.8 billion on such goods, but then this amount dropped to $42 billion in 2001 and increased by a modest 5% in 2002 to $44.2 billion. (See Table 2.2.)

One major change in the way Americans spent their money on computers was the rise in sales of notebook, or laptop, models. The NPD Group, a private market research firm, reported that in May 2003 the total dollar value of notebook computer sales exceeded that of desktop computers for the first time, accounting for 54% of the month's $500 million in retail computer sales. Just three years earlier, in January 2000, notebooks had accounted for just 25% of sales. At the same time, sales of flat-panel liquid crystal diode (LCD) monitors also topped sales of conventional cathode ray tube (CRT) monitors for the first time. These trends were expected to continue over time.

America Goes Digital

According to the CEA, digital products were finding increasing favor with consumers, especially devices that recorded video, images, or music. Blank media and accessories constituted the fastest-growing category during 2003, as manufacturers shipped recordable CDs and

TABLE 2.1

Annual expenditures of all consumer units and percent changes, consumer expenditure survey, 2000–02

				Percent change	
Item	2000	2001	2002	2000–2001	2001–2002
Number of consumer units (000's)	109,367	110,339	112,108		
Income before taxes*	$44,649	$47,507	$49,430		
Average age of reference person	48.2	48.1	48.1		
Average number in consumer unit:					
Persons	2.5	2.5	2.5		
Earners	1.4	1.4	1.4		
Vehicles	1.9	1.9	2.0		
Percent homeowner	66	66	66		
Average annual expenditures	$38,045	$39,518	$40,677	3.9	2.9
Food	5,158	5,321	5,375	3.2	1.0
At home	3,021	3,086	3,099	2.2	.4
Away from home	2,137	2,235	2,276	4.6	1.8
Housing	12,319	13,011	13,283	5.6	2.1
Apparel and services	1,856	1,743	1,749	-6.1	.3
Transportation	7,417	7,633	7,759	2.9	1.7
Health care	2,066	2,182	2,350	5.6	7.7
Entertainment	1,863	1,953	2,079	4.8	6.5
Personal insurance and pensions	3,365	3,737	3,899	11.1	4.3
Other expenditures	4,001	3,939	4,182	-1.5	6.2

*Income values are derived from "complete income reporters" only

SOURCE: "Annual Expenditures of All Consumer Units and Percent Changes, Consumer Expenditure Survey, 2000–2002," in *Consumer Expenditures in 2002,* U.S. Bureau of Labor Statistics, 2003, http://www.bls.gov/news.release/pdf/cesan.pdf (accessed September 10, 2004)

TABLE 2.2

Personal consumption expenditures on recreation, 1998–2002

(In billions of dollars)

	1998	1999	2000	2001	2002
Recreation	**505.8**	**546.1**	**585.7**	**604**	**628.3**
Books and maps (d.)	28.8	31.5	33.7	34.6	36.9
Magazines, newspapers, and sheet music (n.d.)	32.1	33.5	35	35	35.3
Nondurable toys and sport supplies (n.d.)	51.3	54.7	56.6	57.6	59
Wheel goods, sports and photographic equipment, boats, and pleasure aircraft (d.)	48.3	52.6	57.6	59.2	60.6
Video and audio goods, including musical instruments, and computer goods (d.)	99.7	108.1	116.6	115.5	119.1
Video and audio goods, including musical instruments (d.)					
Computers, peripherals, and software (d.)	37	40.4	43.8	42	44.2
Radio and television repair (s.)	4.1	4.1	4.2	4	4
Flowers, seeds, and potted plants (n.d.)	16.4	17.1	18	18	18
Admissions to specified spectator amusements	26.2	28.4	30.4	32.2	34.6
Motion picture theaters (s.)	7.2	7.9	8.6	9	9.6
Legitimate theaters and opera, and entertainments of nonprofit institutions (except athletics) (s.)	9.2	9.9	10.3	10.9	11.5
Spectator sports[1] (s.)	9.8	10.6	11.5	12.4	13.5
Clubs and fraternal organizations[2] (s.)	17.1	18	19	20	21.1
Commercial participant amusements[3] (s.)	63.1	68.8	75.8	79.6	83.5
Pari-mutuel net receipts (s.)	4.4	4.9	5	5.1	5.3
Other[4] (s.)	114.4	124.3	133.9	143.2	151.1

Note: Consumer durable goods are designated (d.), nondurable goods (n.d.), and services (s.).
[1]Consists of admissions to professional and amateur athletic events and to racetracks
[2]Consists of current expenditures (including consumption of fixed capital) of nonprofit clubs and fraternal organizations and dues and fees paid to proprietary clubs
[3]Consists of billiard parlors; bowling alleys; dancing, riding, shooting, skating, and swimming places; amusement devices and parks; golf courses; skiing facilities; marinas; sightseeing; private flying operations; casino gambling; recreational equipment rental; and other commercial participant amusements
[4]Consists of lotteries, pets and pet care services, cable TV, film processing, photographic studios, sporting and recreation camps, video rentals, Internet access fees, and recreational services not elsewhere classified

SOURCE: Adapted from "Personal Consumption Expenditures by Type of Expenditure," in *National Income and Product Accounts Tables,* U.S. Department of Commerce, Bureau of Economic Analysis, December 16, 2003, http://www.bea.doc.gov/bea/dn/nipaweb/TableView.asp?SelectedTable=73&FirstYear=1998&LastYear=2002&Freq=Year (accessed July 14, 2004)

TABLE 2.3

Total factory sales of consumer electronics, 1999–2002, estimated 2003, and projected 2004

(In millions of dollars)

	1999	2000	2001	2002	Estimated 2003	Projected 2004
Analog direct-view color TV	6,199	6,503	5,130	5,782	4,769	4,332
Analog projection TV	1,632	1,481	1,060	733	315	144
Monochrome TV	20	15	15	12	9	5
Digital direct-view and projection TV	295	1,355	2,485	3,574	4,009	4,690
LCD TV	61	107	101	246	651	1,049
Plasma TV	116	515	1,457	2,226		
TV combinations	1,014	968	790	993	718	763
Videocassette players	15	14	5	4	2	2
VCR decks	2,333	1,869	1,058	826	374	273
Camcorders	2,448	2,838	2,236	2,361	2,105	1,959
Direct to home satellite systems	957	790	1,175	1,116	1,380	1,278
Personal video recorders	46	77	144	57	193	251
Separate component DVD players	1,099	1,717	2,097	2,427	3,050	2,859
Set-top Internet access devices	145	193	195	119	63	47
Total	**16,264**	**17,926**	**16,607**	**18,766**	**19,095**	**19,878**
Home & portable audio products						
Rack audio systems	148	84	42	17	9	4
Compact audio systems	1,695	1,776	1,357	965	656	538
Separate audio components	1,530	1,545	1,261	1,202	960	867
Home theater-in-a-box	229	331	794	896	860	932
Portable equipment	1,987	2,156	1,846	1,526	1,289	1,162
Portable MP3 players	100	80	100	205	556	706
Home radios	348	351	326	300	289	245
Total	**6,036**	**6,323**	**5,726**	**5,111**	**4,619**	**4,454**
Mobile electronics						
Aftermarket autosound	2,070	2,169	2,098	2,211	1,904	1,882
Mobile video & navigation	273	293	429	422	517	
Wireless telephones	6,066	8,995	8,651	8,106	9,163	11,504
PDAs	875	1,265	1,077	875	759	657
Family radio services	306	418	461	251	235	201
Pagers	660	750	790	810	729	675
Aftermarket vehicle security	205	218	266	265	260	255
Radar detectors	165	170	170	134	123	120
Factory installed autosound	2,610	2,700	2,850	2,950	3,245	3,569
Total	**12,957**	**16,958**	**16,656**	**16,032**	**16,840**	**19,379**
Home information products						
Cordless telephones	1,808	1,562	1,960	1,261	1,139	976
Corded telephones	483	386	294	266	251	223
Telephone answering devices	1,044	984	1,062	1,060	1,181	1,148
Caller ID devices	64	54	35	20	11	8
Fax machines	455	386	349	297	242	160
Personal word processors	240	240	97	36	13	6
Personal computers	16,390	16,400	12,960	11,523	12,458	13,093
Computer printers	4,500	5,116	5,245	4,829	4,196	3,799
Aftermarket computer monitors	1,505	1,908	2,173	1,670	1,497	1,492
Modems/fax modems	1,460	1,564	1,564	1,445	1,419	1,386
Digital cameras	1,207	1,825	1,972	2,794	3,421	4,184
Other computer peripherals	1,440	1,950	2,150	2,256	2,425	2,563
Computer software	3,930	4,480	5,062	4,961	5,060	5,162
Total	**34,525**	**36,854**	**34,924**	**32,419**	**33,312**	**34,200**
Blank media						
Blank audio cassettes	208	162	129	98	87	70
Blank video cassettes	590	351	357	602	569	507
Blank computer media	900	1,200	1,550	1,600	1,800	2,025
Total	**1,698**	**1,713**	**2,036**	**2,300**	**2,456**	**2,602**
Accessories & batteries						
Electronic accessories	1,398	1,356	1,378	1,500	1,635	1,782
Batteries	3,620	4,943	4,590	4,960	5,406	5,730
Total	**5,018**	**6,299**	**5,968**	**6,460**	**7,041**	**7,512**
Electronic gaming						
Electronic gaming hardware	2,250	2,700	3,250	3,750	3,188	2,709
Electronic gaming software	5,100	5,850	6,725	7,375	7,744	8,131
Total	**7,350**	**8,550**	**9,975**	**11,125**	**10,932**	**10,840**
Home security	1,660	1,750	1,820	1,965	2,055	2,123
Grand total	**85,507**	**96,373**	**93,711**	**94,177**	**96,350**	**100,988**

SOURCE: "Total Factory Sales of Consumer Electronics," in *U.S. Consumer Electronics Sales & Forecasts, 1999–2004*, Consumer Electronics Association, 2004

FIGURE 2.1

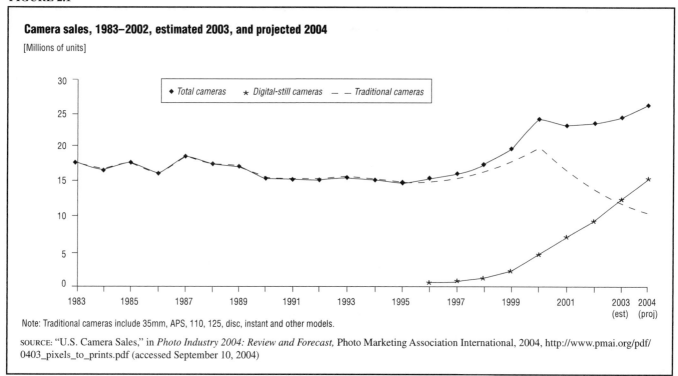

Camera sales, 1983–2002, estimated 2003, and projected 2004

[Millions of units]

Note: Traditional cameras include 35mm, APS, 110, 125, disc, instant and other models.

SOURCE: "U.S. Camera Sales," in *Photo Industry 2004: Review and Forecast,* Photo Marketing Association International, 2004, http://www.pmai.org/pdf/0403_pixels_to_prints.pdf (accessed September 10, 2004)

DVDs, batteries, and other accessories with a wholesale value of $9.5 billion, up about 8% from $8.8 billion in 2002. Other growth categories included mobile electronics, up 5% from $16 billion in 2002 to $16.8 billion in 2003; home security products, up 4.6% to nearly $2.1 billion; home information products, up 2.8% to $33.3 billion; and video hardware, up 1.8% to $19.1 billion. Sales of electronic gaming declined 1.7% to $10.9 billion, and home audio fell 9.6% to $4.6 billion. (See Table 2.3.)

Making projections for 2004, the CEA anticipated demand for cellular telephones, onboard navigation systems, and car audio systems to boost sales of the mobile electronics category by more than 15% to $19.4 billion, and forecast blank media sales to grow by 6.5% to $2.6 billion, while video equipment sales were expected to increase 4.2% to $19.9 billion. (See Table 2.3.)

Video Equipment and Cameras

Sales of new flat-screen, high-definition televisions were growing as prices came down and more digital and high-definition television channels were made available. According to a survey conducted by the NPD Group in March 2004, 6% of televisions sold during that month were flat-screen LCD models and 1% were the plasma type, while 9% were projection televisions. With the cost of such equipment still considerably higher than that of conventional analog models, the market penetration of such equipment rose sharply with income. In households earning less than $50,000 per year, 6% reported having projection equipment and less than 1% plasma, while in households with income greater than $100,000, 19% claimed ownership of projection TVs and 4.3% had plasma sets.

In several video and imaging device categories, the sales growth of new digital products far outstripped that of their analog predecessors. Digital videodisc (DVD) player sales continued to grow rapidly, while sales of analog videocassette recorders (VCRs) fell sharply. Another popular new device was the digital camera, which allowed instant viewing of photographs and gave users the option of either printing or e-mailing copies. In addition to offering improvements or new capabilities in imaging, the new technology also permitted the devices to be smaller, sleeker, lighter, and more portable.

In 2003, according to the Photo Marketing Association International report *Photo Industry 2004: Review and Forecast,* sales of digital cameras topped those of film cameras for the first time. During the year Americans bought an estimated 12.5 million digital cameras versus 12.1 million film models. For 2004 the organization projected sales of 15.7 million digital cameras versus just 10.6 million film cameras. (See Figure 2.1.) Sixteen percent of digital cameras bought in 2002 were purchased as replacements for film cameras, and half of consumers surveyed reported that they would buy a digital camera as a replacement for their film camera if it were to break.

According to *Photo Industry 2004: Review and Forecast,* one-time-use film cameras continued to be the industry's best seller, hitting an estimated 211 million units sold in 2003, up from 162 million in 2000 and just fifty-four million in 1995. (See Figure 2.2.) The total number of rolls of film purchased during the year was dropping, however, to an estimated 816 million in 2003 from 888 million in 2002, which included single-use cam-

FIGURE 2.2

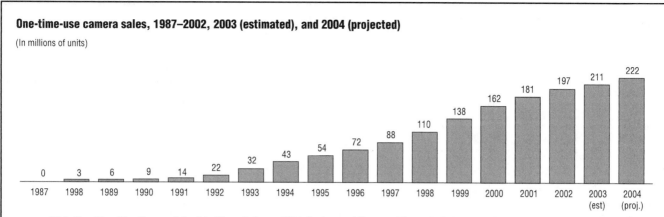

One-time-use camera sales, 1987–2002, 2003 (estimated), and 2004 (projected)

(In millions of units)

SOURCE: "U.S. One-Time-Use Camera Sales," in *Photo Industry 2004: Review and Forecast,* Photo Marketing Association International, 2004, http://www .pmai.org/pdf/0403_pixels_to_prints.pdf (accessed September 12, 2004)

FIGURE 2.3

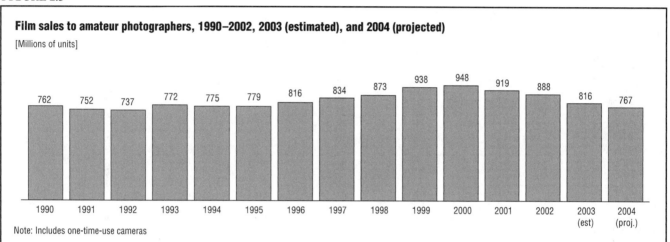

Film sales to amateur photographers, 1990–2002, 2003 (estimated), and 2004 (projected)

[Millions of units]

Note: Includes one-time-use cameras

SOURCE: "U.S. Amateur Film Sales," in *Photo Industry 2004: Review and Forecast,* Photo Marketing Association International, 2004, http://www.pmai.org/ pdf/0403_pixels_to_prints.pdf (accessed September 12, 2004)

era sales. (See Figure 2.3.) At the end of 2003, 31% of U.S. households owned digital cameras, and this was expected to increase to 42% by the end of 2004.

Telephone surveys conducted by the CEA and published in *U.S. Consumer Electronics Sales & Forecasts, 1999–2004,* found that U.S. households have growing numbers of video products of all kinds. In 2004, 98% of homes had color televisions and more than two-thirds had a TV with stereo sound. Fifteen percent of American households had DVD players at the beginning of 2001, but by January 2004 fully half did. Direct-to-home satellite systems also grew in popularity—in January 2001, 16% of homes had one, but by January 2004, 24% of households had them. In 2004, 54% of Americans had camcorders, up from 39% three years earlier. (See Table 2.4.)

Audio

At the same time that video equipment sales were increasing, sales of audio products were falling. Accord-

ing to the CEA in *U.S. Consumer Electronics Sales & Forecasts, 1999–2004,* from 2002 to 2003 sales of portable audio equipment dropped from $1.5 billion to $1.3 billion in wholesale dollars, sales of separate audio components fell from $1.2 billion to $960 million, and compact audio system sales dropped from $965 million to $656 million. Home theater-in-a-box systems held relatively steady, slipping from $896 million to $860 million, while the one bright spot was sales of MP3 players, which can store hundreds of songs digitally in a unit smaller than the size of a pack of cigarettes. Sales in this category increased from $205 million in 2002 to $556 million in 2003, and the CEA projected they would rise further in 2004, to $706 million. (See Table 2.3.)

Although wholesale revenues were falling, the CEA found that between January 2001 and January 2004 the number of American households with audio products increased. During this period the number of homes with personal portable compact disc players grew from 28% to

TABLE 2.4

Household penetration of consumer electronics products, January 2001–January 2004

(By percent)

	January 2001	June 2001	January 2002	June 2002	January 2003	June 2003	January 2004
All television	98	98	98	98	98	98	98
Color TV	98	98	98	98	98	98	98
DTV	1	1	2	3	4	5	8
VCR decks	94	94	94	94	92	89	87
Monochrome TV	41	40	40	39	39	38	37
Color TV with stereo	69	70	70	70	70	71	71
Camcorder	39	40	42	46	49	52	54
Projection TV	15	15	15	16	18	18	19
All LCD TV	12	12	12	13	13	14	14
TV/VCR combinations	21	22	22	22	23	25	25
DVD player	15	21	25	29	35	41	50
Direct-to-home satellite	16	16	18	20	21	22	24
Mobile electronics							
Electronic car alarm	30	31	31	31	31	31	31
Wireless telephones	59	63	64	66	68	69	70
Pager	21	20	19	18	17	17	17
Car CD player	30	35	40	45	52	54	54
Home office products							
Corded phone	96	96	96	96	96	96	96
All CD including CD-ROM	75	76	77	78	78	79	80
Telephone answering device	77	77	78	78	78	78	78
Cordless phone	81	81	81	81	81	81	81
Personal computers	58	59	60	61	62	64	66
Computer printers	54	56	57	57	58	61	64
Computer with CD-ROM	57	59	60	60	61	62	62
Digital camera	18	20	22	25	28	31	33
Multi-line phone	23	23	23	24	25	25	25
Modem or fax/modem	55	55	58	59	60	62	64
Home fax machines	12	12	12	12	12	11	11
Caller ID equipment	27	28	29	30	31	32	32
Audio products							
Home radios	98	98	98	98	98	98	98
MP3 players	2	3	4	7	8	10	13
Home CD players	57	57	57	57	57	57	57
Rack or compact audio system	43	43	43	43	42	41	40
CD boombox	40	42	44	47	52	57	61
Personal portable CD player	28	30	33	36	40	46	52
Home theater system	23	24	25	27	28	30	32

SOURCE: "U.S. Household Penetration of Consumer Electronics Products," in *U.S. Consumer Electronics Sales & Forecasts, 1999–2004,* Consumer Electronics Association, 2004

52%, and those with home theater audio systems jumped from 23% to 32%. Personal MP3 players such as the Apple iPod increased in penetration over the three years as well, from 2% of homes to 13%. (See Table 2.4.)

Video Games

After a peak sales year of $11.1 billion (wholesale) in 2002, video game sales dropped in 2003 to $10.9 billion and were projected to fall slightly again during 2004 to $10.8 billion, according to the CEA. (See Table 2.3.) A study of retail purchases by the marketing information company NPD Group, found that consumers spent $11.2 billion at retail on video games and equipment in 2003, representing a drop of 4% over 2002's record $11.7 billion. A 27% decline in console hardware sales was a major factor in the decline, with growth occurring in other categories including console software, up 14%, portable game software, up 19%, and portable gaming hardware, which increased 54% to $750 million, up from $490 million in 2002.

SPORTING GOODS SALES

Sports Apparel

Many Americans devote part of their leisure time to pursuits related to personal health and fitness. Participants in physical fitness activities or in sports such as softball or skiing often purchase highly specialized apparel and equipment. According to the Sporting Goods Manufacturers Association (SGMA) in *Shoppers Bought More, Spent Less on Sports Apparel in 2003* (May 2004), retail sales of all sports apparel totaled $37 billion in 2003, down slightly from the $37.8 billion tallied in 2002. Sports apparel sales represented about 22% of the $166.1 billion Americans spent on apparel of all kinds during 2003. (See Table 2.5.)

Despite the decline in revenues, the total number of sports apparel items purchased in 2003 increased by 3%. This discrepancy was attributed to a 5% drop in prices, to an average of $8.35 per item. This amount was more than a dollar less than the average price for all apparel of

TABLE 2.5

Consumer spending for apparel, 2003

(Dollars in billions)

	Annual 2002	Annual 2003	Change 2002–03
All apparel	**$175.14**	**$166.14**	**-5.10%**
Total sports apparel	**37.789**	**37.009**	**-2.10%**
Men's	13.458	13.153	-2.30%
Women's	17.013	15.707	-7.70%
Children's	7.318	8.149	11.40%
Active sports apparel	**11.32**	**11.485**	**1.50%**
Men's	5.065	4.909	-3.10%
Women's	4.543	4.576	-0.70%
Children's	1.713	2.001	16.80%

Total sports apparel: Designed for, or that could be used in, active sports
Active sports apparel: Purchased with intent to use in an active sport

SOURCE: "Consumer Spending for Apparel," in *Shoppers Bought More, Spent Less on Sports Apparel in 2003,* SGMA International, May 12, 2004, http://www.sgma.com/press/2004/press1084472907-17845.html (accessed September 10, 2004). Data from Source: NPD Group/NPD Fashionworld consumer data estimates

$9.66. One-third of the total number of items purchased were T-shirts, with the rest consisting of such items as swimwear, outerwear, socks, underwear, hats, and polo, golf, and rugby shirts.

According to the SGMA report, less than a third of the sports apparel purchased was used in active play, accounting for just $11.5 billion of the $37 billion total. (See Table 2.5.) The average cost of these items was less than the $8.35 sports apparel average—just $6.45 each.

Athletic Footwear

In 2003, according to research performed by the NPD Group/NPD Fashionworld for the SGMA, retail sales of athletic footwear in the United States reached $16.4 billion, up 4.2% from 2002. Running shoes accounted for some 28% of the athletic footwear market, with sales of basketball shoes increasing by 6.2%, almost triple the 2.2% sales increase for all running shoes. As with athletic apparel, NPD/SGMA observed that less than half of athletic shoes were purchased primarily for use in sports or exercise. The total number of athletic shoes sold during the year was 448.3 million pairs, approximately three for every two Americans. Men's shoes accounted for 197 million pairs, women's 126.5 million, and children's shoes 124.8 million. The average price per pair was $36.48, a figure that was 9% lower than the 1998 average of $40.07.

Sports Equipment

The SGMA reported in its *Recreation Market Report* (2004) that the wholesale value of sports equipment shipments rose slightly from 2002 ($17.4 billion) to 2003 ($17.5 billion). In 2003 the largest category was exercise equipment and machines ($3.8 billion), followed by golf equipment ($2.4 billion). Camping gear topped $1.7 bil-

lion, and firearms and hunting equipment wholesale shipments were worth $1.9 billion in 2003, while shipments of fishing gear slightly exceeded $1 billion. In team sports, the three largest categories during 2003 were baseball/softball ($473 million), basketball ($377 million), and soccer ($240 million). (See Table 2.6.)

Exercise Equipment

According to the SGMA, by 2000 adults in half of all American households owned at least one piece of exercise equipment, and it was used regularly in two out of three of them. Roughly equal numbers of men and women owned fitness equipment. Those twenty-five to thirty-four owned 24% of the equipment; those thirty-five to forty-four, 23%; fifty-five and over, 22%; forty-five to fifty-four, 18%; and eighteen to twenty-four, 13%. The most frequently owned equipment was free weights, followed by treadmills and stationary bikes.

Research conducted by the National Sporting Goods Association, a retail trade association, found that in 2001 more females (52%) than males (39%) purchased fitness equipment. Nearly one-third of purchases were made by consumers ages thirty-one to forty-four, 29% were made by persons ages forty-five to sixty-four, and 22% of exercise equipment purchases were made by adults ages twenty-five to thirty-four.

Industry observers attributed the strength of the exercise and fitness market to the growing number of older Americans who wanted to stay healthy and fit. This trend was expected to continue as an aging U.S. population, intent on lifetime fitness, drove the market.

Recreational Transport Expenses

In its *Recreation Market Report,* the SGMA announced that wholesale recreational transport sales, which included bicycles, pleasure boats/motors, recreational vehicles, and snowmobiles, totaled $18.5 billion in 2003. Sales of pleasure boats and motors grew from $9.4 billion in 2002 to $9.6 billion in 2003, while sales of personal watercraft, such as Kawasaki's Jet Ski brand, increased from $581 million to $597 million. Sales of other recreational vehicles (not including motor homes) increased from $5.6 billion in 2002 to $5.8 billion in 2003. (See Table 2.6.)

The National Marine Manufacturers Association (NMMA) estimated in *2003 Recreational Boating Abstract* that in 2003 seventy-two million Americans participated in recreational boating, up 6% from the sixty-eight million who participated in 2001. Americans owned about 1.6 million sailboats and approximately 2.5 million miscellaneous craft, such as canoes and rowboats. In 2003 the average cost of a sailboat was $40,077 and inboard cruisers averaged a hefty $372,830, while the typical personal watercraft cost $8,890 and a canoe just $573. (See

TABLE 2.6

SGMA International recreation market report, 2004

(Dollars in millions)

Item	2003	2002
Archery	$260	$250
Paintbal	390	370
Total baseball/softball	$473	$468
Bats	170	170
Gloves & mits	124	12
Baseballs	63	64
Batting gloves	36	38
Softballs	30	30
Protective/other	50	45
Total basketball	$377	$380
Basketballs/accessories	210	205
Backboards	167	175
Billiards	255	241
Bowling	200	225
Total camping	$1,720	$1,669
Coolers/cheast	269	266
Tents/shelters	275	243
Sleeping bags (exc. slumber)	151	173
Jugs/containers	80	80
Backpacks (exc. daypacks)	67	72
Other	878	835
Total exercise	$3,795	$3,775
Exercise—consumer	3,085	3,075
Treadmils	1,000	990
Home gyms	305	300
Exercise cycles	200	205
Free weights	180	175
Exercise benches	160	150
Abmachines	155	150
Ski machines	110	120
Eliptical machines	140	120
Aero gliders	80	110
Stair climbing machines	45	55
Other consumer	710	700
Exercise—institutional	710	700
Fire arms & hunting	$1,900	$1,900
Fishing	1,030	1,000
Footballs & sets	125	120
Total golf	$2,420	$2,383
Clubs	1,180	1,130
Balls	720	753
Ice skates & hockey	$215	$205
Inline rollerskates only	11	158
Inline accessories	35	50
Optical goods	600	575
Racquetball	18	20
Skateboards	130	135
Scuba & skin diving	240	235
Snow skiing, alpine	277	283
Snowskiing, x-country	35	38
Snowboards	50	45
Soccer	141	168
Table tennis	20	20
Total tennis	$210	$228
Racquets	90	100
Balls	70	78
Other	50	50
Volleyball (balls, sets)	60	63
Water sports — ski equip.	128	122
Other water sports equip.	322	306
Miscellaneous (e.g. lawn games, darts, indoor games, boxing, cricket, field hockey, gymnastics, handball, lacrosse, martial arts, paddle ball, polo, rugby, sleds, toboggans, track & field, squash)	260	250
Team/institutional (not listed above)	1,560	1,550
Total sports equipment	$17,546	$17,426
Sports apparel		
Active wear:		
Tops	$12,715	$13,275
Swimwear	1,960	2,000
Sweatshirts	1,265	1,265
Sweatpants/shorts	685	675
Outerwear	1,100	1,065
Shorts	830	815
Socks	870	795
Pants/slacks	315	455
Caps/hats	380	410
Underwear/intimate	500	480
Sport/exercise bras	190	180
All other	1,510	1,445
Total active wear	$22,320	$22,860
Team uniforms	505	530
Total sports apparel	$22,825	$23,390
Athletic footwear		
Running	$2,765	$2,710
Basketball	2,070	1,950
Cross–training/fitness	1,060	1,200
Walking	555	655
Low performance	640	535
Hiking	435	405
Tennis	450	385
Sport sandals	195	190
Recreational boots	170	160
Skate boarding	130	145
Aerobic	150	135
All other sport/athletic	1,105	865
Total athletic footwear	$9,725	$9,335
Total sporting goods equipment, sports apparel, & athletic footwear	$50,096	$50,151
Recreational transport		
Pleasure boats & motors	9,629	9,383
Recreational vehicles (except motor homes)	5,763	5,584
Bicycles & accessories	2,543	2,595
Personal water craft	597	581
Total recreational transport	$18,532	$18,143
Total sports equipment, sports apparel, athletic footwear, and recreational transport industries	$68,628	$68,294

SOURCE: "SGMA Recreation Market Report–2004 Edition," in *Recreation Market Report*, SGMA International, 2004, http://www.sgma.com/reports/2004/report1088435204-26671.html (accessed September 10, 2004)

TABLE 2.7

Number and value of boats sold, 1997–2003

	1997	1998	1999	2000	2001	2002	2003
Outboard boats:							
Total units sold	200,000	213,700	230,200	241,200	217,800	212,000	**207,100**
Retail value	$1,421,400,000	$1,547,188,000	$1,988,928,000	$2,306,577,000	$2,195,859,600	$2,280,908,000	**$2,742,825,960**
Average unit cost	$7,107	$7,240	$8,640	$9,563	$10,082	$10,759	**$13,244**
Outboard motors:							
Total units sold	302,000	314,000	331,900	348,700	299,100	302,100	**305,400**
Retail value	$2,006,186,000	$2,155,610,000	$2,602,096,000	$2,901,881,400	$2,411,045,100	$2,478,838,900	**$2,554,533,570**
Average unit cost	$6,643	$6,865	$7,840	$8,322	$8,061	$8,205	**$8,365**
Boat trailers:							
Total units sold	181,000	174,000	168,000	158,500	135,900	141,200	**130,600**
Retail value	$190,050,000	$189,660,000	$190,008,000	$184,494,000	$181,698,300	$200,645,200	**$202,012,080**
Average unit cost	$1,050	$1,090	$1,131	$1,164	$1,337	$1,421	**$1,547**
Inboard boats-ski/wakeboard boats:							
Total units sold	6,100	10,900	12,100	13,600	11,100	10,500	**11,100**
Retail value	$136,408,200	$253,348,700	$308,429,000	$366,438,400	$352,569,300	$398,811,000	**$403,289,640**
Average unit cost	$22,362	$23,243	$25,490	$26,944	$31,763	$37,982	**$36,332**
Inboard boats-cruisers:							
Total units sold	6,300	6,700	7,000	10,300	10,800	11,800	**9,300**
Retail value	$1,669,103,100	$1,704,245,500	$1,799,420,000	$2,925,756,200	$3,758,475,600	$4,336,559,000	**$3,467,322,720**
Average unit cost	$264,937	$254,365	$257,060	$284,054	$348,007	$367,505	**$372,830**
Sterndrive boats:							
Total units sold	92,000	77,700	79,600	78,400	72,000	69,300	**69,200**
Retail value	$2,068,528,000	$1,746,696,000	$2,054,476,000	$2,253,843,200	$2,216,448,000	$2,192,929,200	**$2,221,116,840**
Average unit cost	$22,484	$22,480	$25,810	$28,748	$30,784	$31,644	**$32,097**
Canoes:							
Total units sold	103,600	107,800	121,000	111,800	105,800	100,000	**86,700**
Retail value	$61,124,000	$64,033,200	$67,034,000	$64,508,600	$57,449,400	$56,900,000	**$49,644,420**
Average unit cost	$590	$594	$554	$577	$543	$569	**$573**
Kayaks:							
Total units sold	N/A	N/A	N/A	N/A	$357,100	340,300	**324,000**
Retail value	N/A	N/A	N/A	N/A	$176,764,500	$157,558,900	**$151,048,800**
Average unit cost	N/A	N/A	N/A	N/A	$495	$463	**$466**
Inflatables:							
Total units sold	N/A	N/A	N/A	N/A	N/A	N/A	**30,500**
Retail value	N/A	N/A	N/A	N/A	N/A	N/A	**$67,417,200**
Average unit cost	N/A	N/A	N/A	N/A	N/A	N/A	**$2,210**
Personal water craft:							
Total units sold	176,000	130,000	106,000	92,000	80,900	79,300	**80,600**
Retail value	$1,135,904,000	$868,530,000	$771,044,000	$720,176,000	$641,456,100	$697,681,400	**$716,501,760**
Average unit cost	$6,454	$6,681	$7,274	$7,828	$7,929	$8,798	**$8,890**
Jet boats:							
Total units sold	11,700	10,100	7,800	7,000	6,200	5,100	**5,600**
Retail value	$144,389,700	$167,033,800	$132,678,000	$123,641,000	$118,692,800	$107,997,600	**$115,268,160**
Average unit cost	$12,341	$16,538	$17,010	$17,663	$19,144	$21,176	**$20,584**
Sailboats:*							
Total units sold	14,400	18,400	21,600	22,600	20,600	17,700	**16,700**
Retail value	N/A	N/A	N/A	$754,252,400	$706,139,303	$669,290,100	**$669,290,100**
Average unit cost	N/A	N/A	N/A	$33,374	$34,279	$37,813	**$40,077**

*Data from the Sailing Company's Annual Sailing Business Review

SOURCE: "Table 2.1. The Retail Boating Market 1997 to 2003 Total Units Sold, Total Retail Value, and Average Retail Unit Cost," in *2003 Recreational Boating Abstract,* National Marine Manufacturers Association, 2004, http://www.nmma.org/facts/boatingstats/2003/files/Abstract.pdf (accessed September 10, 2004)

Table 2.7.) The NMMA estimated that Americans spent more than $25.6 billion on retail expenditures for boating in 2003, up from $19.3 billion in 1997.

TRAVEL COSTS

Travel and tourism is the largest services export industry in the United States. It is also the third largest retail sales category and one of America's largest employers. An estimated 7.2 million U.S. residents worked in the travel and tourism industry in 2002, resulting in $157 billion in payroll. The Travel Industry Association of America (TIA) calculated that one out of every eighteen people in the U.S. civilian labor force was employed as a result of direct travel spending in the United States.

Although the travel industry suffered significant losses following the events of September 11, 2001, which came on the heels of an economic downturn, the TIA projected that domestic and international travelers would spend an estimated $552 billion in 2003, up from $537.2 billion in 2002. International travel accounted for $65.1 billion, and international visitors spent an estimated $80.7 billion traveling in the United

States during the year, including $15.6 billion in travel fares alone.

The TIA reported that travel-related purchases made via the Internet rose dramatically during the early years of the twenty-first century. In 2003 an estimated 64.1 million people used the Internet to check prices or schedules or to find other information about travel destinations. More than two-thirds of these, or 42.2 million, booked some portion of their travel package online, with 29% of that number doing all their travel booking on the Web, up from 23% the year before. The average amount spent by online travel bookers was $2,600, up more than 10% from the $2,300 average spent in 2002. The TIA further reported that 75% of online travel planners had purchased airline tickets via the Internet in 2003; that same year 71% had booked accommodations online, and 43% had ordered rental cars. Other purchases made online included tickets to cultural events and complete travel packages.

The TIA predicted that tourism would continue to grow. By 2005 total domestic person trips were expected to top 1.2 million, and nearly forty-five million international travelers were expected to visit the United States. Travel price inflation was expected to increase 2.2%, mainly because of higher hotel rates and gasoline prices.

AMUSEMENT PARK EXPENDITURES

Americans have always enjoyed such amusement parks and attractions as Busch Gardens, Disneyland, and Six Flags. Big amusement parks and theme parks featuring children's rides, roller coasters, and water slides have existed in the United States since the early years of the twentieth century. According to the International Association of Amusement Parks and Attractions, in 2003 the approximately six hundred parks and attractions in the United States had 322 million visitors and took in revenues of $10.3 billion, up from 317 million visitors and $9.6 billion in revenues in 2000.

SPENDING ON TOYS AND CRAFTS

Buying and playing with toys is a popular activity in the United States. In the past, the toy industry considered children from birth to age fourteen as its prime audience. Today, the prime toy-purchasing years are birth to ten years of age.

While some toys may sell very well one year and then disappear the next, other toys sell consistently from year to year. These enduringly popular best-sellers are the basis of the toy business and include games (such as Monopoly and Scrabble) and preschool and infant toys such as plush stuffed animals and trains.

The United States is the largest market for toys in the world, followed by western Europe, Asia, and Japan. U.S. toy sales in 2003 declined to $30.7 billion from $31.6 bil-

TABLE 2.8

Toy industry sales, 2002–03

Supercategory	Annual 2002	Annual 2003	Percent change
Action figures and accessories	$1.4B	$1.2B	−14.6
Arts and crafts	$2.3B	$2.4B	5.1
Building sets	$766M	$625M	−18.4
Dolls	$2.7B	$2.8B	3.5
Games/puzzles	$2.2B	$2.4B	10.8
Infant/preschool	$2.9B	$2.6B	−11.7
Learning and exploration	$473M	$477M	0.9
Outdoor and sports toys	$2.5B	$2.4B	−5.3
Plush	$1.5B	$1.4B	−5.5
Vehicles	$2.2B	$2.0B	−11.1
All other toys	$2.4B	$2.5B	2.8
Total traditional toy industry	**$21.3B**	**$20.7B**	**−2.9**
Video games	$10.3B	$10.0B	−2.8

Note: There may be variances due to rounding.

SOURCE: The NPD Group/NPD Funworld/Consumer Panel, *2003 vs. 2002 State of the Industry,* Toy Industry Association, Inc., http://www.toy-tia.org/ Content/NavigationMenu/Press_Room/Statistics3/State_of_the_Industry/ State_of_the_Industry.htm (accessed July 10, 2004)

lion in 2002. In 2003 the leading category in toy sales, as reported by the Toy Industry Association, was video games ($10 billion). Other strong sellers were dolls/accessories ($2.8 billion), infant/preschool toys ($2.6 billion), arts and crafts for children ($2.4 billion), games/puzzles ($2.4 billion), vehicles ($2 billion), plush stuffed toys ($1.4 billion), and action figures/accessories ($1.2 billion). (See Table 2.8.)

Spending on crafts and hobbies grew to $29 billion in 2002, up from $25.7 billion in 2001, according to the Hobby Industry Association (www.hobby.org). Needlecrafts, painting and finishing supplies, floral crafts, and general crafts all experienced increased sales. According to statistics presented on the Hobby Industry Association Web site, more than 80% of households have "at least one family member engaged in crafts/hobbies," and the average crafter spends about 7.5 hours per week on his or her hobby.

SPENDING ON BOOKS

According to the Book Industry Study Group (BISG), consumers spent about $37.9 billion to purchase books in 2003, a figure that was projected to rise 2.9% to $39 billion in 2004. Of this total, retail sales of adult trade books accounted for an estimated $8.4 billion in 2003, which would rise to $8.5 billion in 2004, while juvenile trade book sales of $3.4 billion in 2003 were expected to increase to $3.7 billion in 2004. According to the American Booksellers Association, the average retail price of a new hardcover book was declining, hitting $22.75 in 2003, down from $23.73 in 1998. In addition to buying books, many people also borrowed them from libraries, purchased used copies, and shared, loaned, or passed books on to friends or family.

Reflecting the gradual decline in reading that was found by a Harris poll conducted in late 2003, the market research firm Ipsos-Insight reported in 2003 that book sales figures had remained relatively stagnant during the preceding five years. Among the group that historically purchased the most books, households earning $50,000 per year or more, sales had in fact declined. This was true despite the expansion of such chains as Barnes & Noble and Borders and the emergence of such Internet "e-tailers" as Amazon.com.

Ipsos-Insight found that 22.5% of book purchases in 2002 were made at large bookstore chains, while book clubs accounted for 19.2%, independent stores and small chains 15.5%, warehouse clubs 6.8%, mass merchandisers 5.5%, used bookstores 4.8%, and the rest divided among variety stores, supermarkets, drugstores, and other types of retail outlets. Internet sales, nonexistent in 1995, continued to grow steadily, up from 7.1% in 2000 to 8.1% in 2002.

The U.S. publishing industry as a whole saw wholesale revenues of $23.4 billion in 2003, as estimated by the Association of American Publishers in a press release dated March 31, 2004. Sales of trade books rose 1.2% from 2002, to $5.1 billion, while adult trade hardbound titles dropped 2.4% to $2.5 billion, and paperbound sales declined 0.6% to $1.5 billion. Sales of juvenile hardbound books increased 28.6%, to $698 million, while juvenile paperbacks dropped 5.2% to $448.6 million. Sales of book club titles fell 9%, to $1.3 billion, and mass-market paperbacks declined 1.7% to $1.2 billion. The biggest growth area was religious titles, which increased 50.2% to $1.3 billion.

Other major categories included elementary/high school educational books, which increased 2.5% to $4.3 billion; higher education titles, which rose 3.6% to $3.4 billion; professional and scholarly books, which grew by 3.6% to $4 billion; and standardized tests, which increased 12.4% to $592 million.

SPENDING ON COMPACT DISCS AND DVDS

In 2003 Americans spent more on digital videodiscs (DVDs) than they did on compact discs (CDs) for the first time ever. According to the "2003 Consumer Profile" released by the Recording Industry Association of America, manufacturers shipped sound recordings with a retail value of $11.9 billion during the year, down from $12.6 billion in 2002 and $13.7 billion in 2001. (See Table 4.9 in Chapter 4.) The decline in sales was attributed to the impact of illegal Internet file-sharing, as well as the increasing competition for entertainment dollars that had led retailers, and some manufacturers, to reduce prices.

A consumer survey performed in 2004 by the NPD Group found that one-third of respondents cited price as an "important" or "very important" factor when deciding to buy a CD. The average price of CDs was in fact drop-ping, from $13.79 per disc in the first quarter of 2003 to $13.29 in the first quarter of 2004, according to NPD.

A growing number of music consumers were also downloading music online legally via such Web sites as Apple's iTunes and the relaunched Napster.com. By mid-2004 each offered more than 700,000 licensed songs, which were available from iTunes for ninety-nine cents each or from Napster via a $9.95 monthly subscription.

Purchases of DVDs, meanwhile, were growing dramatically, with retail sales in 2003 topping $12 billion, according to the Video Software Dealers Association. This was up $3.9 billion, or 46%, from 2002. An additional $4.3 billion was spent on DVD rentals, an increase of 53% over 2002. While many DVDs were rented from such chains as Blockbuster or Hollywood Video, growing numbers were obtained from online vendors such as Netflix and Wal-mart.com, which, for a monthly fee of approximately $20, allowed users to borrow an unlimited number of discs provided they kept no more than three at a time.

At the end of 2003 the average retail price of a DVD was $20.21, while the average video store rental cost just $3.20, according to the Video Software Dealers Association. Americans bought seventeen discs per DVD player during the year, a nearly threefold increase over the highest reported rate for video cassettes of six per player in 1996.

COSTS OF WILDLIFE-RELATED RECREATION

Many Americans enjoy participating in recreation that involves wildlife. Fishing and hunting are some of the most popular forms of recreation in the United States, and increasing numbers of people enjoy watching, photographing, and feeding wild animals and birds. According to the U.S. Fish and Wildlife Service, more than eighty-two million U.S. residents fished, hunted, and observed wildlife in 2001.

The U.S. Department of the Interior's *2001 National Survey of Fishing, Hunting, and Wildlife-Associated Recreation* found that in 2001 Americans spent more than $108 billion on wildlife-related recreation. Fishing accounted for approximately 32% of that expense, wildlife-watching activities accounted for 36%, and hunting for 19%. Another 13% was unspecified. (See Figure 2.4.) Of the expenditure by sportspersons, 59% was for equipment, 28% was trip-related, and 13% was for other items. (See Figure 2.5.)

Americans who enjoyed watching wildlife spent an estimated $38.4 billion in 2001. Of that amount, 63% was for equipment, 20% was trip related, and 17% was other (such as magazines, membership dues, and contributions to conservation or wildlife-related organizations). (See Figure 2.6.) Although the number of participants had declined somewhat, those who did participate spent more—on more expensive equipment—than previously.

FIGURE 2.4

Expenditures for wildlife-related recreation, 2001

Total expenditures: $108 billion

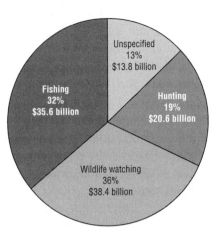

SOURCE: "Expenditures for Wildlife-Related Recreation," in *2001 National Survey of Fishing, Hunting, and Wildlife-Associated Recreation,* U.S. Department of the Interior, Fish and Wildlife Service, and U.S. Department of Commerce, 2002, http://www.census.gov/prod/2002pubs/FHW01.pdf (accessed September 10, 2004)

FIGURE 2.5

Expenditures related to hunting and fishing, 2001

Total expenditures: $70.0 billion

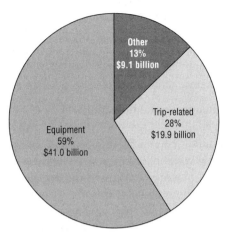

SOURCE: "Expenditures by Sportspersons," in *2001 National Survey of Fishing, Hunting, and Wildlife-Associated Recreation,* U.S. Department of the Interior, Fish and Wildlife Service, and U.S. Department of Commerce, 2002, http://www.census.gov/prod/2002pubs/FHW01.pdf

FIGURE 2.6

Expenditures by wildlife-watching participants, 2001

Total expenditures: $38.4 billion

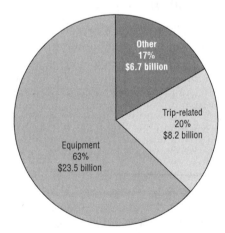

SOURCE: "Expenditures by Wildlife-Watching Participants," in *2001 National Survey of Fishing, Hunting, and Wildlife-Associated Recreation,* U.S. Department of the Interior, Fish and Wildlife Service, and U.S. Department of Commerce, 2002, http://www.census.gov/prod/2002pubs/FHW01.pdf (accessed September 10, 2004)

Expenditures by wildlife recreationists, including funds generated by licenses and taxes on fishing and hunting equipment, finance many conservation efforts throughout the United States. The U.S. Fish and Wildlife Service calls wildlife recreationists "the nation's most ardent conservationists" because they not only underwrite conservation efforts but also take the time to introduce children and adults to the pleasures of the outdoors and wildlife.

BUYING COLLECTIBLES

At the end of the 1990s, collectibles, including limited-edition plates and figurines, accounted for $5.5 billion of the $20.9 billion giftware market. This category was growing at an annual rate of more than 10% and represented 26% of total giftware sales. Industry observers credited the "cocooning trend," with its emphasis on the importance of the home as a place of leisure and entertainment, as a prime driver of increasing sales of collectibles. They also cited the investment value of collectibles and the concept of "family collecting" for helping fuel sales growth as baby boomers found collecting a satisfying way to spend time with their children.

In the early twenty-first century, however, sales of collectibles declined. Unity Marketing, in its *Collectibles Industry Report, 2002,* noted that traditional collectibles industry revenues fell 9% in 2001 to $6.5 billion, from $7.1 billion in 2000. The figurine and sculpture category, which was the industry's largest, saw sales drop by 20% during 2001, to $1.9 billion at the retail level. Industry observers attributed the decline to the economic downturn heightened by the events of September 11, 2001.

In addition to those who collected figurines and plates, other Americans were acquiring "blue-chip" items such as stamps, coins, antiques, and artwork, while others were caught up in fads that rode a wave of massive popularity, and then, when the market became oversaturated, began to fill the clearance shelves of stores or the dollar bins at flea markets. Examples of the latter included items that started out as toys and ended up collected feverishly by adults when they appeared to have potential as "investments," Beanie Babies by Ty Inc. being a prime example.

ONLINE AUCTIONS

One popular way that Americans purchase collectible items is via online auctions. The leading auction Web site, eBay.com, has grown rapidly since it was founded in 1995. By mid-2004 eBay had sixty-five million registered users in the United States, along with thirty million more internationally. Of the ninety-five million users who were registered, 41.2 million had bid, bought, or listed an item for sale during the previous year.

During 2003 eBay users purchased $20 billion worth of goods at auction from an estimated 160,000 sellers. Items listed for sale numbered 971 million, up 52% from the 638 million listed in 2002. The top ten categories, in terms of dollar volume, were: vehicles, $7.5 billion; consumer electronics, $2.6 billion; computers, $2.4 billion; books/movies/music, $2 billion; clothing and accessories, $1.8 billion; collectibles, $1.5 billion; toys, $1.5 billion; home and garden, $1.3 billion; and jewelry and gemstones, $1.3 billion. Other companies also operated online auction sites, and many vendors of collectibles sold items through their own Web sites as well.

PAYING TO TAKE A RISK

Weekend daredevils may encounter a variety of insurance problems, depending on the pastime and the danger involved. People who participate in extreme sports and high-risk recreational pursuits may find themselves forced to pay high rates for insurance coverage or be unable to get such coverage at all. When approached by persons who participate in risky activities, insurance companies may decline to insure them, exclude accidents related to the dangerous activity, postpone coverage until after a specific event, or require a physical examination to renew such a policy. In some cases, they may deem the activity and relative risk as negligible or slight and offer the policy at no additional cost.

Some insurance companies have added questions about high-risk behaviors to their applications for prospective policyholders. Participation in extreme sports can add hundreds or thousands of dollars in annual premiums. Pursuits that involve great speed—auto, motorcycle, and boat racing—tend to make insurers most apprehensive. Disability insurers are more likely than other carriers to reject such high-risk applicants. Disability claims have increased sharply, with some insurers losing money and others leaving the business.

Sports associations sometimes step in to provide insurance when other carriers will not. The Professional Association of Diving Instructors offers certified scuba divers medical insurance. The U.S. Hang Gliding Association has a $1 million liability policy to cover a glider who sails into bystanders. The American Motorcycle

TABLE 2.9

Average annual admission price for movies, selected years 1980–2003

| Year | Average annual admission price | % Change | | % Change |
		Previous period	2003 vs.	Consumer Price Index
2003	**$6.03**	**3.8%**	-	**1.9**
2002	5.81	2.7	3.8%	2.4
2001	5.66	4.9	6.6%	1.6
2000	5.39	6.1	11.8	3.4
1999	5.08	16.8	18.6	2.7
1995	4.35	4.8	38.5	1.7
1992	4.15	(1.7)	45.2	2.9
1990	4.23	19.0	42.7	3.3
1985	3.55	31.9	69.8	2.5
1980	2.69	—	124.0	2.7

Note: National Association of Theatre Owners (NATO) average ticket price based on NSNB survey and reflects average price paid for all admissions to movie theatres, inclusive of first run, subsequent runs, senior citizens, children, and all special pricing

SOURCE: "Average Annual Admission Price," in *U.S. Entertainment Industry 2003 MPA Market Statistics,* Motion Picture Association of America, Inc., Encino, California, 2004

Association offers its racers some medical coverage and accidental death and dismemberment insurance.

THE COST OF A NIGHT OUT

A survey conducted by a Philadelphia-based online dating service in 2000 compared the cost of a date—dinner and a movie—in various cities in the United States. New York was the most expensive city with an average cost of $135, followed by Chicago ($128) and San Francisco ($124). Las Vegas was the least expensive of the fourteen major cities ranked, with dinner and a movie averaging just $74. When the cost of a baby-sitter is added to the cost of an evening out, the price may be prohibitive for many American families.

The high cost of an evening out is considered one of the market forces driving the booming business of video and DVD movie rentals. At the end of 2003 the Motion Picture Association of America reported in *U.S. Entertainment Industry 2003 MPA Market Statistics* that the average price of a movie ticket had risen to $6.03, up 22 cents from the year before (see Table 2.9) and almost double the average DVD rental price of $3.20. If split between two or more people, the cost of seeing a movie dropped well below $2 per person when it was viewed at home.

Family outings can also be quite expensive. Theme park admission fees have increased dramatically over the years: In 1955 a family of four (two parents and two children) paid just $8 for admission to Disneyland, while in 2004 the same family paid $179. In 2004 admission for two adults and two children to Six Flags Magic Mountain in California cost $94, entrance to Colorado's Hyland Hills Water World was $104, and tickets for a family of four to visit Cedar Point in Sandusky, Ohio, cost $138.

CHAPTER 3
OUTDOOR RECREATION

THE LURE OF THE OUTDOORS

Americans love the outdoors. Millions of Americans spend their free time participating in outdoor activities. A Harris poll conducted by Humphrey Taylor in 2003 found that of forty-six leisure-time activities cited by Americans when they were asked to list their two or three favorites, approximately a third were activities or sports in which participants were directly involved with nature.

A survey exploring Americans' preferences in this category conducted by Roper Starch Worldwide for the Recreation Roundtable, *Outdoor Recreation in America 2003,* found that the top outdoor recreation activities that interviewees had participated in during the preceding year were fitness or recreational walking, driving for pleasure, swimming, picnicking, fishing, bicycling, and jogging. Other high-ranking choices included camping, hiking, outdoor photography, and bird watching. (See Table 3.1.)

While the popularity of many activities remained constant from 2001 to 2003, there were changes in some categories. The percentage of those who cited driving for pleasure increased 7%, from 36% to 43%, while the popularity of recreational walking dropped 3%, from 49% to 46%. Overall, six of the tracked activities showed an increase in participation from 2001, while twenty-one showed a decline. (See Table 3.1.)

Although the total number of Americans who participated in outdoor recreation at least once during the year fell only slightly overall, the frequency of participation declined significantly, according to *Outdoor Recreation in America 2003.* The number of Americans who participated in outdoor activities in 2001 at least once a month was 43%, but this number fell to 36% in 2003. Also, the number who said they participated in some form of outdoor recreation less often than once a month jumped, from 28% in 2001 to 41% in 2003.

The Sporting Goods Manufacturers Association (SGMA) has observed that for most Americans, partici-

pation in outdoor activities, even when these activities are among their favorite things to do, is infrequent and often associated with vacation, travel, or summer camp. With increasingly busy lives, many Americans do not take time to reconnect to the natural world and participate in outdoor activities. Still, many Americans do find the time to pursue some form of outdoor recreation, and the SGMA's 2004 edition of its annual *Sports Participation Topline Report* (see Table 1.6 in Chapter 1) offered statistics and insight about outdoor enthusiasts including:

- In 2003 the number of recreational swimmers (96.4 million) increased by more than 4% from 2002.

- In 2003 tent campers (41.9 million) outnumbered recreational vehicle (RV) campers (nineteen million) more than two to one.

- Although overall participation in fishing had declined slightly since 1993, there were almost fifty-three million freshwater, fly, and saltwater anglers in the United States.

- The number of Americans participating in horseback riding increased by more than 9% in 2003 from the previous year, to sixteen million.

- The popularity of trail running had increased by 16% since 1998, to 6.1 million participants.

- Americans' favorite outdoor water sports in 2003 were canoeing, jet skiing, and snorkeling, each with more than ten million participants.

- The top two outdoor winter activities in 2003 were ice skating, with 17 million participants, and downhill skiing, with 13.6 million.

WHO ENGAGES IN OUTDOOR ACTIVITIES?

According to *Outdoor Recreation in America 2003,* there was a correlation between education and income and

TABLE 3.1

Participation in outdoor recreation activities, 1994–2003

	1994 %	1995 %	1996 %	1997 %	1998 %	1999 %	2000 %	2001 %	2003 %
Walking for fitness/recreation	NA	45	39	42	47	42	57	49	46
Driving for pleasure	40	36	33	34	39	35	41	36	43
Swimming	35	31	28	31	33	40	39	40	41
Picnicking	33	29	24	26	30	32	36	36	38
Fishing	26	24	22	20	22	28	26	28	28
Bicycling	21	20	16	19	19	22	23	23	22
Running/jogging	19	16	13	12	16	16	18	21	19
Campground camping	16	16	12	12	15	21	17	18	18
Hiking	18	18	12	15	17	15	19	22	18
Outdoor photography	15	15	10	13	15	12	17	17	17
Birdwatching	14	11	8	11	10	11	16	18	16
Wildlife viewing	18	15	10	14	16	15	16	20	16
Visiting cultural sites	NA	NA	12	14	18	16	16	17	15
Golf	11	12	11	11	12	12	13	12	13
Motorboating	10	9	5	8	9	11	9	12	10
Backpacking	13	12	8	7	10	10	9	10	9
Canoeing/kayaking	6	5	4	5	5	7	5	7	8
Hunting	8	7	7	5	7	8	8	8	8
RV camping	8	8	6	7	7	9	9	9	8
Wilderness camping	NA	NA	NA	NA	NA	NA	8	8	7
Horseback riding	6	5	5	4	4	6	5	6	6
Motorcycling	7	5	6	4	4	6	5	6	6
Offroad vehicle driving	5	5	5	5	7	7	7	7	6
Target shooting	8	6	5	4	5	7	6	6	6
Tennis	9	9	7	8	5	6	8	8	6
Mountain biking	5	5	4	4	4	6	5	5	5
Personal watercraft (e.g. jet skis)	NA	NA	NA	3	5	5	5	6	5
Downhill sking	6	6	5	5	5	4	4	5	4
Water-skiing	6	6	3	4	4	6	4	6	4
In-line skating	NA	4	4	5	6	5	5	6	3
Rock climbing	4	4	3	3	4	3	4	4	3
Rowing	3	2	1	2	1	1	2	2	3
Sailing	4	3	3	3	2	3	2	4	3
Snorkeling/scuba diving	4	3	3	3	3	4	3	4	3
Cross-country skiing	2	3	2	2	2	1	2	2	2
Snowboarding	NA	NA	NA	NA	1	3	2	3	2
Snowmobiling	2	3	2	1	2	2	2	2	2

Note: NA denotes not asked

SOURCE: Roper ASW, "Outdoor Recreation Participation in 2003," in *Outdoor Recreation in America 2003: Recreation's Benefits to Society Challenged by Trends,* The Recreation Roundtable, January 2004, http://www.funoutdoors.com/files/ROPER%20REPORT%202004_0.pdf (accessed September 10, 2004)

rates of outdoor activity participation. College graduates participated in an average of 5.9 activities, compared to 3.7 for those with a high school diploma or less. Households with income above $75,000 per year reported 5.8 activities, while those earning $30,000 or less reported 3.8.

Participation rates differed for Americans of different ethnic backgrounds. Whites engaged in an average of 5.2 different activities, while Hispanics reported 3.5 and African Americans 2.3. Americans in the Midwest and West were far more likely to participate in outdoor activities than those in the Northwest and South. Northeasterners participated in an average of just 3.6 outdoor activities during the year and southerners 3.8, compared to the national average of 4.7. Those in the Midwest reported participation in seven different activities annually, while westerners reported 4.7 and had the lowest number reporting no activity during the year—just 6%, half the national average.

Participation rates varied between different age groups. In 2003, 19% of Americans aged eighteen to twenty-nine participated in outdoor activities several times per week, down by almost a third from the 27% who participated in 2001. Monthly participation in this age group dropped from 51% to 41%, and the number who said they participated less than monthly, or never, almost doubled from 21% to 38%. The decline in participation was less marked in the other age groups surveyed, although the oldest Americans, those sixty and above, showed a similar drop among the most frequent participants, while the number who engaged in a monthly activity remained unchanged. (See Table 3.2.)

A Family Affair

Recreation often starts with the family, and many Americans began the recreational activities they enjoy as adults when they were children. Parents who emphasized and participated in outdoor activities raised children who were more likely to become participants in and supporters of outdoor activities. Families with children reported higher

TABLE 3.2

Frequency of outdoor recreation participation by age, 2001 and 2003

	Most frequent participants (several times per week), as % of all in category			Participated at least monthly, as % of all in category			Least frequent participants (never, less than monthly), as % of all in category		
	2003	2001	Change	2003	2001	Change	2003	2001	Change
All ages	21	26	−5	36	43	−7	41	28	+13
18–29	19	27	−8	41	51	−10	38	21	+17
30–44	24	27	−3	40	45	−5	34	25	+9
45–59	22	22	0	30	45	−15	46	30	+16
601	18	27	−9	31	31	0	48	40	+8

SOURCE: Roper ASW, "Outdoor Recreation Participation in 2003," in *Outdoor Recreation in America 2003: Recreation's Benefits to Society Challenged by Trends,* The Recreation Roundtable, January 2004, http://www.funoutdoors .com/files/ROPER%20REPORT%202004_0.pdf (accessed September 10, 2004)

outdoor recreation participation rates than those without. Individual members of families reported an average of 5.4 activities per year and had significantly higher rates than the average for such activities as swimming, picnicking, tent camping, walking, fishing, camping, and bicycling.

VISITING THE GREAT OUTDOORS

National and State Parks

One of the best ways to enjoy the outdoors is to visit America's national parks. Since Congress established Yellowstone National Park in 1872, the United States has created a system of national parks occupying huge tracts of land. In 2004 the 83.6-million-acre National Park System encompassed 388 parks, monuments, preserves, memorials, historic sites, recreational areas, seashores, and other areas. In addition to providing recreation for more than 266 million visitors each year, the parks preserve habitats ranging from arctic tundra to tropical rain forest and protect many thousands of North American plant and animal species. (See Table 3.3.)

The park system is administered by the National Park Service (NPS), a Department of Interior agency. Established in 1916, the park service employed more than fourteen thousand permanent personnel in 2003 along with approximately four thousand temporary or seasonal workers. An additional twenty-five thousand people worked for some 630 concessionaires, private businesses that the NPS contracted with to provide lodging, transportation, food, shops, and other services in 128 of its park units.

The National Park Service manages national parks, such as Yosemite National Park in California and Yellowstone National Park, mostly in Wyoming; national monuments, such as the Washington Monument and the Lincoln Memorial in Washington, D.C.; and national commemorative sites, such as the Gettysburg battlefield in Pennsylvania, the Vicksburg battlefield in Mississippi, and the Ellis Island Immigration Museum in New York. The system also includes some lakes, rivers, and

seashores. The most popular sites to visit in 2003 included the Blue Ridge Parkway in the Appalachian Mountains, with 18.3 million visitors; the Golden Gate National Recreation Area near San Francisco, with 13.9 million; and the Great Smoky Mountains National Park, located on the border between North Carolina and Tennessee, with 9.4 million. (See Table 3.4.)

NPS sites are found in forty-nine of the fifty states (all but Delaware), the District of Columbia, American Samoa, Guam, Puerto Rico, and the Virgin Islands. In 2003 sites in California received the most visits (34.2 million), followed by those in the District of Columbia (22 million), Virginia (21.9 million), and North Carolina (20.4 million). (See Table 3.5.)

Camping enables visitors to stay overnight in the national parks; during 2002 nearly 3.4 million tent campers, over 2.4 million RV campers, and about 2.5 million backcountry campers stayed on NPS grounds. Not surprisingly, park visitation was greatest in the summer months, in 2003 peaking at about 1.3 million visits per day in July. It was lowest in January, when just under 368,000 Americans visited NPS sites on an average day. (See Figure 3.1.)

In addition, many millions more visited national forests or lands administered by the Bureau of Land Management for car or motorcycle tours, hunting, fishing, boating, and winter recreational activities. Others traveled to state, county, and city parks and recreation areas.

Volunteering Outdoors

America's public lands rely to a significant extent on volunteers to perform many vital tasks, including serving as guides, helping restore wildlife habitats, and assisting with geological or archaeological surveys. More than 125,000 volunteers spent time working for the NPS in 2002, donating more than 4.5 million hours of service, which gave the parks the equivalent of two thousand additional full-time workers.

TABLE 3.3

Recreation visits to National Park Service areas, by type of area, 2003

Areas administered by type	Recreational visit	Areas reporting visits	Areas administered
International historic site	0	0	1
National battlefield	1,533,005	10	11
National battlefield park	2,278,347	3	3
National battlefield site	0	0	1
National historic site	9,238,593	74	77
National historical park	25,054,246	37	41
National lakeshore	3,659,566	4	4
National memorial	23,115,959	28	29
National military park	5,352,739	9	9
National monument	19,987,662	69	74
National park	63,430,778	57	57
National parkway	31,079,207	4	4
National preserve	2,140,881	18	18
National recreation area	47,727,743	17	18
National reserve	79,879	1	2
National river	3,800,063	4	5
National scenic trail	0	0	3
National seashore	18,902,919	10	10
National wild and scenic river	797,120	5	10
Parks (other)	7,920,934	9	11
National Park Service total	**266,099,641**	**359**	**388**

SOURCE: "Table 1. 2003 Recreation Visits by Type of Area," in *National Park Service Statistical Abstract 2003,* National Park Service, 2004, http://www.nature.nps.gov/socialscience/docs/Abstract-Final2003.pdf (accessed September 10, 2004)

TABLE 3.4

Ten most visited units of the National Park System, 2003, and ten most visited national parks, 2003

10 most visited units of the National Park System (2003)

Park unit	Recreational visits
1. Blue Ridge Parkway	18,344,049
2. Golden Gate National Recreation Area	13,854,750
3. Great Smoky Mountains National Park	9,366,845
4. Gateway National Recreation Area	8,567,769
5. Lake Mead National Recreation Area	7,915,581
6. George Washington Memorial Parkway	6,043,508
7. Natchez Trace Parkway	5,555,984
8. Delaware Water Gap National Recreation Area	5,059,410
9. Gulf Islands National Seashore	4,939,771
10. Grand Canyon National Park	4,124,900

10 most visited national parks (2003)

Park unit	Recreational visits
1. Great Smoky Mountains National Park	9,366,845
2. Grand Canyon National Park	4,124,900
3. Yosemite National Park	3,378,664
4. Olympic National Park	3,225,327
5. Rocky Mountain National Park	3,067,256
6. Yellowstone National Park	3,019,375
7. Cuyahoga Valley National Park	2,879,591
8. Zion National Park	2,458,792
9. Acadia National Park	2,431,062
10. Grand Teton National Park	2,355,693

SOURCE: "10 Most Visited Units of the National Park System (2003)" and "10 Most Visited National Parks (2003)," National Park Service, 2004, http://www.nps.gov/pub_aff/refdesk/10MVUNP2003.pdf (accessed September 9, 2004)

FIGURE 3.1

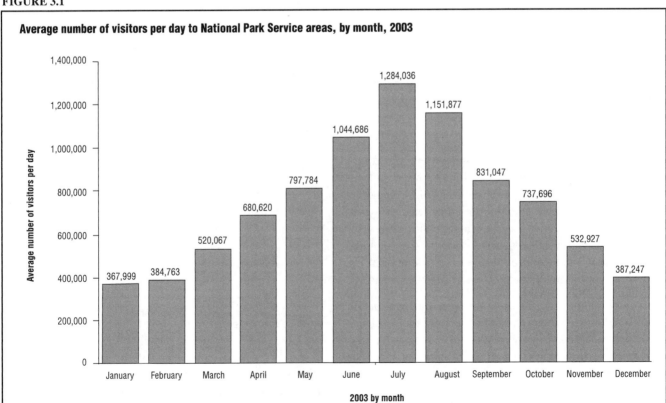

Average number of visitors per day to National Park Service areas, by month, 2003

SOURCE: "Figure 5. 2003 Average Number of Visitors per Day to NPS Areas," in *National Park Service Statistical Abstract 2003,* National Park Service, 2004, http://www.nature.nps.gov/socialscience/docs/Abstract-Final2003.pdf (accessed September 10, 2004)

TABLE 3.5

Recreation visits to National Park Service areas by state, district, or territory, 2003

State	Visits 2002	Visits 2003	Percent change	State	Visits 2002	Visits 2003	Percent change
Alabama	576,081	751,516	30.5%	Montana	4,020,282	3,824,659	−4.9%
Alaska	2,150,215	2,189,717	1.8%	Nebraska	180,752	171,623	−5.1%
American Samoa	1,938	0	−100.0%	Nevada	5,748,490	6,023,706	4.8%
Arizona	10,227,286	10,555,767	3.2%	New Hampshire	34,239	30,907	−9.7%
Arkansas	2,433,642	2,402,262	-1.3%	New Jersey	5,861,776	5,637,151	−3.8%
California	33,769,299	34,177,138	1.2%	New Mexico	1,818,551	1,825,305	0.4%
Colorado	5,157,377	5,596,277	8.5%	New York	15,719,928	14,790,501	−5.9%
Connecticut	16,113	15,455	−4.1%	North Carolina	22,594,035	20,379,780	−9.8%
District of Columbia	24,373,893	22,027,057	−9.6%	North Dakota	524,469	550,924	5.0%
Florida	8,925,852	9,633,446	7.9%	Ohio	3,523,384	3,229,075	−8.4%
Georgia	6,271,091	6,230,747	−0.6%	Oklahoma	1,954,370	1,707,819	−12.6%
Guam	152,881	1,698	−98.9%	Oregon	887,439	937,962	5.7%
Hawaii	4,700,740	4,748,544	1.0%	Pennsylvania	8,298,179	7,829,923	−5.6%
Idaho	481,163	473,906	−1.5%	Puerto Rico	1,278,407	1,198,105	−6.3%
Illinois	390,076	383,025	−1.8%	Rhode Island	58,243	54,482	−6.5%
Indiana	2,245,373	2,204,802	−1.8%	South Carolina	1,562,178	1,500,968	−3.9%
Iowa	266,873	263,022	−1.4%	South Dakota	4,012,981	4,089,458	1.9%
Kansas	126,408	133,039	5.2%	Tennessee	7,987,931	7,933,421	−0.7%
Kentucky	3,407,104	3,376,946	−0.9%	Texas	5,007,121	4,940,516	−1.3%
Louisiana	757,148	684,248	−9.6%	Utah	8,189,745	7,780,053	−5.0%
Maine	2,558,572	2,431,062	−5.0%	Vermont	31,940	33,037	3.4%
Maryland	3,271,583	3,443,049	5.2%	Virgin Islands	853,916	975,862	14.3%
Massachusetts	9,847,828	9,072,916	−7.9%	Virginia	25,006,802	21,904,953	−12.4%
Michigan	1,619,565	1,554,218	−4.0%	Washington	7,665,032	7,123,463	−7.1%
Minnesota	531,542	521,229	−1.9%	West Virginia	1,938,035	1,742,833	−10.1%
Mississippi	6,950,837	6,867,017	−1.2%	Wisconsin	309,204	311,118	0.6%
Missouri	5,256,509	4,291,744	−18.4%	Wyoming	5,765,463	5,542,191	−3.9%
National Park Service total					**277,299,880**	**266,099,641**	**−4.0%**

SOURCE: "Table 2. 2003 Recreation Visits by State," in *National Park Service Statistical Abstract 2003*, National Park Service, 2004, http://www.nature.nps.gov/socialscience/docs/Abstract-Final2003.pdf (accessed September 10, 2004)

A 2003 survey by Roper Starch Worldwide for the Recreation Roundtable found that 21% of Americans said they would be interested in volunteering their time to do work on publicly owned land. Of those who expressed interest, nearly a quarter said they had given of their time during the previous year. Those who expressed the most interest in volunteering tended to be those who actively participated in outdoor recreation—57% of canoers and kayakers, 52% of skiers, 47% of both backpackers and climbers, 46% of wildlife viewers, 44% of hikers, and 43% of mountain bikers, said they would be interested in donating their time to work on public lands.

Rails to Trails

Many railways around the country have been abandoned by the railroads. Almost every state has turned some of that acreage into public trails for hiking, jogging, biking, and even horseback riding. According to information published on the Web site of the Washington, D.C.–based nonprofit Rails-to-Trails Conservancy (RTC) (www.railtrails.org), the ten states that had done the most converting of rail mileage as of 2004 were Wisconsin (1,394 miles), Michigan (1,311), Minnesota (1,244), Pennsylvania (1,185), New York (583), Washington (578), Iowa (546), Ohio (536), Illinois (490), and West Virginia (442). The most popular individual trail was the W&OD Railroad Trail in Virginia with about three mil-

lion users per year, followed by the Minuteman Bikeway in Massachusetts with an estimated two million users per year; the Pinellas Trail in Florida and the Iron Horse State Park Trail in Washington, each with 1.2 million; and the East Bay Bicycle Path in Rhode Island, with 1.1 million annual users.

WILDLIFE AS RECREATION

America is a huge country with many millions of square miles of natural wilderness and a rich tradition of enjoying nature. Many Americans find wildlife-associated recreation a source of immense pleasure, and some of the most popular recreational activities involve wildlife and wild terrain.

According to data gathered by the U.S. Departments of the Interior and Commerce in a survey conducted in 2001, more than 30% of Americans were involved in wildlife-related recreation activities and participation had increased by 5% since 1996. (See Table 3.6 and Table 3.7.) Participation varied by state, with Alaska reporting the highest proportion of participants (70%). Other states with high levels of participants included Vermont (67%), Minnesota (65%), Montana (63%), Oregon (59%), Wyoming (59%), South Dakota (58%), Washington (56%), Iowa (55%), New Hampshire (53%), Arkansas (52%), Idaho (52%), and Oklahoma (51%). (See Table 3.6.)

TABLE 3.6

Participants in wildlife-related recreation by participant's state of residence, 2001

(Population 16 years old and older. Numbers in thousands)

Participant's state of residence	Population	Total participants		Sportspersons		Wildlife-watching participants	
		Number	Percent of population	Number	Percent of population	Number	Percent of population
United States, total	**212,298**	**82,302**	**39**	**37,805**	**18**	**66,105**	**31**
Alabama	3,427	1,323	39	726	21	965	28
Alaska	454	320	70	205	45	241	53
Arizona	3,700	1,296	35	437	12	1,107	30
Arkansas	1,999	1,038	52	621	31	778	39
California	25,982	6,873	26	2,486	10	5,491	21
Colorado	3,215	1,518	47	679	21	1,213	38
Connecticut	2,536	996	39	331	13	883	35
Delaware	599	220	37	94	16	170	28
Florida	12,171	3,857	32	2,158	18	2,856	23
Georgia	6,096	1,932	32	1,136	19	1,326	22
Hawaii	916	195	21	114	12	126	14
Idaho	972	507	52	306	31	388	40
Illinois	9,244	3,148	34	1,507	16	2,492	27
Indiana	4,558	2,179	48	914	20	1,786	39
Iowa	2,201	1,212	55	580	26	983	45
Kansas	2,017	942	47	491	24	735	36
Kentucky	3,121	1,547	50	703	23	1,264	40
Louisiana	3,306	1,326	40	829	25	840	25
Maine	1,005	607	60	256	26	520	52
Maryland	4,078	1,546	38	571	14	1,311	32
Massachusetts	4,837	1,726	36	521	11	1,493	31
Michigan	7,587	2,950	39	1,325	17	2,424	32
Minnesota	3,688	2,388	65	1,437	39	1,993	54
Mississippi	2,111	851	40	533	25	579	27
Missouri	4,206	2,010	48	1,076	26	1,612	38
Montana	699	438	63	279	40	362	52
Nebraska	1,266	623	49	308	24	498	39
Nevada	1,454	439	30	194	13	334	23
New Hampshire	954	506	53	175	18	450	47
New Jersey	6,300	1,993	32	669	11	1,694	27
New Mexico	1,337	595	45	256	19	471	35
New York	14,201	3,990	28	1,493	11	3,524	25
North Carolina	5,918	2,330	39	982	17	1,884	32
North Dakota	483	228	47	170	35	135	28
Ohio	8,645	3,407	39	1,513	17	2,768	32
Oklahoma	2,587	1,308	51	730	28	1,042	40
Oregon	2,630	1,545	59	611	23	1,286	49
Pennsylvania	9,303	4,169	45	1,648	18	3,522	38
Rhode Island	765	280	37	96	13	242	32
South Carolina	3,080	1,375	45	674	22	1,079	35
South Dakota	559	326	58	176	31	251	45
Tennessee	4,317	2,109	49	903	21	1,706	40
Texas	15,445	4,515	29	2,745	18	3,088	20
Utah	1,554	736	47	468	30	572	37
Vermont	479	319	67	125	26	287	60
Virginia	5,471	2,535	46	970	18	2,168	40
Washington	4,516	2,537	56	932	21	2,234	49
West Virginia	1,447	694	48	353	24	517	36
Wisconsin	4,059	2,489	61	1,141	28	2,159	53
Wyoming	377	223	59	138	37	172	46

Note: Detail does not add to total because of multiple responses. U.S. totals include responses from participants residing in the District of Columbia.

SOURCE: "Table 50. Participants in Wildlife-Related Recreation by Participant's State of Residence: 2001," in *2001 National Survey of Fishing, Hunting, and Wildlife-Associated Recreation,* U.S. Department of the Interior, Fish and Wildlife Service, and U.S. Department of Commerce, 2002, http://www.census.gov/prod/2002pubs/FHW01.pdf (accessed September 10, 2004).

Not surprisingly, states with ample opportunities for wildlife recreation—observing wildlife, photographing, and feeding birds or other wildlife—reported higher levels of participation than states better known for other environmental attractions. For example, Hawaii, which is better known for its beaches, hotels, and resorts, reported that just 21% of its population engaged in wildlife recreation. Similarly, Nevada, with its urban tourism attracting employees and visitors to the cities of Las Vegas and Reno, reported that just 30% of its residents participated in wildlife recreation. (See Table 3.6.)

National Survey

The mission of the U.S. Fish and Wildlife Service (FWS) is to conserve and enhance the nation's fish, wildlife, and habitat. For conservation efforts to be effec-

TABLE 3.7

Wildlife watching participants by days and expenditures, 1996–2001

(Population 16 years old and older. Numbers in thousands)

	1996		2001[1]		1996–2001 Percent change
	Number	Percent	Number	Percent	
Wildlife watching, total	**62,868**	**100**	**66,105**	**100**	**5**
Residential	60,751	97	62,928	95	4*
Observe wildlife	44,063	70	42,111	64	24*
Photograph wildlife	16,021	25	13,937	21	213*
Feed wild birds or other wildlife	54,122	86	53,988	82	0
Visit public parks or areas	11,011	18	10,981	17	0
Maintain plantings or natural areas	13,401	21	13,072	20	2*
Nonresidential	23,652	38	21,823	33	28*
Observe wildlife	22,878	36	20,080	30	212
Photograph wildlife	12,038	19	9,427	14	2 22
Feed wildlife	9,976	16	7,077	11	2 29
Days, nonresidential	313,790	100	372,006	100	19*
Observing wildlife	278,683	89	295,345	79	6*
Photographing wildlife	79,342	25	76,324	21	24*
Feeding wildlife	89,606	29	103,307	28	15*
Wildlife-watching expenditures, total (2001 dollars)	**$29,062,524**	**100**	**$33,730,868**	**100**	**16***
Trips	10,250,604	35	8,162,439	24	2 20*
Equipment	16,785,440	58	23,616,982	70	41
Wildlife-watching equipment	8,783,405	30	6,850,971	20	2 22*
Auxiliary equipment	853,374	3	716,900	2	2 16*
Special equipment	7,148,661	25	16,049,111	48	125
Other	2,026,480	7	1,951,447	6	24*

[1]All 2001 expenditures are adjusted to make them comparable to 1991 estimates
*Not different from zero at the 5 percent level

SOURCE: "1996–2001 Wildlife Watching Participants, Days, and Expenditures," in *2001 National Survey of Fishing, Hunting, and Wildlife-Associated Recreation,* U.S. Department of the Interior, Fish and Wildlife Service, and U.S. Department of Commerce, 2002, http://www.census.gov/prod/2002pubs/FHW01.pdf (accessed September 10, 2004)

tive, the FWS needs to know how people use fish and wildlife resources. Since 1955 the FWS has conducted a periodic survey of fishing, hunting, and wildlife-related recreation. The 2001 FWS survey and report was the tenth such study conducted to determine how often recreationists participated and how much they spent on their activities.

The *2001 National Survey of Fishing, Hunting, and Wildlife-Associated Recreation* (Washington, DC: U.S. Department of the Interior, Fish and Wildlife Service, and U.S. Department of Commerce, 2002), found that more than eighty-two million Americans participated in some form of wildlife-related activity in 2001.

During 2001, according to the survey, 34.1 million people in the United States fished, 13 million hunted, and 66.1 million enjoyed other forms of wildlife-watching recreation, including photographing or feeding animals. Among anglers, hunters, and nonconsuming participants (those who did not capture or kill the animals or fish), many of those who participated in one activity often engaged in the other activities as well. For example, in 2001 more than two-thirds (71%) of hunters also fished, and more than one-quarter (27%) of anglers hunted.

Trends

According to the *2001 National Survey of Fishing, Hunting, and Wildlife-Associated Recreation,* the number of Americans fishing in 2001, 34.1 million, decreased only slightly from 1996, when there were 35.2 million anglers. The number of hunters, thirteen million, also dropped from fourteen million in 1996. Despite these declines, an examination of trends revealed that the number of anglers outpaced U.S. population growth at a rate of two to one from 1955 to 2001. Although the number of hunters increased by 31% during the same period, this rate of growth did not keep pace with U.S. population growth. (See Figure 3.2.)

Participation in wildlife watching grew to 66.1 million in 2001, from 62.9 million in 1996. The percentage of people who took trips away from their homes to observe, feed, or photograph wildlife fell by 19% from 1980 (the first year it was measured) to 2001. The number of people who enjoyed these activities within one mile of their homes (62.9 million) increased by 4% from 1996. (See Table 3.7 and Figure 3.3.)

Expenditures

In 2001 Americans spent about $108 billion, representing about 1% of the gross domestic product, on wildlife-related recreation. Fishing accounted for approximately 32% of that expenditure, wildlife-watching activities, 36%, and hunting, 19%. (Another 13% was unspecified.) (See Figure 2.4 in Chapter 2.) Of the money spent, 59% was for equipment, 28% was trip-related, and 13% fell into the "other" category.

Who Participates in Wildlife Sports?

In 2001 the greatest number of wildlife enthusiasts lived in California, Texas, New York, Florida, and Illinois. (See Table 3.6.) According to *2001 National Survey of Fishing, Hunting, and Wildlife-Associated Recreation,* the greatest percentage and the largest number of anglers and hunters were between the ages of thirty-five and fifty-four. (See Table 3.8.) The majority were male: 74% of the anglers and 91% of the hunters. Of those who watched wildlife, 54% were female, while 34% of all women watched wildlife at their residences. Most hunters were white (96%), while 2% were black and 2% were members of other races. Among anglers, 93% were white, 5% were black, 1% were Asian, and 1% were other races. Among those who participated in nonresidential wildlife-watching activities, 95% were white, 3% were black, 1% were Asian, and 1% were other races.

Among anglers, 35% had a high school education, 27% had one to three years of college, and 26% had four

FIGURE 3.2

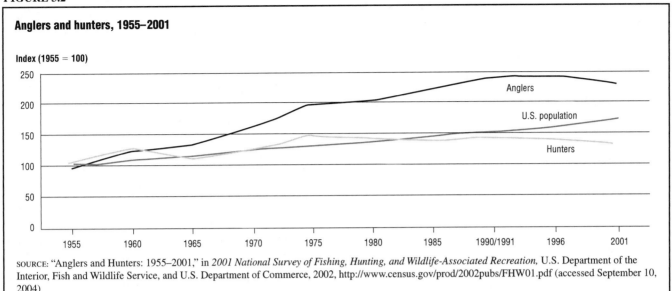

Anglers and hunters, 1955–2001

Index (1955 = 100)

SOURCE: "Anglers and Hunters: 1955–2001," in *2001 National Survey of Fishing, Hunting, and Wildlife-Associated Recreation,* U.S. Department of the Interior, Fish and Wildlife Service, and U.S. Department of Commerce, 2002, http://www.census.gov/prod/2002pubs/FHW01.pdf (accessed September 10, 2004)

FIGURE 3.3

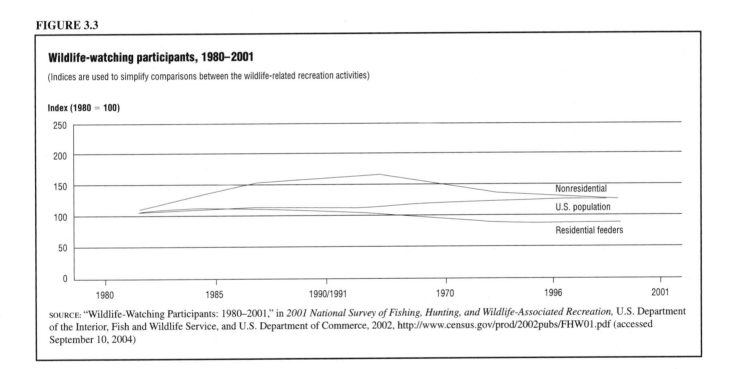

Wildlife-watching participants, 1980–2001

(Indices are used to simplify comparisons between the wildlife-related recreation activities)

Index (1980 = 100)

SOURCE: "Wildlife-Watching Participants: 1980–2001," in *2001 National Survey of Fishing, Hunting, and Wildlife-Associated Recreation,* U.S. Department of the Interior, Fish and Wildlife Service, and U.S. Department of Commerce, 2002, http://www.census.gov/prod/2002pubs/FHW01.pdf (accessed September 10, 2004)

years of college or more. Only 12% had fewer than twelve years of school. Among hunters, 38% had a high school diploma, 26% had one to three years of college, 22% had four years of college or more, and only 14% had fewer than twelve years of school. For those who enjoyed wildlife-watching activities, 27% had a high school diploma, 27% had one to three years of college, and 37% had four or more years of college. Only 8% had less than a high school education.

Hunting

In 2001, thirteen million Americans sixteen years and older enjoyed hunting a variety of game animals within the United States. In order of preference, hunters sought big game (deer, elk, bear, and wild turkey), small game (squirrels, rabbits, pheasants, quail, and grouse), migratory birds (doves, ducks, and geese), and other animals (groundhogs, raccoons, foxes, and coyotes). Hunters spent $20.6 billion on trips and equipment during 2001. (See Table 3.9.) Collectively, they hunted 228 million days and took two hundred million trips.

People living in the west north-central states were most likely to hunt (12%), while residents of the Pacific states (2%) and the New England (4%) and middle and south Atlantic states (5% each) were least likely. (See Figure 3.4.) Nearly all (95%) hunted within their resident state; only 2.1 million hunted out of state.

TABLE 3.8

Anglers, by gender and age, 2001

Total, both sexes	**34.1million**
Male	25.2 million
Female	8.9 million
Total, all ages	**34.1million**
16 and 17	1.3 million
18 to 24	2.9 million
25 to 34	6.6 million
35 to 44	9.0 million
45 to 54	6.9 million
55 to 64	4.2 million
65 and older	3.1 million

SOURCE: "Anglers–by Gender and Age," in *2001 National Survey of Fishing, Hunting, and Wildlife-Associated Recreation*, U.S. Department of the Interior, Fish and Wildlife Service, and U.S. Department of Commerce, 2002, http://www.census.gov/prod/2002pubs/FHW01.pdf (accessed September 10, 2004)

Animal rights advocates have sometimes tried to characterize hunters as wanton, unfeeling killers. Hunters and hunters' organizations have worked to counter this negative image by teaching ethics to hunters, actively promoting the contributions that hunters make to conservation, and defending hunting as a time-honored American tradition. The campaign to improve hunting's reputation coincided with state initiatives to restrict specific types of hunting, such as the baiting of bears in Michigan and Washington and airborne hunting of wolves in Alaska.

Fishing

In 2001 more than thirty-four million U.S. residents enjoyed a variety of fishing activities throughout the United States. Collectively, anglers fished 557 million days and took 437 million fishing trips. Freshwater species were fished for by 84% of anglers, while saltwater fish were fished for by 26%. (There was some overlap because of those who fished for both.) Anglers spent $35.6 billion on fishing-related expenses during the year. Of that amount, 41% was trip-related, 48% went for equipment, and 11% was for other expenses.

Wildlife-Watching Activities

Wildlife-watching activities, including observing, feeding, and photographing wildlife, are popular in the United States. These activities were termed either "residential" (within a mile of one's home) or "nonresidential" (at least one mile from home) in the FWS survey. In 2001, 31% (66.1 million) of the American population sixteen years and older enjoyed watching wildlife. Each participant spent an average of $738 for a total of $38.4 billion. Of the total spent, 61% was for equipment, 21% was trip-related, and 17% went for other expenses.

Among the nearly sixty-three million people who enjoyed wildlife-watching activities in their own communities (residential), 82% fed birds, 64% observed wildlife,

TABLE 3.9

Total hunters and hunting days, trips, and expenditures, 2001

Hunters	13.0 million
Big game	10.9 million
Small game	5.4 million
Migratory bird	3.0 million
Other animals	1.0 million
Days	228 million
Big game	153 million
Small game	60 million
Migratory bird	29 million
Other animals	19 million
Trips	200 million
Big game	114 million
Small game	46 million
Migratory bird	24 million
Other animals	15 million
Expenditures	$20.6 billion
Big game	10.1 billion
Small game	1.8 billion
Migratory game	1.4 billion
Other animals	0.2 billion
Unspecified	7.1 billion

Note: Detail does not add to total because of multiple responses and nonresponse

SOURCE: "Total Hunting," in *2001 National Survey of Fishing, Hunting, and Wildlife-Associated Recreation*, U.S. Department of the Interior, Fish and Wildlife Service, and U.S. Department of Commerce, 2002, http://www.census.gov/prod/2002pubs/FHW01.pdf (accessed September 10, 2004)

21% photographed wildlife, and 17% visited public areas, such as parks, within one mile of their homes. Another 20% maintained plantings for wildlife or natural areas for the primary purpose of benefiting wildlife. Among those who took trips away from home for the primary purpose of observing, feeding, or photographing wildlife, 30% observed, 14% photographed, and 11% fed the animals. (See Table 3.7.)

Residents from the west north-central (41%), east south-central (34%), and New England (36%) states were most likely to enjoy local wildlife activities. Residents of the mountain (15%) and west north-central states (14%) were most likely to travel to participate in wildlife activities. Almost equal proportions of males and females enjoyed wildlife-watching activities.

Whale Watching

Whale watching grew dramatically as a form of wildlife watching recreation during the 1990s. The whales supported an industry pouring millions of dollars into many coastal economies, particularly those of New England, California, and Hawaii.

According to the International Fund for Animal Welfare study *Whale Watching 2001*, by Eric Hoyt, whale watching in the United States generated an estimated $158 million in direct spending and $357 million in total related expenditures in 1998, and there were more than 4.3 million U.S. whale watchers. In New England alone,

FIGURE 3.4

Hunting participation, 2001

(National participation rate: 6%)

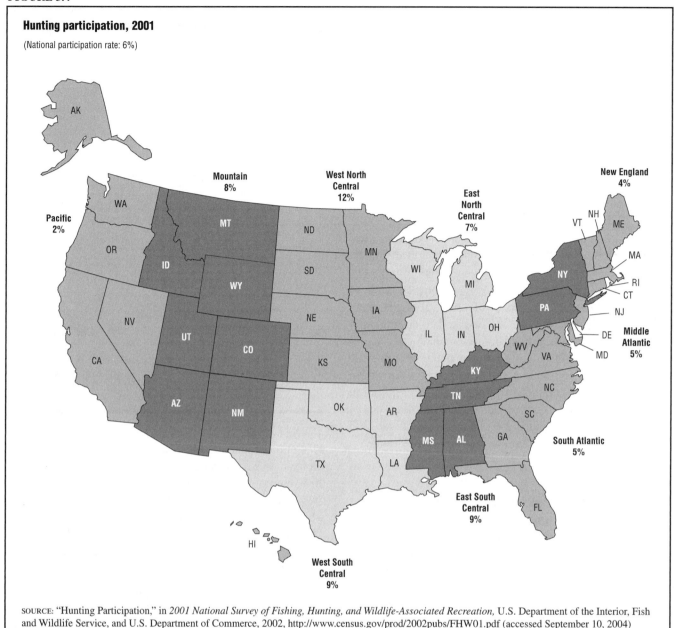

SOURCE: "Hunting Participation," in *2001 National Survey of Fishing, Hunting, and Wildlife-Associated Recreation,* U.S. Department of the Interior, Fish and Wildlife Service, and U.S. Department of Commerce, 2002, http://www.census.gov/prod/2002pubs/FHW01.pdf (accessed September 10, 2004)

tourists spent more than $30 million in direct expenditures to visit whales in their natural environment. Humpback, fin, and minke whales could be seen there, along with the highly endangered North Atlantic right whale.

In California the gray whale, now removed from the endangered species list, was the star of the West Coast's whale-watching industry, and blue and humpback whales could be seen as well. Hawaii offered humpback, short-finned pilot, and sperm whales. In addition to transporting ecotourists, commercial whale-watching vessels also served as forums for educational outreach and scientific research.

"Canned Hunting"

During the 1990s a controversial form of commercial exploitation of wildlife, known as "canned hunting," swept across the country. Beginning in Texas, by 2004 canned hunting occurred in most states in the United States. In a canned hunt, the "hunter" pays a set fee and steps into an enclosure where an animal—boar, ram, bear, lion, tiger, zebra, buffalo, rhinoceros, or antelope—is confined. The hunter then kills the animal with the weapon of his or her choice. The animals are easily cornered. Some have been domesticated or raised in facilities where they have become friendly to humans, even walking up to them.

In 2003 the Fund for Animals listed a total of 298 canned hunt operations around the United States that it had identified through advertising brochures, magazine ads, or Web sites, and estimated that there were many more it had not been able to discover. The states it found to have the most canned hunts were Texas, with sixty-two;

TABLE 3.10

Recreational boats in use, by boat type, 1997–2003

Year	Outboard boats (millions)	Inboard boats (millions)	Sterndrive boats (millions)	Personal watercraft (millions)	Sailboats (millions)	Other (millions)	Total (millions)
1997	8.13	1.59	1.58	1.00	1.65	2.29	16.23
1998	8.19	1.61	1.62	1.10	1.67	2.45	16.65
1999	8.21	1.63	1.67	1.18	1.65	2.49	16.82
2000	8.29	1.66	1.71	1.24	1.64	2.50	17.03
2001	8.34	1.69	1.74	1.29	1.63	2.51	17.20
2002	8.38	1.71	1.77	1.35	1.61	2.53	17.36
2003	8.42	1.74	1.79	1.42	1.60	2.53	17.49

SOURCE: "Table 1.3. Recreational Boats in Use by Boat Type 1997 to 2003," in *2003 Recreational Boating Statistical Abstract,* National Marine Manufacturers Association, 2004, http://www.nmma.org/facts/boatingstats/2003/files/Abstract.pdf (accessed September 10, 2004)

Michigan, with twenty-four; Pennsylvania, with twenty-one; and Florida, with seventeen.

No federal laws restrict canned hunts, although in late 2001 Senator Joseph Biden, a Democrat from Delaware, introduced legislation that would make it illegal to "knowingly transfer, transport, or possess in interstate or foreign commerce a confined exotic mammal for the purposes of allowing the killing or injuring of that animal for entertainment" or for the collection of a "trophy," but it did not reach the Senate floor for a vote.

By 2004 Arizona, California, Connecticut, Hawaii, Maryland, Massachusetts, Minnesota, Montana, Nevada, Oregon, Washington, and Wyoming had banned canned hunts for all mammals, while Delaware, Georgia, Mississippi, North Carolina, Utah, Virginia, and Wisconsin had banned canned hunts for many or most mammals, with certain exceptions permitted in each state.

Investigations have revealed that zoos across the nation have sold animals they consider surplus either directly to canned-hunt facilities or to dealers who sell animals to auctions patronized by canned-hunt organizers. Some pressure has been exerted on zoos to acknowledge their responsibility for the animals they discard.

BOATING

Many Americans enjoy boating. The National Marine Manufacturers Association (NMMA) estimated in its *2003 Recreational Boating Statistical Abstract* that in 2003 seventy-two million Americans participated in recreational boating and almost 17.5 million boats were in use. Close to thirteen million Americans were registered boaters in 2002, according to the U.S. Coast Guard. Michigan (1,000,337), Florida (922,597), California (896,090), Minnesota (834,974), Texas (624,390), and Wisconsin (619,924) led in the number of registered boaters.

The NMMA estimated that in 2003, Americans owned about 8.4 million outboard motorboats, 1.8 million sterndrive boats, 1.7 million inboard motorboats, 1.6 million sailboats, 1.4 million personal watercraft, and approximately 2.5 million miscellaneous craft, such as canoes and rowboats. (See Table 3.10.) According to the NMMA, Americans spent about $30 billion on boating in 2003, up from $21.7 billion in 1998.

MOTORCYCLING—CHANGING TIMES

Motorcycling is not only a means of transportation but also a popular recreational activity. In 2002 the U.S. Department of Transportation reported that just under five million motorcycles were registered in the United States. The Motorcycle Industry Council reported that motorcycle sales increased 6.4% during 2003, to a total of approximately 996,000 cycles sold during the year.

The Motorcycle Owner—a Profile

In 1980 the average age of registered motorcyclists was twenty-six; by 1990, thirty-two; and by 2003, forty-four, according to research firm J.D. Power and Associates. Although men bought the vast majority of motorcycles, they are proving increasingly attractive to women as well. In 2003 more than one in ten new motorcycles were purchased by women, an increase of 30% from 1998. Of these, half were first-time buyers, compared with just one man in five who was buying his first bike.

In the early twenty-first century, the industry catered more to baby boomers with disposable incomes and a yen for adventure. Manufacturers introduced a line of bigger, safer, and more expensive machines with plenty of extras—wide-body, big-windshield cruising bikes—aimed at customers more interested in comfort than performing daredevil acrobatics.

By 2003 very expensive bikes were reviving the industry. The recovery of Harley-Davidson from the edge of bankruptcy was based on marketing to older, more affluent consumers looking for excitement in their lives. The median age of a Harley buyer in 2003 was approximately forty-seven, up from forty-four in 1999, and his median income was $80,000, up from less than $75,000 in 1999.

RECREATIONAL VEHICLES

Recreational vehicles (RVs) include a variety of vehicles, such as motor homes, travel trailers, folding camping trailers, truck campers, and van conversions. Motor homes and vans are motorized, while the others must be towed or mounted on other vehicles. According to the Recreational Vehicle Industry Association (RVIA), in 2003 there were approximately 7.2 million RVs in the United States—one for every twelve vehicle-owning households. There were an estimated thirty million RV enthusiasts, including renters of RVs.

RV owners cite freedom, flexibility, comfort, family appeal, affordability, and versatility as the reasons they choose to purchase RVs. Sports enthusiasts value the ability of bringing snowmobiles, motorcycles, and bicycles with them for their outdoor adventures. Fans of this type of vehicle claim that family vacations in a RV improve family relationships and communication.

According to a 2001 study conducted by the University of Michigan, RV ownership increased 7.8% between 1998 and 2001 and grew by 38% between 1980 and 2001. The RVIA reported that shipments of RVs in 2003 were worth $12 million at retail, up from $10 million in 2001. The average price of a folding camping trailer was $6,824; of a conventional towable travel trailer, $16,631; and of a full-size motor home, $143,834.

Some also chose to rent RVs from one of more than 460 rental outlets located around the United States. Rentals of motor homes, the model most commonly chosen, cost between $90 and $200 per day in 2003, according to the RVIA, while folding camping trailers and travel trailers cost between $28 and $85 per day. Rentals of RVs were popular and the rental category was growing, with the RVIA predicting it would increase by 34% during 2004.

RVs Go High Tech

RVs are being outfitted with increasingly sophisticated technology. According to the RVIA, popular electronic items found on RVs included flat-screen televisions, satellite dishes, video game systems, computers, surround-sound CD and DVD players with individual headphones, and global positioning systems. Many also came equipped with automatic leveling systems and closed-circuit television cameras to facilitate backing up the large vehicles, and "slideouts," moving walls that increase an RV's interior space once it is stopped by as much as three and one-half feet. More than 90% of fifth-wheel travel trailers and large motor homes contained slideouts, according to the RVIA.

Who Owns RVs?

The University of Michigan study described the typical RV owner as a forty-nine-year-old married man with an annual household income of $56,000. RV owners were likely to be homeowners, and they tended to spend their disposable income on travel, averaging 4,500 miles during twenty-eight to thirty-five days of travel per year. The highest number of RVs were owned by those age fifty-five and older, 10% of whom possessed one, according to the University of Michigan.

Shifting U.S. demographics—the aging of baby boomers—will likely add to the growth of the RV industry. Increasing numbers of single people, especially women, are also taking to the road in RVs. The University of Michigan study projected that eight million U.S. households would own an RV by 2010, an increase of 15%, outpacing the projected 10% growth in U.S. households.

THRILL CHASING—EXTREME SPORTS

Growing numbers of people have begun participating in high-risk recreational activities. Young adults dominate the thrill seekers, but older people are jumping in as well. Skydiving, hang gliding, rock climbing, mountaineering, bungee jumping, white-water rafting, and other extreme sports have all shown huge increases in participation.

The U.S. Parachute Association (USPA) reported that its membership had grown to more than thirty-four thousand in 2003 and that between 130,000 and 150,000 people went skydiving in a typical year. A USPA membership survey conducted in 2002 reported that 84.1% of member skydivers were men, half of whom were under the age of forty. Almost half of USPA members said they had jumped more than 250 times in their lives, with a third having jumped between twenty-six and 250 times. The ranks of parachutists came from a diverse group of occupations, but the most common field cited was the military (10.1%), followed by business management (9%), building trades (7.9%), the computer industry (7%), engineering (6.8%) and medicine (6.3%).

The Sporting Goods Manufacturers Association's (SGMA) *Sports Participation Topline Report* for 2004 reported that 2.2 million Americans participated in mountain or rock climbing during 2003. Participation had grown almost 4% from the year earlier. Rock-climbing gyms were also beginning to spring up around the country. Participation in artificial wall climbing grew by almost 84% from 1998 to 2003, to 8.6 million participants. (See Table 1.6 in Chapter 1.)

Another popular new extreme sport was paintball, in which participants staged mock battles with air-powered guns that shot paint-filled projectiles. According to the SGMA, total sales of paintball equipment increased by more than 5% between 2002 and 2003, to $390 million. (See Table 2.6 in Chapter 2.) The organization also found that in 2003, there were 9.8 million paintball players, up 13% from 2002 and a 66% increase since 1998. (See Table 1.6 in Chapter 1.)

Advocates of extreme sports continued to search for new challenges in the early twenty-first century. Skydiving had grown to include several new forms, including sky surfing, free flying, and aerial ballet, for those who thought simply jumping from fifteen thousand feet was too easy. Bungee jumping had also been expanded to include bridge, aerial, structure, and earth jumping.

One explanation for the rising popularity of extreme sports was the heightened awareness of them created by the media. Movies and advertising often featured mountain climbers or skydivers in dramatic, breathtaking scenes. In addition, many participants reported a life-affirming "adrenaline rush," and some experts suggested that extreme sports enthusiasts enjoyed the appearance of living on the edge.

Others believed that the improved safety of extreme sports as a result of technological advances and training had stimulated this growth. Equipment was well engineered to ensure that bungee cords and parachutes were highly unlikely to fail, and modern sports medicine could prepare participants with conditioning programs and exercises and assist them in recovering after mishaps.

Sports manufacturing industry experts predicted that the popularity of extreme sports would grow as young adults' earnings continued to rise. Furthermore, traditional obstacles to participation, such as gender and age, were rapidly disappearing because Americans remained physically active longer.

AMUSEMENT AND THEME PARKS

Theme and amusement parks, in general, saw a drop in attendance in the early twenty-first century. According to *Amusement Business* magazine, attendance at the nation's top fifty parks fell 1.6% in 2003, to almost 168 million people, following a slightly smaller decline in 2002. Factors cited for the drop included the depressed U.S. economy, the war on terrorism and in Iraq, and bad weather during the early part of the summer season.

Many adults may also be wearying of the very things that give young adults such a thrill: high-tech, action-packed adventure. In addition, theme parks are becoming increasingly expensive to attend. According to *Amusement Business,* the average price in 2004 for an adult admission to a park was $44.99, up by $1.59 from 2003. An online poll conducted by the same magazine in April of that year found that 84% of respondents believed amusement park prices were too high.

Several theme parks reported attendance increases between 2002 and 2003, including Walt Disney World's EPCOT in Florida, up 4%; Disney's California Adventure, up 13%; SeaWorld Florida, up 4%; and Cedar Point and Paramount's Kings Island, both in Ohio, up 3% each. Atten-dance at most amusement parks, however, declined during 2003, according to data compiled by *Amusement Business.*

Those experiencing drops included Disney MGM Studios in Florida, down 2% from 2002; Universal Studios Hollywood, down 12%; and Busch Gardens in Florida and Adventuredome at Circus Circus in Las Vegas, both down 4%. Knott's Berry Farm in California also experienced a 4% drop, and Morey's Piers in New Jersey had a 5% falloff.

Because children are generally accompanied by adults to theme parks, the parks have begun seeking novel ways to appeal to adult visitors. The parks of the future will likely anticipate the needs and preferences of their older customers. They may feature fewer thrill rides and place greater emphasis on serene, comfortable surroundings, such as fountains, seats, and garden settings.

Similarly, parks are expected to cater to families' preferences for wholesome pastimes rather than competitive or violence-oriented activities. Legoland, a Carlsbad, California, park that debuted in 1998, invites visitors to build structures with plastic blocks and appeals to families seeking lively, creative recreation.

FAIRS AND CARNIVALS

Americans have long loved agricultural fairs that feature displays of prize-winning farm animals, crafts, vegetables, and baked goods, along with midways filled with rides and food vendors selling such treats as elephant ears and corn dogs. Traveling carnival operators that provide the midway attractions for such fairs also set up shop in temporary locations such as school or church parking lots to bring this quintessential form of American outdoor entertainment to those in urban areas.

The top five fairs in North America in 2003, according to *Amusement Business,* were the State Fair of Texas, with more than three million visitors; the Houston Livestock Show and Rodeo, with 1.7 million; the Minnesota State Fair, with 1.7 million; the Los Angeles County Fair, with 1.3 million; and the Canadian National Exhibition in Toronto, with 1.3 million.

Overall attendance at the top fifty fairs was more than 43.2 million, down slightly from the almost forty-four million counted in 2002 and very close to the figure reported for 2001. The 2003 decline was primarily attributed to new counting methods at several fairs, which saw large drops in reported attendance although revenue figures had stayed the same. Several fairs did record poor results because of weather and other circumstances, however, including the Canadian National Expositions in Toronto and Ottawa and the Michigan State Fair in Detroit, all of which were forced to cancel portions of their schedules because of a massive power outage that struck the eastern half of North America in August 2003.

The carnival operators that supplied the rides at the top fifty North American fairs reported a slight drop in business during 2003, with their total customers falling from 38.1 million to 37.4 million. The leading carnival operator, Conklin Shows, served 6.7 million customers at eight major fairs during 2003.

GARDENING

For some Americans, outdoor activities are as close as their own backyard. According to the National Gardening Association (NGA), in 2003 eighty-four million U.S. households (78%) had at least one gardener, up from seventy-two million in 1994. Gardening participation varied from year to year, based on home ownership rates, the number of sunny days during the growing season, and portrayals of gardening in the media.

A survey conducted by the NGA in 2001 found that flower gardening was more popular than vegetable gardening in the United States, with four out of ten households growing flowers, compared to three out of ten raising vegetables. Householders ages thirty-five to fifty-four (51%) were most likely to live in a flower-gardening household; middle-aged and older households were more likely to grow vegetables. On average, 31% of all households grew vegetables. The NGA predicted that the huge number of baby-boomer households entering the prime gardening ages would likely boost the overall number of flower-gardening households by 17% and vegetable-gardening households by 18.5% by 2010.

Surveyed gardeners reported that they gardened for the pleasure of being outdoors, the aesthetic pleasure gardening provided, the relaxation, and the exercise. In addition to providing pleasure as a recreational activity, gardening also offers an array of health benefits. It provides an ideal form of moderate exercise, and tilling the soil can help soothe jagged nerves, relieve stress, and reconnect people to the natural, seasonal rhythms of the earth.

The exercise benefits of gardening vary. Strenuous tasks such as mowing with a push mower, mixing compost into the soil, using heavy power tools, and chopping wood are as vigorous as tennis, jogging, and weight lifting. More sedate activities, such as watering the lawn, trimming shrubs with power tools, raking, or riding a power mower, burn fewer calories but still offer opportunities to bend, stretch, and strengthen joints.

For many older adults, gardening proves to be an enjoyable way to incorporate exercise and creativity into their lives. For others, it is therapeutic. Hospitals, assisted-living facilities, nursing homes, and adult day care, retirement, and recreation centers offered programs ranging from botany classes and garden clubs to horticultural therapy (gardening as a means of helping to heal illness and promote well-being).

THE FUTURE OF OUTDOOR RECREATION

According to the middle-series projections of the U.S. Census Bureau, the total population of the United States will increase 49% between 2000 and 2050. Most of the growth, however, was expected to be among the older ages and minorities, neither of which have had historically high rates of participation in active sports. A rapidly increasing share of young adults would be black, Hispanic, or Asian. In general, minorities have had less discretionary income than whites, especially older whites.

Despite these inhibiting factors, outdoor recreation activity was projected to grow over the next half-century, according to J. M. Bowker, Donald B. K. English, and H. Ken Cordell in their 1999 study *Projections of Outdoor Recreation Participation to 2050*. The five fastest growing activities as measured by number of participants were projected to be cross-country skiing (up 95%), downhill skiing (up 93%), visiting historic places (up 76%), sightseeing (up 71%), and biking (up 70%). The five slowest growing activities were projected to be rafting (up 26%), backpacking (up 26%), off-road vehicle driving (up 16%), primitive camping (up 10%), and hunting (projected to decline 11%).

CHAPTER 4
THE ARTS AND MEDIA

ARTS ACTIVITIES

Many Americans like to spend their free time experiencing the fine arts. Some attend opera, ballet, or classical music performances, others go to art museums or galleries, and many curl up with a good book.

The National Endowment for the Arts (NEA) *2002 Survey of Public Participation in the Arts* (2004) found that 39.4% of the American adult population, or 81.2 million people, had attended a classical music, jazz, opera, or ballet performance; musical or play; or visited an art museum or gallery during the previous year. This percentage was down slightly from the 41% of adults who participated in the arts in 1992 (the last time the survey was taken), although the total number of participants was up by five million.

When the number of Americans who participated in these "benchmark" activities (which did not include elementary or high school performances) was added to those who watched other types of dance performances, visited art/craft fairs, visited historic sites, read literature, viewed or listened to performing arts on television or radio, personally performed or created art, took art classes, or owned art, the percentage increased to 76% of adults, or 157 million Americans.

The most popular arts activity among Americans was reading literature, (plays, poetry, novels, or short stories), which was done by 46.7% of adults, or 95.3 million people. It was followed by visiting art/craft fairs or festivals, at 33.4% (68.4 million); visiting historic sites (parks/historic buildings/neighborhoods), 31.6% (64.7 million); visiting art museums or galleries, 26.5% (54.3 million); musical plays, 17.1% (35.1 million); nonmusical plays, 12.3% (25.2 million); classical music concerts, 11.6% (23.8 million); and jazz performances, 10.8% (22.2 million). (See Table 4.1.)

Those who attended arts performances or visited historic sites typically went at least twice per year. Visitors to

historic sites tended to visit an average of 3.6 different ones, while those who liked art museums and galleries visited 3.5 times. Fans of modern and other nonballet types of dance saw two performances during 2002, while jazz lovers went to 3.1 performances and classical music listeners, 3.1. Other popular repeat activities included attending art/craft fairs and festivals (2.4 visits per person), musical plays (2.3), and plays (2.3). (See Table 4.2.)

In general, attendance at various arts events was highest among whites. One exception was jazz performances, which a greater proportion of African-Americans attended compared to their percentage of the total U.S. population. Many activities also appealed more to women than men, most notably ballet, for which more than two-thirds of the attendees were female. People between the ages of thirty-five and forty-four were somewhat more likely to attend arts events, with those ages forty-five to fifty-four close behind. Higher levels of education and greater income were also linked to greater participation and attendance at arts events. (See Table 4.3.)

CREATING ART

The NEA survey asked respondents about their participation in personally performing or creating art in 2002. The study revealed that the highest rates of personal participation were in weaving/sewing (16%), photography (11.5%), painting/drawing (8.6%), and writing (7%). The survey also found that almost 5% of the adult population sang publicly in a choir or chorale. The lowest rates of participation were in jazz (1.3%), opera (0.7%) and ballet (0.3%). These low rates were not unexpected because these disciplines are demanding and require extensive training. Participation in almost every category had declined since 1992, save for slight increases in those reporting that they composed music or danced ballet. (See Table 4.4.)

As with attending arts performances and events, in many categories whites were more likely to participate in

TABLE 4.1

Adults participating in the arts at least once in a 12-month period, 1982, 1992, 2002

	Percent of adults attending/visiting/reading			Millions of adults attending/visiting/reading		
	1982	1992	2002	1982	1992	2002
Performing arts						
Music						
Jazz[1]	9.6%	10.6%	10.8%	15.7	19.7	22.2
Classical music[1]	13.0	12.5	11.6	21.3	23.2	23.8
Opera[1]	3.0	3.3	3.2	4.5	6.1	6.6
Plays						
Musical plays[1]	18.6	17.4	17.1	30.5	32.3	35.1
Nonmusical plays[1]	1.9	13.5	12.3	19.5	25.1	25.2
Dance						
Ballet[1]	4.2	4.7	3.9	6.9	8.7	8.0
Other dance[2]	NA	7.1	6.3	NA	13.2	12.1
Visual arts						
Art museums/galleries[1]	22.1	26.7	26.5	36.2	49.6	54.3
Art/craft fairs and festivals	39.0	40.7	33.4	63.9	75.6	68.4
Historic sites						
Parks/historic buildings/neighborhoods	37.0	34.5	31.6	60.6	64.1	64.7
Literature						
Plays/poetry/novels/short stories	56.9	54.0	46.7	93.3	100.3	95.3
Any benchmark activity	39.0	41.0	39.4	66.5	76.2	81.2

[1]Denotes "benchmark" art activity.
[2]"Other dance" refers to dance other than ballet, including modern, folk, and tap. "Other dance" was not included in the 1982 survey.
Note: Figures may differ slightly from those shown in other reports and notes due to rounding.

SOURCE: "Table 1. U.S. Adults Participating in the Arts at Least Once in a 12-Month Period: 1982, 1992, 2002," in *2002 Survey of Public Participation in the Arts*, National Endowment for the Arts, 2004, http://www.arts.gov/pub/NEASurvey2004.pdf (accessed September 9, 2004)

TABLE 4.2

Average number of attendances to an arts event and total number of attendances, 1992 and 2002

	1992			2002		
	Audience in millions	Average number of attendances per attender	Total number of attendances in millions	Audience in millions	Average number of attendances per attender	Total number of attendances in millions
Performing arts						
Music						
Jazz[1]	19.7	2.9	57.1	22.2	3.1	68.8
Classical music[1]	23.2	2.6	60.3	23.8	3.1	72.8
Opera[1]	6.1	1.7	10.4	6.6	2.0	13.3
Plays						
Musical plays[1]	32.3	2.3	74.5	35.1	2.3	79.3
Non-musical plays[1]	25.1	2.4	60.2	25.2	2.3	58.7
Dance						
Ballet[1]	8.7	1.7	14.8	8.0	1.7	13.5
Other dance[2]	13.2	3.0	39.6	12.1	2.0	24.6
Vlisual arts						
Art museums/galleries[1]	49.6	3.3	163.7	54.3	3.5	190.6
Art/craft fairs and festivals	75.6	2.7	204.1	68.4	2.4	164.2
Historic sites						
Parks/historic buildings/ neighborhoods	64.1	3.8	243.6	64.7	3.6	231.0

[1] Denotes benchmark activity
[2] "Other dance" refers to dance other than ballet, including modern, folk, and tap

SOURCE: "Table 7. Average Number of Attendances and Total Number of Attendances, 1992 and 2002," in *2002 Survey of Public Participation in the Arts*, National Endowment for the Arts, 2004, http://www.arts.gov/pub/NEASurvey2004.pdf (accessed September 9, 2004)

TABLE 4.3

Demographic distribution of adults who participated in the arts at least once in the 12-month period ending August 2002

	U.S. population (millions)	U.S. population (Percent)	Any benchmark activity	Jazz	Classical music	Opera	Musicals	Nonmusical plays	Ballet	Art museum	Other dance	Literature	Historic sites	Art fairs and festivals
Gender														
Male	98.7	47.9%	44.2%	47.7%	42.7%	42.2%	39.1%	40.1%	31.6%	44.5%	38.2%	38.6%	46.4%	38.8%
Female	107.2	52.1	55.8	52.3	57.3	57.8	60.9	59.9	68.4	55.5	61.8	61.4	53.6	61.2
Total	**205.9**	**100.0**	**100.0**	**100.0**	**100.0**	**100.0**	**100.0**	**100.0**	**100.0**	**100.0**	**100.0**	**100.0**	**100.0**	**100.0**
Race and ethnicity														
Hispanic	22.7	11.0	6.5	6.3	5.2	6.1	4.5	5.5	4.6	6.7	9.7	6.2	6.0	6.7
White*	150.1	72.9	80.5	77.0	86.2	86.4	85.4	84.1	88.2	81.2	79.0	80.3	83.1	83.0
African-American*	23.7	11.5	8.1	13.5	4.5	3.8	6.9	6.6	4.5	6.4	7.6	9.1	6.5	6.8
Other*	9.5	4.6	4.9	3.1	4.1	3.6	3.2	3.7	2.7	5.7	3.7	4.3	4.4	3.5
Total	**205.9**	**100.0**	**100.0**	**100.0**	**100.0**	**100.0**	**100.0**	**100.0**	**100.0**	**100.0**	**100.0**	**100.0**	**100.0**	**100.0**
Age														
18–24	26.8	13.0	11.8	12.7	8.8	8.3	11.3	12.0	8.8	11.6	12.8	11.9	11.7	11.4
25–34	36.9	17.9	18.0	18.0	14.0	17.0	16.2	15.5	16.2	18.1	16.7	18.3	18.9	18.0
35–44	44.2	21.5	23.0	25.8	19.8	18.9	23.9	22.6	27.2	22.2	23.6	21.4	24.3	23.8
45–54	39.0	18.9	22.1	24.4	24.9	24.0	21.4	23.4	25.1	23.5	24.0	20.9	22.8	22.0
55–64	25.9	12.6	13.0	10.3	17.0	16.8	14.5	14.1	10.8	13.2	12.0	13.2	12.6	13.2
65–74	17.6	8.5	7.7	6.1	9.3	10.7	8.3	9.1	7.4	7.6	7.3	8.3	6.6	8.0
75 and over	15.5	7.5	4.4	2.7	6.2	4.4	4.5	3.3	4.4	3.8	3.6	5.9	3.1	3.5
Total	**205.9**	**100.0**	**100.0**	**100.0**	**100.0**	**100.0**	**100.0**	**100.0**	**100.0**	**100.0**	**100.0**	**100.0**	**100.0**	**100.0**
Education														
Grade school	11.6	5.6	1.1	0.5	0.7	0.4	0.5	0.5	0.6	1.0	2.0	1.7	1.1	1.4
Some high school	20.1	9.8	3.4	2.4	1.6	2.6	2.4	2.9	1.9	2.8	2.7	4.9	3.5	4.1
High school graduate	63.8	31.0	19.5	15.2	12.2	8.3	16.5	14.4	9.3	16.6	16.5	25.0	19.9	23.9
Some college	56.9	27.6	31.4	31.5	27.5	24.1	31.3	28.6	27.7	30.2	31.8	31.3	32.0	31.7
College graduate	36.1	17.5	28.5	31.5	33.1	35.5	30.8	31.9	32.3	30.7	27.3	23.7	28.3	25.8
Graduate school	17.4	8.5	16.2	18.9	24.9	29.1	18.5	21.7	28.1	18.6	19.7	13.4	15.2	13.1
Total	**205.9**	**100.0**	**100.0**	**100.0**	**100.0**	**100.0**	**100.0**	**100.0**	**100.0**	**100.0**	**100.0**	**100.0**	**100.0**	**100.0**
Income														
Less than $10K	14.4	7.0	4.1	3.6	4.4	3.2	3.4	3.4	3.0	3.6	3.2	5.3	3.4	4.5
$10K to $20K	22.7	11.0	6.8	6.0	5.5	6.4	5.8	5.4	5.8	6.3	7.3	9.8	5.6	7.7
$20K to $30K	25.0	12.1	8.7	7.8	7.2	7.0	6.7	6.6	8.1	8.1	8.0	10.8	8.7	9.7
$30K to $40K	24.2	11.8	11.5	13.1	11.3	10.7	10.2	10.6	9.1	11.2	12.4	12.2	11.5	12.7
$40K to $50K	17.6	8.5	9.4	9.0	10.5	7.1	8.9	9.4	8.8	8.9	8.6	9.7	9.6	9.7
$50K to $75K	34.7	16.9	21.3	19.3	19.7	20.2	23.2	21.2	20.4	21.1	22.0	20.8	22.6	22.2
$75K and over	45.8	22.2	38.2	41.2	41.5	45.3	41.8	43.5	44.8	40.7	38.5	31.6	38.6	33.5
Total	**205.9**	**100.0**	**100.0**	**100.0**	**100.0**	**100.0**	**100.0**	**100.0**	**100.0**	**100.0**	**100.0**	**100.0**	**100.0**	**100.0**

*Not including Hispanics

Note: Total may not equal 100% due to rounding

SOURCE: "Table 8. Demographic Distribution of U.S. Adults Who Attend/Visit/Read at Least Once in the 12-Month Period Ending August, 2002," in 2002 Survey of Public Participation in the Arts, National Endowment for the Arts, 2004, http://www.arts.gov/pub/NEASurvey2004.pdf (accessed September 9, 2004)

TABLE 4.4

Adults performing or creating art at least once in a 12-month period, 1992 and 2002

	Percent of adults personally performing or creating		Millions of adults personally performing or creating	
	1992	2002	1992	2002
Performing arts				
Music				
Jazz	1.7 %	1.3 %	3.2	2.7
Classical music	4.2	1.8	7.8	3.7
Opera	1.1	0.7	2.0	1.4
Choir/chorale[1]	6.3	4.8	11.7	9.8
Composing music	2.1	2.3	3.9	4.7
Plays				
Musical plays	3.8	2.4	7.1	4.9
Nonmusical plays	1.6	1.4	3.0	2.9
Dance				
Ballet	0.2	0.3	0.4	0.6
Other dance[2]	8.1	4.2	15.0	8.6
Visual arts				
Creating art				
Painting/drawing	9.6	8.6	17.8	17.6
Pottery/jewelry	8.4	6.9	15.6	14.1
Weaving/sewing	24.8	16.0	46.1	32.7
Photography	11.6	11.5	21.6	23.5
Own original art	22.1	19.3	41.1	39.5
Literature				
Plays/poetry/novels/ short stories	7.4	7.0	13.7	14.4

[1] Only includes those singing in a public performance or rehearsing for one
[2] "Other dance" refers to dance other than ballet, including modern, folk and tap

SOURCE: "Table 15. U.S. Adults Performing or Creating Art at Least Once in a 12-Month Period: 1992 and 2002," in *2002 Survey of Public Participation in the Arts,* National Endowment for the Arts, 2004, http://www.arts.gov/pub/NEASurvey2004.pdf (accessed September 9, 2004)

the performing and creating of art than those of other races, as were women. African-Americans, who made up 11.5% of the U.S. population, reported higher rates of participation in choirs/chorales (22%) and acting in plays (17.6%), while 11.2% of Hispanics reported participating in creating "other dance," slightly more than their 11% percent share of the population. There was also a strong correlation between greater participation in performing/creating and higher education and income levels. (See Table 4.5.)

Online Content Creation

In addition to creating and performing art in more traditional ways, many Americans now express themselves online. According to a spring 2003 Pew Internet & American Life Project (Pew/Internet) survey, *Content Creation Online,* 44% of the nearly two-thirds of American adults who used the Internet (fifty-three million) had created online content. The most common activity was posting photographs to Web sites, done by 21% of Internet users, followed by posting written material (17%), posting comments to an online newsgroup (10%), contributing material to Web sites run by businesses (8%), and contributing material to Web sites run by such organizations as church-

es or professional groups (7%). Another 6% of Internet users had posted artwork to Web sites, while 5% had posted audio files, 4% had posted material to Web sites created for their families, 3% had put video files on Web sites, and 2% maintained Web diaries or "blogs."

According to Pew/Internet, 13% of Internet users maintained their own Web sites, and 7% had "Web cams" on their computers to allow other Internet users to view them or their surroundings. Many of those who created online content did so infrequently—42% of those with Web sites said they added new content less often than every few weeks. Only 10% said they added content on a daily basis. (See Table 4.6.)

Online content creators were almost equally split between men and women, and three-fourths had attended or graduated from college. More than three-fourths were also under the age of fifty, while only 4% were older than sixty-five. Whites made up 77% of online content creators, 9% were African American, and 9% were Hispanic—roughly the same proportions as the population as a whole. (See Table 4.7.)

ART MUSEUMS

The Association of Art Museum Directors (AAMD) reported in its 2004 *State of the Nation's Art Museums* that attendance at American art museums was generally up in 2003. Forty-three percent of museum directors reported that their attendance had increased during the year, while 28% said it had not changed and 29% said it had decreased. Forty percent said they had increased educational programming, while 48% had made no changes and only 12% had decreased it. Most reported no change in artwork acquisitions, although 16% reported an increase and 8% reported a decline.

The AAMD also reported that funding was generally improving. Fifty-six percent of museum directors reported that individual giving was up from 2002 levels, while 39% said foundation support was up, and 35% indicated there had been no change. Corporate support was up for a third, unchanged for a third, and down for another third, while government support dropped for 46% and increased for only 19%, although this was an improvement when compared with the results for 2002.

THEATER, CONCERTS, AND OPERAS

Before there were movies, television, and radio, there was live theater. The first American theater, with actors, scenery, and numerous play productions, came to the American colonies from England in 1750. By the beginning of the nineteenth century, every major city had at least one theater company performing plays.

Taking the Show on the Road

As the American population grew and spread westward, so did the number of theaters. From New York City,

TABLE 4.5

Demographic distribution of adults personally participating in the arts at least once in the 12-month period ending August 2002

	U.S. adult population		Jazz	Classical	Opera	Choir/ Chorale	Musical play	Act in plays	Ballet	Other dance	Music composition	Painting	Writing	Photography	Pottery	Sewing	Own art	Purchased art recently
	Millions	Percent																
Gender																		
Male	98.7	47.9%	65.1%	40.0%	37.4%	38.2%	37.6%	44.3%	14.1%	38.3%	72.9%	35.7%	39.5%	45.0%	34.2%	7.1%	44.7%	45.0%
Female	1 07.2	52.1	34.9	60.0	62.6	61.8	62.4	55.7	85.9	61.7	27.1	64.3	60.5	55.0	65.8	92.9	55.3	55.0
Total	**205.9**	**100.0**	**100.0**	**100.0**	**100.0**	**100.0**	**100.0**	**100.0**	**100.0**	**100.0**	**100.0**	**100.0**	**100.0**	**100.0**	**100.0**	**100.0**	**100.0**	**100.0**
Race and ethnicity																		
Hispanic	22.7	11.0	4.6	4.4	6.7	6.6	3.8	10.4	6.6	11.2	3.0	8.7	6.3	6.5	8.2	8.6	4.0	5.1
White*	150.1	72.9	83.0	87.1	80.8	68.1	87.4	68.4	76.5	72.7	78.0	79.9	78.2	81.2	80.6	80.3	87.3	85.4
African-American	23.7	11.5	10.8	2.4	6.2	22.0	6.6	17.6	13.1	9.7	14.6	7.4	12.1	7.6	6.9	6.8	5.3	6.4
Other*	9.5	4.6	1.6	6.0	6.4	3.4	2.2	3.6	3.7	6.4	4.4	3.9	3.4	4.7	4.3	4.3	3.4	3.1
Total	**205.9**	**100.0**	**100.0**	**100.0**	**100.0**	**100.0**	**100.0**	**100.0**	**100.0**	**100.0**	**100.0**	**100.0**	**100.0**	**100.0**	**100.0**	**100.0**	**100.0**	**100.0**
Age																		
18–24	26.8	13.0	18.7	17.9	12.6	13.4	14.0	27.4	41.0	19.0	31.8	23.3	23.3	14.6	17.6	8.5	6.4	8.9
25–34	36.9	17.9	15.8	14.0	14.6	14.8	15.9	17.5	12.6	19.4	25.3	21.3	20.2	19.3	20.3	14.6	14.3	19.0
35–44	44.2	21.5	24.5	21.3	18.3	21.6	19.4	26.3	26.4	20.1	21.3	20.1	20.4	26.2	22.9	20.4	23.2	24.5
45–54	39.0	18.9	28.2	26.5	23.2	20.1	22.0	15.4	9.2	19.1	14.8	18.0	18.2	19.9	20.7	22.0	25.4	24.0
55–64	25.9	12.6	7.2	10.6	14.9	14.7	13.9	8.3	6.7	10.4	5.0	9.9	8.9	11.5	10.2	15.1	16.0	14.2
65–74	17.6	8.5	3.2	6.7	9.5	9.6	7.7	3.9	0.4	7.6	1.4	4.7	5.0	6.0	5.7	11.0	8.9	7.2
75 and over	1 5.5	7.5	2.5	3.0	6.9	5.8	7.0	1.2	3.8	4.5	0.3	2.7	3.9	2.5	2.6	8.5	5.8	2.2
Total	**205.9**	**100.0**	**100.0**	**100.0**	**100.0**	**100.0**	**100.0**	**100.0**	**100.0**	**100.0**	**100.0**	**100.0**	**100.0**	**100.0**	**100.0**	**100.0**	**100.0**	**100.0**
Education																		
Grade school	11.6	5.6	0.5	0.2	0.9	1.3	0.6	0.1	n a	0.9	1.5	1.1	0.8	0.8	1.3	4.2	0.8	0.6
Some high school	20.1	9.8	1.9	1.5	2.1	5.3	2.1	6.6	5.8	8.2	4.7	5.9	3.9	3.9	5.6	6.8	2.4	1.9
High school graduate	63.8	31.0	10.2	10.4	16.9	22.4	16.7	18.1	15.2	21.1	19.5	22.6	18.0	21.9	27.6	29.0	16.3	12.9
Some college	56.9	27.6	37.3	27.6	31.2	34.7	32.3	35.3	37.7	37.6	36.8	37.3	35.8	32.3	36.3	31.7	31.1	29.9
College graduate	36.1	17.5	30.1	35.0	25.2	23.5	27.1	29.5	21.2	20.5	24.4	22.3	26.2	26.3	20.2	19.0	29.7	31.5
Graduate school	17.4	8.5	19.8	25.3	23.7	12.8	21.2	10.3	20.3	11.6	13.2	10.8	15.2	14.8	8.9	9.3	19.8	23.2
Total	**205.9**	**100.0**	**100.0**	**100.0**	**100.0**	**100.0**	**100.0**	**100.0**	**100.0**	**100.0**	**100.0**	**100.0**	**100.0**	**100.0**	**100.0**	**100.0**	**100.0**	**100.0**
Income																		
Less than $10K	14.4	7.0	3.2	6.2	3.9	5.4	4.2	2.9	15.7	5.9	9.8	6.5	8.5	4.4	7.3	7.5	2.9	2.3
$10K to $20K	22.7	11.0	8.1	5.5	10.3	12.3	6.8	8.4	n/a	9.5	11.4	9.9	9.5	7.4	9.6	13.2	5.8	4.2
$20K to $30K	25.0	12.1	6.8	4.0	4.0	11.3	6.7	11.1	19.8	15.0	9.7	11.4	10.6	7.8	10.9	13.2	7.3	6.5
$30K to $40K	24.2	11.8	13.5	16.0	9.0	14.9	13.8	17.5	4.8	14.6	15.1	14.4	13.8	11.6	12.8	13.4	11.7	10.5
$40K to $50K	17.6	8.5	10.2	14.9	10.1	10.6	13.3	16.4	12.4	9.8	10.1	10.2	9.9	11.3	9.2	10.4	9.3	7.5
$50K to $75K	34.7	16.9	21.1	25.0	19.8	21.8	20.3	20.7	14.6	21.1	19.6	18.0	18.4	21.3	21.7	19.4	22.0	22.9
$75K and over	45.8	22.2	37.1	31.4	42.9	23.7	35.0	23.1	32.7	24.1	24.2	29.6	29.2	36.2	28.5	23.0	41.0	46.0
Total	**205.9**	**100.0**	**100.0**	**100.0**	**100.0**	**100.0**	**100.0**	**100.0**	**100.0**	**100.0**	**100.0**	**100.0**	**100.0**	**100.0**	**100.0**	**100.0**	**100.0**	**100.0**

Note: Percentages may not equal 100% due to rounding
*Not including Hispanics

source: "Table 17. Demographic Distribution of U.S. Adults Personally Participating in the Arts at Least Once in the 12-Month Period Ending August 2002," in 2002 Survey of Public Participation in the Arts, National Endowment for the Arts, 2004, http://www.arts.gov/pub/NEASurvey2004.pdf (accessed September 9, 2004)

TABLE 4.6

Frequency with which people maintaining their own Web sites update their sites, 2003

Several times a day	4%
About once a day	6%
3–5 days a week	7%
1–2 days a week	11%
Every few weeks	25%
Less often	42%
Do not know/refused	5%

Population = 202

SOURCE: Amanda Lenhart, John Horrigan, and Deborah Fallows, "How Often Do You Post Material on Your Web Site?" in *Content Creation Online,* Pew Internet & American Life Project, February 29, 2004, http://www.pewinternet .org/pdfs/PIP_Content_Creation_Report.pdf (accessed August 7, 2004)

TABLE 4.7

Demographics of Internet content creators, 2003

Men	51%
Women	49%
Race/Ethnicity	
Whites	77%
Blacks	9%
Hispanics	9%
Age	
18–29	28%
30–49	48%
50–64	20%
65 +	4%
Household income	
Less than $30,000	19%
$30,000–$50,000	21%
$50,000–$75,000	17%
$75,000 +	31%
Education level	
Did not graduate from high school	6%
High school graduate	19%
Some college	29%
College degree +	46%
Type of home Internet connection	
Dial up	63%
Broadband	37%

Population for Internet users = 1,555. In the Race/Ethnicity category 6% of respondents fall into the "other" category

SOURCE: Amanda Lenhart, John Horrigan, and Deborah Fallows, "Who Creates Content," in *Content Creation Online,* Pew Internet & American Life Project, February 29, 2004, http://www.pewinternet.org/pdfs/PIP_Content_ Creation_Report.pdf (accessed July 7, 2004)

the leading theater center, hundreds of companies took their performers on the road to bring entertainment to settlers all across the country. Until the early 1900s the theater—which included opera, drama, comedy, and musical shows—was America's principal form of entertainment. An original American theater type was the showboat, which sailed up and down the Mississippi River entertaining passengers, the gamblers who made a living on the river, and the residents of the towns where the boats docked.

Broadway

The modern period on Broadway began in New York City with the founding of the Theater Guild in 1918. It was the first commercially successful art theater to produce plays of the same caliber and quality as those produced in Europe. Other theaters soon opened, and they prospered right up to the stock market crash of 1929. The nation recovered from the Great Depression that followed, but theater did not because more and more people were going to see motion pictures or staying home to listen to the radio and, later, watch television.

By the turn of the twenty-first century it had become extraordinarily expensive to put on a Broadway show. In some instances, the extravagant sets and breathtaking special effects overshadowed the play. For example, the show *Sunset Boulevard* involved two separate stages, and in *Miss Saigon,* a real helicopter landed on the stage. The costs involved in staging a successful theatrical performance on Broadway had become almost prohibitive. As a result, fewer and fewer shows were produced there. Financial backers, concerned about minimizing their risks, appeared more willing to finance revivals of shows that were successful in years past or stage plays drawn from movies. Examples of revivals in the early 2000s included classics such as *Fiddler on the Roof* and *Gypsy,* as well as newer fare such as John Kander and Fred Ebb's darkly comic 1970s musical *Chicago.*

In 2004 forty venues were designated as Broadway theaters. In 1980 there were sixty-one new Broadway

shows, by 1991 just twenty-eight new shows had started, and in 1996 thirty-eight shows opened. In the 2003–04 season, there were thirty-nine new shows: twenty-four plays, thirteen musicals, and two "specials." Total box office sales for the 2003–04 season were $771 million, up 6.9% from the previous year, according to industry newspaper *Variety.* Attendance was up almost 2%, to 11.6 million, with the average ticket price rising $3.20 to $66.47.

Touring versions of Broadway shows were successful as well. During the 2002–03 season 12.4 million Americans bought $642 million worth of tickets to see traveling productions of hit shows around the country, according to the League of American Theaters and Producers.

In New York City there were also about 150 "Off-Broadway" and "Off-Off-Broadway" performance spaces, which presented an estimated 1,500 productions annually. Attendance was approximately seven million in 2002, according to the Alliance of Resident Theaters of New York.

Nonprofit Theater

The Theatre Communications Group (TCG; www.tcg.org) represents the interests of nonprofit professional theaters in the United States. At the end of the 2002–03 season, its membership consisted of 454 theater companies in forty-six states and Washington, D.C., up from 228 in 1996. These groups included ensembles, touring companies, children's theater groups, and small companies. During 2002–03 they held 63,330 performances of 4,787 different productions: the classics, modern plays, musicals, new plays by American and foreign playwrights, experimental works, and plays aimed at young audiences. In 1980, 14.2 million people attended TCG members' nonprofit theater productions; in 1994, 20.7 million did; and in the season that ended in 2003, attendance was eighteen million.

The TCG's annual report for 2002–03 noted that 4% of member theaters had budgets of $10 million or more, 7% spent $5–10 million, 6% spent $3–5 million, and 25% spent $1–3 million. The remaining 58% had budgets of less than $1 million. Nonprofit theaters employed forty-two thousand artists, administrators, and production staff in 2002–03.

Going to Concerts and Operas

Research conducted by Audience Insight for fifteen orchestras and the John S. and James L. Knight Foundation found that in 2002 just 17% of adults in the United States reported that they had attended a live classical music performance. Americans attended classical music concerts in a variety of settings, including traditional concert halls, school auditoriums and gymnasiums, churches and synagogues, and outdoor venues.

Although just over 3% of Americans typically attended opera performances each year, opera audiences increased by almost 50% in numbers from 1982 to 2002 (see Table 4.1.) In 2002–03 North America's professional opera companies offered 2,112 performances of 401 fully staged productions. According to OPERA America, a service organization that supports the creation and performance of opera, the ten most frequently produced operas during the 2004–05 season were: *Madama Butterfly* (Puccini), *Don Giovanni,* (Mozart), *La Boheme* (Puccini), *Carmen* (Bizet), *The Marriage of Figaro* (Mozart), *Tosca* (Puccini), *Rigoletto* (Verdi), *Aida* (Verdi), *The Mikado* (Sullivan), and *La Traviata* (Verdi).

Rock and Pop Music

The 2002 NEA survey asked Americans which types of music they liked to listen to. Almost half said they liked classic rock/oldies, while two-fifths said they liked country western, and almost 30% each said they liked blues/R & B, mood music/easy listening, jazz, classical/chamber music, and hymns/gospel music. When asked what their favorite type of music was, 16% said classic rock/oldies, 15% said country, and 14% said they preferred no particular genre.

Given these findings, it was not surprising that the best-attended concerts in America were ones given by well-established rock, country, and popular music performers. According to *Billboard* magazine, the top concert tours of 2003, in order, were those of the Rolling Stones, Bruce Springsteen, Cher, Fleetwood Mac, the Dixie Chicks, the Eagles, the Dave Matthews Band, Aerosmith/Kiss, Metallica's Summer Sanitarium, and Billy Joel/Elton John.

The Rolling Stones' 116-date September 2002 to October 2003 world tour was 99% sold out and attended by 3.4 million people worldwide, according to *Billboard*. It grossed $299.5 million. For his 2003 shows, Bruce Springsteen grossed $181.7 million, and Cher took in $76.3 million at the 116 shows of her two-hundred-date "Farewell Tour" in 2003, which grossed $145 million over two years.

MEDIA USAGE

Media experiences have become a part of the fabric of modern life. In their work and personal lives, Americans are bombarded with images and sounds that convey insistent and powerful messages. According to communications expert Marshall McLuhan, the medium is the message, and each medium presents a different type of experience. Listening to music on a compact disc (CD) player is unlike watching television, playing a video game, surfing the Internet, or reading a book.

Multiple contacts with the media are inescapable aspects of daily life. Televisions flicker in kitchens, living rooms, dens, and bedrooms. Children are mesmerized by video game competitions, and families use the computer to budget, bank, and send e-mail, as well as to surf the Internet and make purchases. Music flows from radios and CD players, while cell phones and personal digital assistants (PDAs) connect people to one another and the Internet.

Americans devote much time to the media, which includes television, radio, recorded music, newspapers, books, magazines, videos/DVDs for rent or purchase, movies in theaters, video games, and online computer services. In general, the less costly a form of consumer media is, the greater the usage of that medium. Since broadcast TV and radio are free to consumers, they have become the most widely used media, followed by subscription video services, recorded music, and online services. The most expensive media on an hourly basis are movies in theaters and videos/DVDs for rent or purchase.

According to the July 2003 survey *Internet and Multimedia 11: New Media Enters the Mainstream*, conducted by Arbitron Edison Research, the average American was then spending three hours and twenty minutes a day watching television, two hours, thirty-nine minutes listening to the radio, thirty-eight minutes reading the newspaper, and one hour, three minutes online. In *Communications Industry Forecast and Report 2004*, a study released in August

2004, the merchant banking firm Veronis Suhler Stevenson projected that by 2008 total media time per consumer would surpass eleven hours a day, reaching approximately seventy-eight hours per week.

The Birth of an Industry

In 1891 Thomas Alva Edison, the American inventor best known for the electric light bulb and phonograph, or "talking machine," applied for a patent on a "kinetoscopic camera." This camera took motion pictures on a band of film that could be seen by looking or "peeping" into a box, which gave these early pictures the name "peep shows." This invention soon gave rise to movie projectors and screens. In 1893 Edison and his partner, W. K. L. Dickson, built the Black Maria, the first movie studio.

As the United States entered the twentieth century, inventions such as the automobile, radio, telephone, and airplane were beginning to change the way people lived. While not everyone could afford all of these modern wonders, almost anyone could pay the price of a ticket to see "moving pictures" wherever there was a theater and a piano. (The first motion pictures were "silent movies." They had no sound and the actors' words were printed on the screen so the audience could follow the plot. A piano player or musical ensemble typically provided background music to make the movie more exciting.)

The first "blockbuster" movie, D. W. Griffith's *The Birth of a Nation* (also known as *The Clansman*), was released in 1915 and concerned the American Civil War and the beginnings of the racist group the Ku Klux Klan. The film's sympathetic treatment of its subject matter outraged African-Americans and some whites, but it went on to make more money than any other film released to that time. World War I gave filmmakers spectacles that audiences wanted to see, and 1,175 war films were made during that time, according to the *American Film Institute Catalog of Motion Pictures Produced in the United States.*

The years following the war saw a period of financial growth for the United States, and this prosperity, along with the emergence of such stars as Charlie Chaplin, Mary Pickford, and Rudolph Valentino, helped the motion picture industry become highly successful. By the mid-1920s, some twenty thousand movie theaters were showing moving pictures in the United States, twice the number as in 1910.

On the technical side, the industry was moving forward, with the first feature-length "talking picture," 1927's *The Jazz Singer,* revolutionizing the art of filmmaking while ending some careers and giving birth to others. The late 1930s saw the perfection of Technicolor, which was used to spectacular effect in such features as *Gone with the Wind* and *The Wizard of Oz,* although many films continued to be made in less-expensive black and white until the mid-1960s.

Movie Business Boom

Motion pictures remained one of America's favorite pastimes throughout the 1930s and 1940s. By 1950, however, television had emerged as a competitor. When it began to surge in popularity, fewer people went to the movies. Weekly attendance dropped from about ninety million people in 1947 to an average of forty-two million in the 1950s and 1960s. Gross sales fell from an all-time record high of $1.5 billion in 1957 to a yearly average of $1.2 billion in the 1950s and rose only slightly in the 1960s.

To respond to the threat of television, movie producers in the 1950s introduced a number of gimmicks such as widescreen and three-dimensional (3-D) movies to lure people back to theaters. Special glasses had to be worn for 3-D films to make it seem as though figures "jumped off" the screen, while widescreen movies simply resized the image for display on a larger, panoramic screen. Though the 3-D craze died off after just a year, the industry retained the widescreen format for all future theatrical releases.

The 1950s also saw an estimated 4,700 drive-in theaters built. These outdoor venues allowed families to park their cars by poles equipped with portable speakers and view the movies on giant screens. Drive-ins solved babysitting problems for parents and were so popular that they accounted for 25% of movie attendance in the 1950s. Teenagers also loved them for other reasons, which led to drive-ins earning the nickname "passion pits."

The number of drive-ins began to fall as suburbs spread out and property became more expensive. By 1971 the total had dropped to 3,720, and the ensuing decades saw an even more rapid decline. In 2003 just 408 remained in the entire country.

The way Americans viewed movies on indoor screens also changed during these years. In 1945 some 20,355 movie theaters existed; by 1960 that number had dwindled to 11,300. In 2003 it stood at 6,066, but because of the rise of the multiplex (multiscreen) theater beginning in the 1970s, the number of actual screens had grown to 35,786, an average of more than six per theater, according to the Motion Picture Association of America (MPAA).

Technological changes were occurring as well. In the late 1970s Dolby Stereo was introduced, and with its effective use in such films as the first *Star Wars* movie, it soon became the standard of the industry. By the late 1990s digital sound had become commonplace, and by the early twenty-first century the era of film itself appeared to be nearing an end. With filmmakers like George Lucas of *Star Wars* fame shooting their features digitally, and with rapid advances in digital projection technology, the number of all-digital screens rose to 171 worldwide in 2003 from 124 in 2002, according to the MPAA. The savings on expensive 35mm movie prints, and the prospect of splice- and scratch-free screenings for the life of a film, were driving factors in the anticipated conversion of the entire industry to an all-digital standard over time.

Box Office Grosses

According to the MPAA, total U.S. box office grosses climbed from the mid-1990s, with 2003 receipts of $9.5 billion, only 0.3% lower than the industry record year of 2002 and 13.2% above the $8.4 billion taken in during 2001. (See Table 4.8.) The increased revenues were largely attributable to growing numbers of admissions, although rising ticket prices also contributed. (See Table 2.9 in Chapter 2.)

The top movie of 2003, *Finding Nemo,* earned a total of $339.7 million at the U.S. box office, according to the MPAA, followed by *Pirates of the Caribbean* ($305.4 million), *Lord of the Rings: Return of the King* (290.4 million), *The Matrix Reloaded* ($281.5 million), and *Bruce Almighty* ($242.6 million).

Moviegoers

According to the MPAA, 167.6 million Americans went to a movie in 2003. Of these, slightly more than one-third went to movies more than once a month, while half went between two and eleven times a year and 15% went less than once every six months. Half of moviegoers were between the ages of twelve and twenty-nine, and although their growth rate remained flat when compared with 2002, the number of moviegoers aged forty to fifty-nine was growing, with attendance in this age group increasing 7% during the year.

In addition to revenues from box office receipts, which were split with theater owners, a movie such as the third entry in the *Lord of the Rings* trilogy also drove sales of the books it was based on, toys, games, clothing, videocassettes, and DVDs. According to Peter Mirsky, an Oppenheimer media analyst, 40% of the earnings for the *Ring* films would come from the box office, while another 35% would be from home video sales, 5% to 10% would come from television showings, and 15% would be derived from licensed merchandise sales.

Digital Videodiscs (DVDs) and Videocassettes

Some industry experts once believed that videocassette recorders (VCRs) and digital videodisc (DVD) players, which made it easy to watch movies at home, would hurt movie box office sales more than television. Others thought that such viewing alternatives would make more money for a film over time. Moviemakers learned that if a movie made money at the box office, it would also make money in video/DVD sales and rentals. In fact, sometimes a movie that was not expected to do well in movie theaters was released directly to video, where it could generate considerable revenue from rentals and purchases.

Although home video was once dominated by the tape-based VCR, by 2004 the higher-quality image and sound of DVDs, and the drop in price of players to an aver-

TABLE 4.8

Movie box office grosses, selected years 1983–2003

Year	Box office gross (in millions)	% Change	
		Previous period	2003 vs.
2003	**$9,488.5**	**−0.3%**	—
2002	9,519.6	13.2	**−0.3%**
2001	8,412.5	9.8	13.2%
2000	7,660.7	2.9	23.9
1999	7,448.0	7.2	27.4
1998	6,949.0	9.2	36.5
1997	6,365.9	7.7	49.1
1996	5,911.5	7.6	60.5
1995	5,493.5	1.8	72.7
1994	5,396.2	4.7	75.8
1993	5,154.2	5.8	84.1
1992	4,871.0	1.4	94.8
1991	4,803.2	(4.4)	97.5
1990	5,021.8	(0.2)	88.9
1989	5,033.4	12.9	88.5
1988	4,458.4	4.8	112.8
1987	4,252.9	12.6	123.1
1986	3,778.0	0.8	151.2
1985	3,749.4	(7.0)	153.1
1984	4,030.6	7.0	135.4
1983	3,766.0	—	152.0

SOURCE: "Box Office Growth," in *U.S. Entertainment Industry 2003 MPA Market Statistics,* Motion Picture Association of America, Inc., Encino, California, 2004

age of $122 (according to the Consumer Electronics Association, or CEA), had made it the hottest format in the video industry. Research conducted by the CEA found that in January 2001, 94% of U.S. households had VCRs and 15% had DVD players, but by January 2004, the number of households with VCRs had fallen to 87%, while 50% had DVD players. (See Table 2.4 in Chapter 2.)

According to Adams Media Research, the number of DVDs sold to dealers in the United States in 2003 was 1.1 billion, up 50.2% from 2002. The number of videocassettes sold was just 293.6 million, down 39% from 2002. By 2003, twenty-nine thousand different titles were available on DVD.

A 2001 Gallup poll found that watching movies at home was a popular way for Americans to spend an evening. Eighty-three percent of all polled respondents and 88% of those who owned a VCR or DVD player said they had viewed a movie at home during the month preceding the poll. Nearly all (96%) young adults ages eighteen to twenty-nine reported viewing an average of almost thirteen movies per month at home. More than 90% of adults ages thirty to forty-nine watched movies at home, but on average they watched about half as many as the younger adults. Rates of home movie viewing as well as the average number of films viewed per month declined with advancing age.

TELEVISION

Television has defined two generations of consumers. It has, however, ceased to possess the unifying power it once had. A TV viewer of the 1950s or 1960s could tune in to comedian Milton Berle or *Gunsmoke* and know that he or she was sharing the moment with nearly every other American. Today, people have many more choices, including cable TV, satellite TV, pay per view, rented videos and DVDs, and computers. The American viewing audience has become fragmented.

The Consumer Electronics Association (CEA) study *U.S. Consumer Electronics Sales & Forecasts, 1999–2004* found that virtually all U.S. households had at least one television and three-quarters had more than one. Nielsen Media Research estimated that as of August 2004 there were 109.6 million TV-owning households in the United States, representing an increase of 1.2 million television households over the previous year.

Effect of the Internet on TV Viewing

Conflicting opinions have been expressed about the effect of Internet use on TV viewing. Some data has suggested that Americans online view less television, while other data has indicated that the time saved by online activities leaves more time to spend watching television. Veronis Suhler Stevenson observed that the projected 192 hours per year Americans would devote to Internet use in 2003 was just a fraction of the 1,610 hours they would spend watching television or the 992 hours spent listening to the radio. They forecast that the time saved using the Internet to perform tasks such as banking, paying bills, and shopping would free up additional hours Americans could devote to other media including television.

Cable and Satellite TV

Cable TV subscribers pay a monthly fee to cable companies to receive not only the regular broadcast networks but also such specialized channels as The History Channel, Animal Planet, the Game Show Network, Nickelodeon (a children's channel), and ESPN (a sports channel). Cable TV subscribers who choose to pay more can also see the latest movies on such premium channels as HBO or Showtime. As of 1995 basic cable channels began to draw more total viewers than the three biggest networks (CBS, NBC, and ABC) in homes that had cable. During prime-time hours, however, the major networks still attracted more viewers than the cable channels, but the cable networks' audiences have only grown over time.

According to Nielsen Media Research, 68.1% of American households with television (73.9 million) subscribed to at least a basic cable TV package in 2003. Almost 37% of TV homes (forty million) subscribed to a premium cable package, which included such channels as HBO. Another 19.4 million households had satellite television. According to *Screen Digest,* 283 different cable and satellite channels were available in 2003.

RADIO

The original form of broadcast media, radio, was developed and refined during the late 1800s and early 1900s, initially gaining use for experimental and governmental purposes. A radio distress signal helped save many lives when the *Titanic* sank in 1912, and radio was used by the military during World War I. The first commercial broadcast was transmitted in 1920 by KDKA in Pittsburgh, and the 1930s and 1940s saw a golden age of radio entertainment, with such classic shows as "The Shadow" and "The Jack Benny Program" heard by millions of Americans across the country.

In 1950 ninety million radios were in use in homes, compared to just ten million televisions. The balance soon shifted, however, and with the widespread adoption of television by Americans, radio was relegated to back-burner status, delivering recorded music, news, farm reports, and weather, but with far fewer entertainment programs. The rise of rock and roll music gave radio a new lease on life, however, and the late 1950s and 1960s were another golden era, this time for AM (amplitude modulation) radio broadcasts featuring personality disc jockeys such as Murray the K and Wolfman Jack. The late 1960s also saw the spread of FM (frequency modulation) radio, which broadcast a high-fidelity stereo signal.

Radio continues to prove a popular medium with Americans in the twenty-first century. In 2004 almost 13,900 radio stations were broadcasting around the country, according to research firm Arbitron, Inc., in *Radio Today—How America Listens to Radio* (2004 edition). Of these, more than 80% were advertiser-supported commercial outlets.

According to Arbitron, the percentage of Americans who listened to radio weekly was roughly the same for every age group, approximately 90% to 95%, with those over sixty-five listening slightly less. People ages thirty-five to forty-four spent the most time listening, approximately twenty hours per week for women and twenty-two hours, forty-five minutes for men. While the number of men and women listening was roughly equal in most age groups, Arbitron found that in the youngest group (ages twelve to seventeen), more girls listened, and they spent more time listening than boys (fifteen hours per week versus eleven and three-quarters hours for boys).

Many Americans listened in the car while driving to or from work. Daily listenership figures peaked at seven A.M., noon, and from three to five P.M. More than one-third of listeners were in cars between six and ten A.M., while 43% were in cars between three and seven P.M. This number dropped to 26.1% from seven P.M. to midnight, according to Arbitron.

Different age groups listened to different types of radio stations. Those between twelve and seventeen preferred contemporary hit radio, urban, and alternative stations, while those eighteen to twenty-four listened mostly to alternative, along with contemporary hit and urban. Between twenty-five and thirty-four, the most popular formats included alternative, rock, Spanish-language, urban, contemporary hit, and adult contemporary. Americans ages thirty-five to forty-four preferred rock, adult contemporary, new adult contemporary/smooth jazz, and oldies. For those ages forty-five to fifty-four, oldies topped the list, followed by new adult contemporary/smooth jazz. Those ages fifty-five to sixty-four preferred classical music, adult standards, new adult contemporary/smooth jazz, and news/talk/information. Americans sixty-five and above preferred adult standards, classical, and news/talk/information.

HOME ELECTRONICS PRODUCTS

America's love affair with consumer electronics has shown no sign of waning. Cellular phones; digital cameras and camcorders; cordless phones; large-screen, flat panel, projection, and high-definition TV sets; video game systems; mobile navigation devices; and home security systems have continued to rank high on the wish lists of many Americans. The CEA forecast that the wholesale value of shipments of consumer electronics would reach a record $100.1 billion in 2004, up from the estimated $96.4 billion worth shipped in 2003.

The CEA credits digital products such as digital televisions (DTVs) with driving industry growth. An estimated four million DTVs were sold in 2003, and in 2004 this figure was expected to rise to more than 5.7 million, with a total value of $8 billion at wholesale. The DTV category included flat panel, plasma, and liquid crystal diode (LCD) TVs. Although falling off in some categories, digital audio sales continued to be strong overall, with sales of MP3 players expected to hit 5.1 million in 2004, up from the estimated 3.8 million sold in 2003. Digital camera sales totaled an estimated 12.5 million in 2003, and were projected to rise to more than 15.3 million in 2004.

Cellular telephones are another highly popular consumer electronics product. The number of wireless telephone subscribers has skyrocketed since the 1990s. The CEA predicted that sales of wireless telephones would grow to 84.6 million units in 2004, representing $11.5 billion worth of factory sales.

Sales of personal computers were also expected to rise in 2004 as consumers upgraded older systems to accommodate new digital media and software requirements. The CEA projected that 17.5 million computers would be sold, up from the estimated 15.9 million sold in 2003. The electronic gaming market, meanwhile, was expected to remain flat, with wholesale sales estimated at $10.9 billion for both 2003 and 2004, as a rise in software

TABLE 4.9

Total dollar value of sound recording sales, 1994–2003

(In millions)

1994	$12,068.00
1995	$12,320.30
1996	$12,533.80
1997	$12,236.80
1998	$13,723.50
1999	$14,584.50
2000	$14,323.00
2001	$13,740.89
2002	$12,614.21
2003	$11,854.40

Figures indicate the overall size of the U.S. sound recording industry based on manufacturers' shipments at suggested list prices

SOURCE: Peter Hart Research, *2003 Consumer Profile*, Recording Industry Association of America, 2004, http://www.riaa.com/news/marketingdata/pdf/2003consumerprofile.pdf (accessed July 7, 2004)

sales was cancelled out by a drop in hardware sales. Home security systems also projected flat or slight sales growth, from just under $2.1 billion in 2003 to slightly more than that figure in 2004.

RECORDED MUSIC

Americans have long been among the most voracious consumers of recorded music in the world. However, the Recording Industry Association of America, the music industry's primary trade association, reported that the total U.S. dollar value of audio recordings was dropping, from $14.6 billion in 1999, to $13.7 billion in 2001, to $11.9 billion in 2003. (See Table 4.9.) The decline was attributed to such factors as widespread illegal downloading of music from the Internet, the falling price of compact discs at retail, and a lack of blockbuster albums from major artists.

In 2003 the most widely purchased type of recorded music was rock, at 25.2%, although its popularity had steadily declined since 1994 when 35.1% of audio recordings sold were in this category. During the same period, interest in country music waned from 16.3% to 10.4%. (See Table 4.10.)

Other categories of music experienced growth. Rap/hip-hop nearly doubled its share of the market, rising from 7.9% in 1994 to 13.3% in 2003, while religious music increased from 3.3% of the total in 1994 to 5.8% in 2003. Most other categories held relatively stable throughout the period. (See Table 4.10.)

The form in which Americans purchased music also changed. In 1994 slightly more than half of audio recordings purchased were CDs (58.4%) and a third were cassette tapes (32.1%). By 2003 cassette purchases had dropped to 2.2% as CDs became the overwhelming format of choice, with 87.8% of the market. In the future, the

TABLE 4.10

Recorded music purchased, by genre, format, age, source, and gender, 1994–2003

	1994 %	1995 %	1996 %	1997 %	1998 %	1999 %	2000 %	2001 %	2002 %	2003 %
Rock	35 .1	33.5	32.6	32.5	25.7	25.2	24.8	24.4	24.7	25..2
Rap/Hip-hop[1]	7.9	6.7	8.9	10.1	9.7	10.8	12.9	11.4	13.8	13.3
R&B/Urban[2]	9.6	11.3	12.1	11.2	12.8	10.5	9.7	10.6	11.2	10.6
Country	16. 3	16.7	14.7	14.4	14.1	10.8	10.7	10.5	10.7	10.4
Pop	10.3	10.1	9.3	9.4	10.0	10.3	11.0	12.1	9.0	8.9
Religious[3]	3.3	3.1	4.3	4.5	6.3	5.1	4.8	6.7	6.7	5.8
Classical	3.7	2.9	3.4	2.8	3.3	3.5	2.7	3.2	3.1	3.0
Jazz	3.0	3.0	3.3	2.8	1.9	3.0	2.9	3.4	3.2	2.9
Soundtracks	1.0	0.9	0.8	1.2	1.7	0.8	0.7	1.4	1.1	1.4
Oldies	0.8	1.0	0.8	0.8	0.7	0.7	0.9	0.8	0.9	1.3
New Age	1.0	0.7	0.7	0.8	0.6	0.5	0.5	1.0	0.5	0.5
Children's	0.4	0.5	0.7	0.9	0.4	0.4	0.6	0.5	0.4	0.6
Other [4]	5.3	7.0	5.2	5.7	7.9	9.1	8.3	7.9	8.1	7.6
Full-length CDs	58 .4	65.0	68.4	70.2	74.8	83.2	89.3	89.2	90.5	87.8
Full-length cassettes	32.1	25.1	19.3	18.2	14.8	8.0	4.9	3.4	2.4	2.2
Singles (all types)	7.4	7.5	9.3	9.3	6.8	5.4	2.5	2.4	1.9	2.4
Music videos/video DVDs	0.8	0.9	1.0	0.6	1.0	0.9	0.8	1.1	0.7	0.6
DVD audio[5]	NA	NA	NA	NA	NA	NA	NA	1.1	1.3	2.7
Digital download[5]	NA	NA	NA	NA	NA	NA	NA	0.2	0.5	1.3
SACD[6]	NA	NA	NA	NA	NA	NA	NA	NA	NA	0.5
Vinyl LPs	0.8	0.5	0.6	0.7	0.7	0.5	0.5	0.6	0.7	0.5
10–14 years	7.9	8.0	7.9	8.9	9.1	8.5	8.9	8.5	8.9	8.6
15–19 years	16 .8	17.1	17.2	16.8	15.8	12.6	12.9	13.0	13.3	11.4
20–24 years	15.4	15.3	15.0	13.8	12.2	12.6	12.5	12.2	11 .5	10.0
25–29 years	12 .6	12.3	12.5	11.7	11.4	10.5	10.6	10.9	9.4	10.9
30–34 years	11 .8	12.1	11.4	11.0	11.4	10.1	9.8	10.3	10.8	10.1
35–39 years	11 .5	10.8	11.1	11.6	12.6	10.4	10.6	10.2	9.8	11.2
40–44 years	7.9	7.5	9.1	8.8	8.3	9.3	9.6	10.3	9.9	10.0
451 years	15.4	16.1	15.1	16.5	18.1	24.7	23.8	23.7	25.5	26.6
Record store	53 .3	52.0	49.9	51.8	50.8	44.5	42.4	42.5	36 .8	33.2
Other store	26 .7	28.2	31.5	31.9	34.4	38.3	40.8	42.4	50.7	52.8
Tape/Recor d club	15.1	14.3	14.3	11.6	9.0	7.9	7.6	6.1	4	4.1
TV, newspaper, magazine ad or 800 number	3.4	4.0	2.9	2.7	2.9	2.5	2.4	3.0	2	1.5
Internet[7]	NA	NA	NA	0.3	1.1	2.4	3.2	2.9	3.4	5.0
Female	47 .3	47.0	49.1	51.4	51.3	49.7	49.4	51.2	50.6	50.9
Male	52 .7	53.0	50.9	48.6	48.7	50.3	50.6	48.8	49 .4	49.1

[1] "Rap": Includes rap (10.4%) and hip-hop (2.9%)
[2] "R&B": Includes R&B, blues, dance, disco, funk, fusion, Motown, reggae, soul
[3] "Religious": Includes Christian, gospel, inspirational, religious, and spiritual
[4] "Other": Includes ethnic, standards, big band, swing, latin, electronic, instrumental, comedy, humor, spoken word, exercise, language, folk, and holiday music
[5] 2001 is the first year that data was collected on DVD audio and digital download purchases
[6] 2003 is the first year that data was collected on SACD purchases
[7] "Internet": Does not include record club purchases made over the Internet

SOURCE: Peter Hart Research, *2003 Consumer Profile,* Recording Industry Association of America, 2004, http://www.riaa.com/news/marketingdata/pdf/2003consumerprofile.pdf (accessed July 7, 2004)

industry was expected to sell more and more music legally downloaded from the Internet, although in 2003 this constituted just 1.3% of sales, up from 0.5% in 2002. Music was also sold on DVD audio discs (2.7%), super-audio CDs (0.5%), and vinyl long-play albums (0.5%), among other specialist formats. (See Table 4.10.)

Americans over age forty-five made more than one-quarter (26.6%) of audio recording purchases in 2003, nearly twice their percentage in 1994. The growth in this age group likely reflected the enduring interest in music of the aging baby-boomer generation. In contrast, young people, once considered the recording industry's strongest supporters, comprised a declining proportion of the market for recordings. Purchases made by consumers ages fif-teen through nineteen dropped from 16.8% in 1994 to 11.4% in 2003, and among young adults ages twenty to twenty-four the number of consumers dropped from 15.4% in 1994 to 10% in 2003. While there were slight variations from year to year, men and women bought recordings in almost equal numbers. (See Table 4.10.)

The places Americans purchased their music was changing as well. In 1994 more than half of music purchases were made in record stores, but by 2003 only a third were. At the same time, sales through other types of stores, including such mass merchandisers as Wal-Mart, grew from less than a third to account for more than half of purchases. Only a small percentage of people (5%) purchased music over the Internet during 2003, while slightly less (4.1%) bought music from a record club such as Columbia House. (See Table 4.10.)

THE INTERNET, CONNECTIVITY, AND CONVERGENCE

An explosion in digital technology coupled with growth of the Internet have combined to produce a wealth of new possibilities for media experiences. It has become possible to move seamlessly from one medium to another in the same delivery platform—televisions or personal computers. Along with computer and TV access to the Internet, consumers can go online via cellular telephones and an expanding array of handheld devices, including personal digital assistants (PDAs).

The study *Internet and Multimedia 11: New Media Enters the Mainstream,* conducted by Arbitron Edison Research in July 2003 looked at practices and preferences of online consumers. The survey found that about 108 million Americans, 45% of the population over age twelve, had on at least one occasion accessed streaming media—that is, listened to audio or watched video online—and nearly half of these (fifty million) had done so within the last month. These online consumers were known as "streamies."

Streamies tended to be male (57%), and nearly a quarter were between the ages of thirty-five and forty-four. Nearly three-quarters were white and more than half reported an income in excess of $50,000 per year. Streamies spent an average of two hours and fifty-six minutes per day watching television, two hours and forty-four minutes listening to radio, one hour and fifty minutes accessing the Internet, and thirty minutes reading the newspaper.

Reported as a percentage of total Internet users, the most frequently viewed types of streaming video content were movie trailers or previews (9%), music videos (7%), highlights of sports events (5%), and short- or full-length movies (3%). Audio users primarily listened to radio station Webcasts, the most popular of which were those featuring contemporary hits. The Internet was a source for a wider variety of radio than many people could get over the airwaves, and stations broadcasting jazz, classical music, or Spanish-language programming were popular as well.

The study also found that 22% of Americans had residential broadband Internet access, while 42% had dial-up connections. Consumers with high-speed connections, as opposed to slower dial-up ones, viewed Internet access as much more essential for the activities of their daily lives and used streaming media more often. They also used the Internet nearly twice as much as those with dial-up connections and used other forms of media less.

Online Advertising and Spam

Use of the Internet was not without its frustrations. While two-thirds of those in the Arbitron Edison Research

TABLE 4.11

What e-mailers consider spam, 2003

Sender or subject matter	% who consider it spam
Unsolicited commercial email (UCE) from a sender you don't know	92%
UCE from a political or advocacy group	74
UCE from a non-profit or charity	65
UCE from a sender with whom you've done business	32
UCE from a sender you have given permission to contact you	11
UCE containing adult content	92
UCE with investment deals, financial offers, moneymaking proposals	89
UCE with product or service offers	81
UCE with software offers	78
UCE with health, beauty, or medical offers	78
Unsolicited email with political messages	76
Unsolicited email with religious information	76
A personal or professional message from one you don't know	74

For items 1–5, sample size = 624; for items 6–13, sample size = 648.

SOURCE: Deborah Fallows, "What Is Spam, Anyway?," in *Spam: How It Is Hurting Email and Degrading Life on the Internet,* Pew Internet &American Life Project, October 22, 2003, http://www.pewinternet.org/pdfs/PIP_Spam_Report.pdf (accessed July 7, 2004)

study said they preferred advertiser-sponsored free content over paid content, they did not like the intrusions of the ads. "Pop-up" advertisements that appeared when accessing certain Web sites were cited by 65% of those online as the most annoying type of Internet advertising, followed by "spam" e-mails from advertisers (9%), commercials during Internet audio or video broadcasts (3%), and Web site banner ads (3%).

According to the October 2003 Pew Internet & American Life Project (Pew/Internet) report *Spam: How It Is Hurting Email and Degrading Life on the Internet,* the definition of spam varied from person to person. While 92% considered unsolicited commercial e-mail (UCE) from a sender they did not know or with adult content to be spam, only 32% considered UCE from a sender they had done business with to be. Slightly more than three-fourths of e-mail users considered UCE with software offers, health, beauty, or medical offers, political messages, or religious information to be spam, while 11% considered UCE from a sender they had given permission to contact them spam. (See Table 4.11.) Women, parents, and older Internet users were more likely to consider a UCE to be spam or to be offended by it, according to Pew/Internet researchers.

While many have decried the spread of spam, the Pew/Internet report found that a third of e-mailers had clicked on a link to investigate the content of a spam e-mail, and 7% had ordered something online as the result of an unsolicited spam e-mail. Another 4% had provided personal information requested in a UCE, and 1% had given money in response to a request. (See Table 4.12.) Twelve percent of e-mail users also said they responded to an e-mail offer, only to find out later that it was phony or fraudulent.

TABLE 4.12

What e-mailers did with spam, 2003

	% respondents
Deleted it immediately without opening	86%
Clicked "remove me"	67
Clicked to get more information	33
Reported unsolicited commercial email (UCE) to email provider	21
Ordered a product or service	7
Reported UCE to consumer or government agency	7
Provided personal info requested in UCE	4
Given money in response to UCE	1

Sample size = 1,272

SOURCE: Deborah Fallows, "How Emailers Interact with Spam," in *Spam: How It Is Hurting Email and Degrading Life on the Internet*, Pew Internet & American Life Project, October 22, 2003, http://www.pewinternet.org/pdfs/PIP_Spam_Report.pdf (accessed July 7, 2004)

FIGURE 4.1

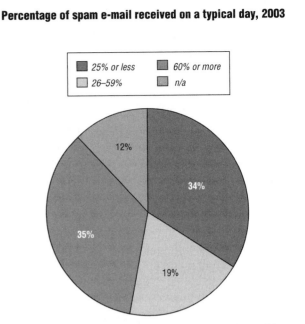

Percentage of spam e-mail received on a typical day, 2003

- 25% or less
- 60% or more
- 26–59%
- n/a

SOURCE: Deborah Fallows, "The Volume and Burdens of Spam," in *Spam: How It Is Hurting Email and Degrading Life on the Internet*, Pew Internet & American Life Project, October 22, 2003, http://www.pewinternet.org/pdfs/PIP_Spam_Report.pdf (accessed July 7, 2004)

The volume of spam received by e-mail users was found to vary widely. While 34% said that spam made up a quarter or less of the e-mail they received each day, an almost equal number (35%) said it comprised 60% or more of their e-mail. (See Figure 4.1.) This posed a problem for people whose e-mail service providers limited the amount of file space they could use—if they did not delete spam messages every day, they were in danger of reaching their storage limit and having incoming messages "bounced."

In 2003 a Center for Democracy and Technology study found that over 97% of the ten thousand incoming spam e-mails that researchers collected came to addresses that had been posted on the Web. Pew/Internet researchers found that 73% of e-mail users said they avoided giving out their e-mail addresses to reduce the amount of spam they got, 69% said they avoided posting their addresses on the Web, and 14% said they tried to use obscure screen names that were harder for spammers' address-generating computer programs to come up with.

Spam has proven to be more than just an annoyance for e-mail users, however—its uncontrolled spread has threatened to slow down Internet traffic worldwide. In July 2004 the United Nations' International Telecommunications Union hosted a meeting in Geneva, Switzerland, to explore ways to stop the spread of spam, noting that it had grown to comprise as much as 85% of all e-mails sent, up from 35% just a year earlier. While many touted bogus products like herbal weight-loss and sexual potency pills, some were sent by criminals hoping to commit fraud by gaining access to people's bank account numbers or other personal information. Only a few hundred people were suspected of sending the vast majority of such e-mails worldwide, according to UN experts.

CHAPTER 5

FOOTBALL, BASEBALL, BASKETBALL, AND OTHER POPULAR SPORTS

Americans love sports, and most children grow up playing team and individual sports during their physical education programs at school and simply for fun. Many men have played baseball or softball at some time in their lives, and some continue to play in community or neighborhood leagues long after they are finished with school. Today, women are playing sports once played mainly by men, such as soccer, baseball, and basketball. Many men and increasing numbers of women are sports fans.

SPECTATOR SPORTS

Historically, football, baseball, and basketball have been called the "holy trinity" of sports in the United States. They make money not only by filling ballparks and arenas with fans but also from televised sports events. The start of each new sports season brings hope to millions of sports fans that their teams will be in the championship games at the end of the year. These sports also fill stadiums with fans to watch middle school, high school, and collegiate competitions as well as professional games.

A December 2003 Gallup poll found that 37% of Americans named football as their favorite sport to watch. Almost a third of this number, 14%, said basketball, followed by 10% who named baseball and 6% who said figure skating. Ice hockey was named by 5%, as was auto racing. (See Figure 5.1.) Golf was named by 3%, and soccer and boxing were cited by 2% each.

While the number of Americans naming football and basketball had held relatively steady over the preceding ten years, the number of baseball fans had declined noticeably. Baseball was once the top spectator sport in America—in 1948, 39% named it their favorite sport to watch, and in 1960, 34% did, with football cited by just 21%. By 1972, however, football had taken the lead, 32% to 24%.

In 2003 about 67.6 million people attended Major League Baseball games and slightly more than 28,000

FIGURE 5.1

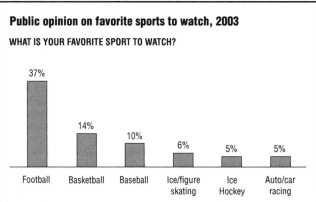

Public opinion on favorite sports to watch, 2003

WHAT IS YOUR FAVORITE SPORT TO WATCH?

SOURCE: Mark Gillespie, "What Is Your Favorite Sport to Watch?" in *Football Reigns as America's Favorite Sport,* http://www.gallup.com/content/default.aspx?ci=10438&pg=1. Copyright © 2004 by The Gallup Organization. Reproduced by permission of The Gallup Organization.

bought tickets to the average game. In the National Basketball Association's 2003–04 season, 20.3 million fans bought tickets, and an average of 17,059 attended each game. The National Hockey League also counted close to 20.3 million tickets sold in 2003–04 and averaged 16,533 per game. The National Football League had 17.1 million ticket buyers in 2003, but with far fewer games the average attendance was 66,726.

Although ratings of televised sports including baseball, basketball, and hockey declined in the early twenty-first century, football held steady. In 2004 approximately seventy-two thousand ticket buyers and 143 million television viewers watched the Super Bowl victory of the New England Patriots over the Carolina Panthers.

Collegiate Athletics

FOOTBALL. College sports are also popular with Americans, and many college teams inspire more devotion than

TABLE 5.1

National Collegiate Athletic Association football attendance, 2003

	Total teams	G	2003 attend.	Avg. PG	Change+ in avg.		Change+ in total	
				Division I-A and I-AA conferences and independents				
1. Southeastern (I-A)	12	83	$6,146,890	$74,059	Up	744	Up	61,734
2. Big Ten (I-A)	11	75	5,264,867	*70,198	Up	261	Dn	190,238
3. Big 12 (I-A)	12	81	*4,565,288	*56,362	Up	1,187	Up	206,470
4. Atlantic Coast (I-A)	9	58	*3,012,392	*51,938	Up	945	Up	54,781
5. Pacific-10 (I-A)	10	62	3,199,732	*51,608	Up	1,610	Dn	100,129
6. Big East (I-A)	8	51	*2,390,358	*46,870	Up	3,179	Up	74,750
7. Div. I-A Indep.#	4	21	940,404	44,781	Up	6,755	Up	103,830
8. Mountain West (I-A)	8	49	*1,607,660	32,809	Dn	2,077	Up	2,905
9. Conference USA (I-A)#	11	67	*2,167,173	*32,346	Up	5,705	Up	382,218
10. Western Athletic (I-A)	10	59	1,455,837	24,675	Dn	384	Up	2,431
11. Mid-American (I-A)	14	84	*1,496,906	17,820	Up	283	Up	76,381
12. Sun Belt (I-A)#	8	42	*602,763	*14,352	Up	795	Up	19,817
13. SW Athletic (I-AA)	10	48	579,976	12,083	Up	1,133	Up	120,065
14. Southern (I-AA)#	9	54	563,433	10,434	Up	647	Up	44,712
15. Ivy (I-AA)	8	42	431,729	10,279	Up	919	Dn	26,893
16. Gateway (I-AA)	8	50	*509,725	*10,195	Up	835	Up	51,103
17. Big Sky (I-AA)	8	49	495,861	10,120	Up	484	Up	42,976
18. Southland (I-AA)#	6	33	31,628	10,049	Up	373	Dn	16,725
19. Mid-Eastern (I-AA)	9	39	388,800	9,969	Up	705	Dn	65,147
20. Atlantic 10 (I-AA)	11	66	535,253	8,100	Up	841	Up	46,439
21. Ohio Valley (I-AA)#	9	48	343,855	7,164	Up	12	Up	36,327
22. Div. I-AA Indep.#	7	41	244,645	5,967	Up	846	Up	34,691
23. Patriot (I-AA)	8	49	*277,167	5,656	Up	445	Up	42,692
24. Big South (I-AA)#	5	29	136,101	4,693	Dn	1,223	Dn	17,710
25. Pioneer (I-AA)	9	54	*210,949	3,906	Up	574	Up	44,367
26. Northeast (I-AA)	8	37	*89,255	*2,412	Up	357	Up	4,983
27. Metro Atlantic(I-AA)#	6	33	62,007	1,879	Dn	243	Dn	5,883
Div. I-A teams	117	732	32,850,270	44,877	—	—	—	—
Div. I-A neutral sites		12	776,619	64,718	—	—	—	—
Div. I-A bowl games		28	1,458,757	52,098	—	—	—	—
Div. I-A . totals #	**117**	**772**	***35,085,646**	***45,447**	**Up**	**1,080**	**Up**	**701,382**
Div. I-AA teams	121	672	5,200,384	7,739	—	—	—	—
Div. I-AA neutral sites		26	855,451	32,902	—	—	—	—
Div. I- AA championship game		1	14,281	14,281	—	—	—	—
Div. I-AA totals #	**121**	**699**	**6,070,116**	**8,684**	**Up**	**791**	**Up**	**544,866**
Div. II teams	150	771	2,744,177	3,559	—	—	—	—
Div. II neutral sites		14	84,443	6,032	—	—	—	—
Div. II championship game		1	7,236	7,236	—	—	—	—
Div. II totals #	**150**	**786**	**2,835,856**	**3,608**	**Up**	**285**	**Up**	**189,044**
Div. III teams	229	1,127	2,097,719	1,861	—	—	—	—
Div. III neutral sites		16	50,129	3,133	—	—	—	—
Div. III championship game		1	5,073	5,073	—	—	—	—
Div. III totals #	**229**	**1,144**	**2,152,921**	**1,882**	**Up**	**123**	**Up**	**153,258**
All NCAA teams	***617**	***3,401**	***46,144,539**	**13,568**	**Up**	**444**	**Up 1,588,324**	

#Did not have same lineup as 2002.
$New national record.
*Record high.

SOURCE: "2003 NCAA College Football Attendance," The National Collegiate Athletic Association Statistics Service, 2004, http://www.ncaa.org/stats/football/attendance/2003/2003footballattendance.pdf (accessed September 10, 2004)

their professional counterparts. Saturday afternoon in autumn in many college towns offers more than just a football game—it gives old college friends a chance to reconnect and colleges the opportunity to pamper wealthy alumni from whom they hope to someday receive donations.

The "tailgate" party is a ritual of college football, and parking lots near stadiums on football Saturdays are typically filled with large recreational vehicles, campers, and station wagons from which food and drinks are dispensed as fans socialize before the game. With autumn leaves crunching underfoot, the scent of grilling burgers fills the

air, and the strains of the school fight song drift in from the marching band warming up nearby. Season tickets to many college teams' football seasons are prized possessions, and they are sometimes handed down from generation to generation.

In 2003 total attendance for National Collegiate Athletic Association (NCAA) Division I-A football was 35.1 million. An additional 11.1 million attended games at smaller schools in the Division I-AA, Division II, and Division III leagues. Average attendance in Division I was 45,447, and for the NCAA as a whole it was 13,568. (See Table 5.1.)

TABLE 5.2

National Collegiate Athletic Association women's basketball attendance, 2003–2004

[NCAA varsity women's teams only; home attendance includes double-headers with men in which separate attendance was taken by halftime of the women's game]

	Total teams	Game or session	2003–04 net attendance	Average per game or session	Change@ in total		Change@ in avg.	
Home attendance, NCAA Div. I	*324	4,273	6,718,289	1,572	Down	177,244	No change	
NCAA Div. I Tournament	—	42	318,666	7,587	Down	15,921	Down	379
Other Div. I neutral sites	—	120	136,422	1,137	Up	14,908	Up	62
NCAA Division I totals	*324	4,435	7,173,377	1,617	Down	178,257	Down	2
Home attendance, NCAA Div. II	269	3,456	1,631,098	472	Up	14,603	Up	9
Home attendance, NCAA Div. III	*415	*4,912	*1,039,547	*212	Up	39,076	Up 4	
Neutral-Site attendance, Divs. II & III	—	154	88,712	576	Up	18,527	Up	99
NCAA Div. II Tournament	—	36	43,309	1,203	Down	11,466	Down	319
NCAA Div. III Tournament	—	44	40,063	911	Down	800	Down	18
National totals	1,008	13,037	10,016,106	768	Down	147,523	Down	6

*Record. Net attendance includes some double-headers with men if attendance is counted by halftime of the women's game. @The 2002–03 figures used for comparisons reflect 2003–04 changes in divisional lineups to provide parallel comparisons (i.e., 2003–04 lineups vs. same teams in 2002–03, whether members or not).

SOURCE: *2003–2004 NCAA Women's Basketball Attendance,* The National Collegiate Athletic Association Statistical Service, 2004, http://www.ncaa.org/stats/ w_basketball/attendance/2003-04/2003-04_attendance.pdf (accessed September 10, 2004)

The football team of the University of Michigan sold out every home game in 2003, boasting average attendance of 110,918 per game, or 103% of the stadium's official seating capacity. Other teams, including Penn State, Tennessee, and Ohio State, also averaged more than 100,000 per home game.

BASKETBALL. College basketball draws millions of fans each year. In 2003 varsity men's basketball drew a total of 30.1 million fans, twenty-five million of whom went to Division I games. The average game in Division I had 5,372 in attendance, with the entire NCAA averaging 2,339. Leading schools included Kentucky, with an average of 22,271 per home game, Syracuse, with 20,921, and Louisville, with 19,037.

SOCCER, BASEBALL, AND OTHER SPORTS. According to the NCAA Web site, more than 40,000 student athletes participate in NCAA competition each year. In addition to football and basketball, other popular college sports included soccer, ice hockey, volleyball, baseball, softball, and lacrosse, a sport gaining enthusiasts in the early twenty-first century. The 2003 NCAA lacrosse championship game was attended by 43,898. According to U.S. Lacrosse, Inc., in 2003 almost 25,000 men and 5,500 women were playing lacrosse.

WOMEN'S ATHLETICS. Title IX of the Education Amendments passed by Congress in 1972 addressed gender equity in college education, and a series of amendments and later legal rulings significantly improved funding for women's sports programs in colleges, which had previously been given little money. As a result, opportunities for women in college athletics were greatly expanded, and their popularity exploded. In 2003–04 attendance at NCAA women's basketball games was ten million for all divisions. Division I schools averaged 1,617 fans per game. (See Table 5.2.)

Professional Wrestling—Is It a Sport?

Professional wrestling enjoyed a dramatic increase in popularity in the 1990s, but then peaked and fell off in the early years of the twenty-first century. World Wrestling Entertainment, Inc. (WWE—formerly known as the World Wrestling Federation) sold 1.8 million tickets to live events in 2003, down from a high of 2.5 million in 2001. Sales of pay-per-view television shows dropped to 5.3 million from eight million.

Wrestling fans tend to be male and young. According to Nielsen Media Research cited by the WWE in 2003, 71% of the television audience for WWE programs was male, and 29% was female. More than half were under the age of thirty-four, with 42% between twelve and twenty-four.

Professional wrestling is really athletic entertainment, since the results of the match are usually predetermined, a fact many Americans formerly did not understand. A 1999 Gallup survey found that eight out of ten Americans believed that the outcomes of most wrestling matches were fixed, compared to less than two out of ten who believed that in 1951. This may be why 81% of Americans, according to the survey, said that wrestling was not a sport. True wrestling fans, however, begged to differ. Among persons describing themselves as wrestling fans (and 18% of Americans did), 44% said that wrestling was, indeed, a sport.

THE WEEKEND WARRIOR— SPORTS PARTICIPATION

Each year, American Sports Data surveys individuals in twenty-five thousand households about their favorite

TABLE 5.3

Most popular team sports, 2003

Team sport	Number of participants Aged 6 and above (in millions)
1. Basketball	35.4
2. Soccer (outdoor)	16.1
3. Softball (regular)	14.4
4. Football (touch/flag)	14.1
5. Volleyball (hard surface)	11
6. Baseball	10.9
7. Volleyball (grass)	8
8. Volleyball (beach)	7.5
9. Football (tackle)	5.8
10. Soccer (indoor)	4.6
11. Cheerleading	3.6
12. Softball (fast-pitch)	3.5
13. Ice hockey	2.8
14. Lacrosse	1.1

SOURCE: *Team Sports—An American Institution,* SGMA Interntational, April 13, 2004, http://www.sgma.com/press/2004/press1081888640-15351 .html (accessed September 9, 2004)

TABLE 5.4

Most popular organized sports among participants age 6 and older, by participation, 2003

Sport	Organized participants in 2003
1 Basketball	8,798,000
2 Outdoor soccer	6,755,000
3 Slow-pitch softball	5,549,000
4 Baseball	5,343,000
5 Court volleyball	3,773,000
6 Tackle football	2,824,000
7 Touch football	1,792,000
8 Indoor soccer	1,784,000
9 Fast-pitch softball	1,715,000
10 Sand/beach volleyball	790,000
11 Grass volleyball	408,000

SOURCE: "The Most Popular Organized Sports in the U.S. Based on Participation—Age 6 and Older," in "Organized Sports Attract Millions of Americans," *Superstudy of Sports Participation*, SGMA International, June 23, 2004, http://www.sgma.com/press/2004/press1088003422-22941 .html (accessed September 9, 2004)

sports and sports activities for the Sporting Goods Manufacturers Association (SGMA). In 2003 the top four activities were recreational swimming, walking, bowling, and bicycling. (See Table 1.6 in Chapter 1.)

When the SGMA ranked those sports that involved team play, it found that the most popular choice was basketball, played by 35.4 million Americans over the age of six. The second most popular sport was outdoor soccer, which was played by fewer than half this number, or 16.1 million. Regular (slow-pitch) softball was played by 14.4 million Americans, followed closely by touch or flag football with 14.1 million participants. (See Table 5.3.)

Organized sports, which required membership in a league or other official body, were also ranked by the SGMA. The results were similar to the team sport results but with several notable differences. Only 8.8 million basketball players were in organized leagues, which showed that close to three-fourths of basketball players participated only in pick-up games. Outdoor soccer had 6.8 million organized participants (just under half the total), slow-pitch softball 5.5 million, and baseball 5.3 million. Other popular organized sports included court volleyball (3.8 million participants), tackle football (2.8 million), touch football (1.8 million), indoor soccer (1.8 million) and fast-pitch softball (1.7 million). (See Table 5.4.)

Other Sports Trends

While some older sports were declining in popularity, newer ones appeared that saw rapid growth. One such example is paintball, where participants stage battles in which they shoot paint markers at each other with air guns. From the time the SGMA began tracking it in 1998, participation in paintball grew by 66%, to 9.8 million participants in 2003. (See Table 1.6 in Chapter 1).

Other sports that increased in popularity included snowboarding (up 269.5% from 1993 to 2003), artificial wall climbing (up 83.9% since 1998), and martial arts (up 28.2% since 1998). Interest in various types of sport shooting was also on the rise, with handgun target shooting growing 14.3% since 1998 and sport clay shooting up 31.9% since 1993. (See Table 1.6 in Chapter 1).

BASEBALL

Participation in baseball, the sport once known as "the national pastime," fell during the final years of the twentieth century. During a sixteen-year period ending in 2003, baseball participation dropped 27.1%, according to the SGMA. (See Table 1.6 in Chapter 1). In that year the number of Americans who played fell to 10.9 million, with the sport ranked as the sixth most popular team sport in the United States (see Table 5.3) and the seventh most popular team sport for youth ages six to seventeen. (See Table 1.10 in Chapter 1.)

While enthusiasm for playing baseball may have waned, the number of Americans who said they "follow" the sport had not changed significantly since the 1930s when Gallup pollsters asked Americans whether they were fans of professional baseball. During the late 1930s, about 40% of Americans followed big league baseball. In the early 1950s, an average of 43% were fans, and a poll conducted in March 2004 reported that 45% of Americans followed baseball. (See Figure 5.2.)

When the Gallup Organization asked self-described baseball fans how closely they followed the sport, however, almost twice as many said they were less interested than they had been three years earlier (30%), than said they followed baseball more (16%). The rest (54%) said

FIGURE 5.2

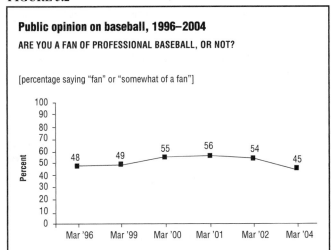

Public opinion on baseball, 1996–2004

ARE YOU A FAN OF PROFESSIONAL BASEBALL, OR NOT?

[percentage saying "fan" or "somewhat of a fan"]

SOURCE: Mark Gillespie, "Are You a Fan of Professional Baseball, or Not?" in *Baseball Fans Overwhelmingly Want Mandatory Steroid Testing*, http://www.gallup.com/content/default.aspx?ci=11245&pg=1 (accessed September 10, 2004). Copyright © 2004 by The Gallup Organization. Reproduced by permission of The Gallup Organization.

their interest had stayed the same. Among sports fans in general, the number who followed baseball less was almost triple the number who followed it more, though more than half said their interest had not changed. The reasons for this drop in interest may include controversy over the use of steroids by star players and the variable quality of play caused by drastic differences in salary expenditures between teams. In 2003 this ranged from the Tampa Bay Devil Rays' $19.6 million to the New York Yankees' $149.2 million.

BASKETBALL

Basketball is a highly popular activity in the United States. It was the most popular participatory team sport in 2003, according to the SGMA (see Table 5.3), and the second most popular spectator sport according to a Gallup poll conducted in December 2003. That poll found that 14% of Americans ranked basketball as their favorite sport to watch. (See Figure 5.1.)

Basketball players were also among the most popular athletes in the United States. According to a 2004 Harris poll by Humphrey Taylor, retired star Michael Jordan was the most popular athlete in America, a position he had held in every Harris poll conducted on the subject since 1993. Other basketball stars on the list included Shaquille O'Neal, Kobe Bryant, and Allen Iverson.

According to the SGMA, a decline in basketball participation started in the late 1990s and continued into 2003, with the number playing the sport at least once during the year dropping to 35.4 million. (See Table 1.6 in Chapter 1.) There were increasing numbers of female players, however, especially at the high school level.

According to the National Federation of State High School Associations, in the 2002–03 school year there were 457,165 female participants, compared to 540,874 male ones. Basketball was the most popular high school sport for girls and the second most popular sport for high school boys after football.

SOCCER

Although soccer has long been popular in Europe, Asia, Central America, and South America, its popularity in North America began growing during the late twentieth century. Two key events that helped boost interest were Olympic soccer tournaments held in Los Angeles, California, in 1984, and in Atlanta, Georgia, in 1996.

In 1994 the U.S. Soccer organization served as the host federation for World Cup USA 1994, a record-breaking event attended by more than 3.5 million fans, and then hosted the most successful women's sporting event to that date: the Women's World Cup 1999, which was held in Pasadena, California, and attended by more than ninety thousand fans. The U.S. women won the 1999 World Cup by defending against the Chinese team in a zero to zero tie through regulation play and overtime and then defeating China five to four in penalty kicks.

Their victory provoked soccer hysteria in the United States as the winning team members appeared on television news programs, at the White House, and on the covers of newspapers and magazines. In 2001 the Women's United Soccer Association was formed as a national league, and although it attracted a number of top American and international players, financial difficulties forced it to suspend operations after the 2003 season, which had featured eight teams playing a total of eighty-four games to 560,000 spectators. A 2004 Harris poll by Humphrey Taylor found that of America's favorite female athletes, the third most popular was soccer star Mia Hamm.

Several other professional soccer leagues, both male and female, have been formed in the United States. The largest, Major League Soccer (MLS), is a male league. It featured ten teams that played a total of 150 games during the 2003 season. Total attendance for the year was 2.2 million, or an average of 14,898 per game. Two expansion teams were to be added for the 2005 season, taking the place of a pair of clubs that had only lasted from the league's first season in 1996 through 2001.

While U.S. soccer had not developed the major spectator following of such sports as baseball and football, it had become extremely popular as a participatory sport. According to the SGMA, 17.7 million Americans over the age of six played soccer at least once during 2003, about the same as in 2002 but down from the nineteen million who participated in 2001. (See Table 1.6 in Chapter 1.)

An SGMA analysis of sports participation found that the number of "core" soccer players—those who played fifty-two or more days per year—was rising, increasing from 3.8 million in 2000 to 4.1 million in 2002. The total number of players over eighteen increased by 30% during that time, from 3.9 million in 2000 to 5.1 million in 2002. Soccer was eighth among the most popular frequently played sports for youth aged six to seventeen, according to the SGMA, with nearly 2.4 million children and teens who played more than fifty-two days per year in 2003. (See Table 1.10 in Chapter 1.)

In 2003 the national organization U.S. Youth Soccer had 3.2 million registered players between the ages of five and nineteen. Youth aged ten to fourteen comprised 48% of U.S. Youth Soccer members, with those under ten making up another 37%. The remaining 15% were between fifteen and nineteen. Some 55% of players were male, and 45% were female. An estimated 75% of all registered soccer players in the United States were members of the organization. Its programs were administered by a network of fifty-five state associations staffed by more than 300,000 coaches and 500,000 volunteers.

BOWLING

In 2003 bowling ranked as America's most popular participant sport, according to the SGMA, with fifty-five million players. (See Table 1.6 in Chapter 1.) However, according to the American Bowling Congress (ABC), the largest organization of bowlers in the United States, serious participation was declining. In 1998 the organization reported total membership in men's, women's, and youth leagues of 4.2 million, but this fell to 3.2 million in 2003. The ABC reported that slightly more men than women bowled and that approximately one-third of bowlers were under the age of seventeen.

In an attempt to increase participation, many bowling centers have been upgraded and modernized to enhance the image of both the sport and the facilities. Although the overall number of bowling alleys and centers declined from 6,857 in 1998 to 6,070 in 2003, according to the ABC, the consolidation of centers resulted in the closing of a number of antiquated bowling lanes, some of which were replaced by new state-of-the-art facilities. Many of these featured attractive decor, updated scoring and playing equipment, quality food service, and other entertainment, and were built in better locations. Some "megacenters" also provided access to golf driving ranges, basketball, skating, billiards, and even microbreweries.

Other changes were being made to reinvigorate the image of bowling and attract the youth market. The industry introduced higher-performance bowling balls at more popular midrange prices and developed products and promotions designed to attract younger players. During cer-

tain times of the week many bowling centers offered "Rock 'n' Bowl" or "Cosmic Bowling"—bowling under ultraviolet lights with lanes, pins, and bowlers set aglow.

Bowling was most popular in the northern industrialized states. Although it had also experienced a drop in participation, Detroit was considered the bowling capital of the United States, and Michigan led the nation in the number of league members, with 289,931 in 2003, although it was only fifth in the number of bowling centers, with 369. Pennsylvania (408), New York (401), Wisconsin (379), and Ohio (376) had the most centers, according to the ABC.

BILLIARDS AND POOL—COMING OF AGE

Billiards is another popular participation sport in the United States. In 2003, 40.7 million Americans played billiards at least once, up 15.4% from 1987 when 35.3 million people played, according to the SGMA in its 2004 *Superstudy of Sports Participation*. (See Table 1.6 in Chapter 1.)

According to a 2001 SGMA survey, about nine million Americans played pool frequently—more than twenty-five times per year—and the number of people who named billiards as a favorite activity increased 22% from 3.6 million in 1990 to 4.4 million in 2000.

The favorable image of billiards was reflected in a changing demographic player profile, one that was younger and more often female than in years past. From 1990 to 2001 the number of players aged twelve to seventeen grew 20%, while the number of female players rose 9.4%. Growing attention to female players was reflected by the ESPN cable network's decision to increase coverage of the Women's Professional Billiard Association Tour for the period 2004 to 2006.

One of the industry's efforts to boost participation was to try to convert casual players into more frequent, serious players. The Billiard Congress of America, the sport's governing body, cultivated a system with more than 450 leagues and fifty thousand members and initiated a national tournament system to generate greater frequency of play in poolrooms across the country.

Pool halls were no longer limited to dark and dreary back rooms of bars. Billiard and pool tables could be found in a variety of sites, including upscale multi-activity entertainment centers, which might include video games, basketball hoops, indoor golf, sports bars, satellite-networked trivia games, and restaurants. Billiards and pool were also springing up in food courts, at large military bases, and in college student centers. Even traditional pool halls had changed; many were better lighted and more "wholesome" in decor. Some did not serve alcohol. These changes had not only increased the availability of billiards and pool but had also made the environment in which they were played more appealing to those who might not try the games otherwise.

TENNIS IS ON THE UPSWING

Through the 1960s, tennis was popular primarily among the affluent. The game became "fashionable" and gained broader participation in the 1970s, but industry experts reported that many tennis players turned to aerobics and other fitness activities in the 1980s. In 1987 the SGMA reported that 21.1 million Americans played tennis. (See Table 1.6 in Chapter 1.)

In the 1990s tennis participation declined further, with the total number of U.S. tennis players six years of age or older falling to 19.3 million in 1993 and then to 16.9 million in 1998. The trend was reversed in the early years of the twenty-first century, however, as participation climbed from a low of 15.1 million in 2001 to 17.3 million in 2003, according to the SGMA. (See Table 1.6 in Chapter 1.)

The increase in participation was attributable in part to a five-year, $50 million program launched during the 1990s. Called USA Tennis Plan for Growth, it offered free lessons around the country. By 2001 more than one million people had received lessons in six hundred cities, and in 2002 it was extended for another five years in an attempt to further boost the number of tennis players.

Another factor helping increase interest in tennis was the widespread popularity of several professional players. In a 2004 Harris poll ranking of favorite female sports stars, the top two named were sisters Venus and Serena Williams, with Anna Kournikova placing sixth and retired star Chris Evert ninth. Although no tennis players made the 2004 list of most popular stars of both sexes, in 2003 the list had included Serena Williams and Andre Agassi.

GOLF

Golf was the fifteenth most popular sport to play in the United States in 2003, according to the SGMA. (See Table 1.7 in Chapter 1.) Although the total number of golfers grew 4% between 1987 and 2003, from 26.3 million to 27.3 million, it was down almost 10% from a high of thirty million in 1998. (See Table 1.6 in Chapter 1.) Professional golf also had a strong following as a spectator sport. A December 2003 Gallup poll found that it was the seventh most popular sport to watch, just behind auto racing and just ahead of soccer.

According to the National Golf Foundation (NGF), the number of "core" golfers (those aged eighteen and older who played a minimum of eight rounds per year) increased from 12.6 million in 2002 to 13.2 million in 2003. They averaged thirty-seven rounds per year. Occasional golfers (one to seven rounds per year) increased by 4% to 14.2 million, while junior players declined by 10% to 5.5 million.

The stereotypical golfer is sometimes seen as an older male, and an NGF profile compiled in 2002 supported this image to some extent. The organization found that 78% of golfers were male, and 33% were over age fifty. Almost half (45%) were between the ages of eighteen and thirty-nine, however.

As of December 31, 2002, there were 15,827 golf facilities in the United States, according to the NGF. Of these, 11,501 were open to the public, with the remainder being private courses.

As an outdoor sport, golf is best enjoyed in warm, sunny weather. Not surprisingly, the states with the most golf courses were Florida (1,073) and California (912). Other top states included Michigan (854), Texas (838), and New York (813). Not all of these were full eighteen-hole courses—the NGF counted only 14,725 eighteen-hole equivalents, with a total of 265,050 golf holes.

Industry experts predict that the aging of America will benefit golf participation, especially as baby boomers reach retirement age, but that cost and convenience of play are major obstacles to growth. The cost of development and maintaining courses translates into a high fee for play, which discourages people of moderate means and those who are just beginning and not yet regular players.

In 2002, according to the NGF, golfers spent $24.3 billion on equipment and fees. Of this total, $19.7 billion was for green fees and golf club dues. "Avid" golfers (twenty-five or more rounds per year), who comprised 23% of all golfers, spent 63% percent of this total.

Golf's popularity among players and spectators has benefited immensely from the remarkable career of golfer Tiger Woods. The young, talented, and charismatic golfer has encouraged young people to take up the sport, and he has become a celebrity known throughout the world. A January 2004 Harris poll by Humphrey Taylor found that public regard for Woods was greater than for every other living athlete save basketball's Michael Jordan. He was the only golfer to make the Harris top ten list.

CHAPTER 6
GAMBLING IN AMERICA

Historically, gambling has been a popular form of recreation in North America. George Washington liked to play cards, and Benjamin Franklin printed and sold playing cards. Americans were so fond of card games that when the British Stamp Act of 1765 put a one-shilling tax on playing cards, people became extremely upset. In fact, anger about the Stamp Act and a tax on tea contributed to support for the American Revolution. During the colonial period, lotteries (a system of raising money by selling numbered tickets and distributing prizes to the holders of numbers drawn at random) were used to raise money to establish the colony of Virginia. In 1777 the Continental Congress held a $5 million lottery to pay for the Revolutionary War.

By the 1800s Americans were known for their gambling. Visitors to this country said it was impossible to talk to a person from Kentucky without hearing the phrase, "I'll bet you!" Large riverboats that traveled up and down the Mississippi and Ohio Rivers carrying passengers or freight almost always had a casino where gamblers played cards and other games of chance. Along the Mississippi River was New Orleans, Louisiana, a city famous for gambling. After the Civil War, adventurers went searching for gold and silver in the West, and virtually every mining town had a few gambling casinos.

Beginning in the 1870s, however, most forms of gambling and all lotteries were outlawed by states, following a scandal in the Louisiana lottery. This state lottery had operated nationwide, and the scandal involved bribery of state and federal officials. In 1890 Congress outlawed the use of the mail for lotteries, and in 1895 it forbade shipments of lottery tickets across state lines.

Although gambling has always been popular in the United States, many people have opposed it because they believed gambling was immoral and posed a threat to both individuals and the community. Some people that became addicted to gambling lost their homes, families, and

careers. Furthermore, during the Prohibition Era (1920–33), when alcohol was outlawed, organized crime moved into the profitable worlds of alcoholic beverages and gambling. Although legal gambling has since regained respectability and is viewed by many Americans as an acceptable activity, the association with organized crime and corruption still taints the activity in the minds of others.

Lotteries began a revival in 1964 when New Hampshire created a state lottery. New York followed suit in 1966. From 1970 to 1975 ten more states established them. In 2004 thirty-eight states and Washington, D.C., operated lotteries.

TYPES OF LEGAL GAMBLING

There are six primary forms of legal gambling in the United States: bingo, lotteries, pari-mutuel betting, off-track betting, organized poker playing, and casinos. Bingo is the most common form of legalized gambling. Lotteries operate in thirty-eight states, Washington, D.C., Puerto Rico, and the Virgin Islands. Forty-three states, Puerto Rico, and the Virgin Islands permit Thoroughbred racing. Poker "card rooms" operate legally in sixteen states. A total of eleven states offer legal casino gambling—ranging from floating riverboats to large commercially run casinos such as those found in Las Vegas or Atlantic City, New Jersey. Twenty-eight states also have Native American gambling facilities, which range from bingo and card-playing operations to full-scale casinos.

HOW AMERICANS GAMBLE THEIR MONEY

In 2002 the U.S. gaming industry had gross revenues of approximately $68.7 billion, according to research cited by the American Gaming Association from industry analysts Christiansen Capital Advisors LLC. More than half of this figure came from casino gambling, $28.1 billion of which was from commercial ventures and $14.2 billion of which was from Indian reservation casinos. Lotteries took in another $18.6 billion, and the rest came from smaller categories, including pari-mutuel betting, with an estimated $4 billion; charitable games and bingo, $2.6 billion; card rooms, $972.5 million; and legal bookmaking, $116.2 million. The total amount Americans wager legally each year has been estimated at more than $800 billion, with illegal gambling through office pools and other unregulated activities put as high as $380 billion by the National Gambling Impact Study Commission Report of 1999.

In a December 2003 poll, the Gallup Organization found that 49% of Americans polled said they had bought a state lottery ticket during the preceding twelve months, while 30% had visited a casino, 15% had participated in an office pool, 14% had played a video poker machine, and 10% said they had bet on professional sports. (See Figure 6.1.) When compared with data collected in 1989 and 1990, the number of casino players had increased by 50%, while those who bet on horse races and college or pro sports had fallen by more than half, bingo players had dropped by almost two-thirds, and the number who bet on boxing matches had fallen by three-fourths.

CASINO GAMBLING

Technically, a casino is any room or rooms in which gaming is conducted. When most Americans think of casinos, they picture lavish hotel and entertainment complexes, such as those in Las Vegas or Atlantic City, New Jersey. Before 1990 only Nevada and Atlantic City permitted casinos, but the 1990s saw regulations eased as states and municipalities sought the jobs and tax revenues that casinos could generate. In 2004 eleven states had commercially run casinos, twenty-eight had casinos operated by Native American tribes, and six had casinos at racetracks. Two additional states, Maine and New York, were planning to introduce the latter. The 443 commercial casinos ranged from large land-based facilities in Nevada, Michigan, New Jersey, and Louisiana to limited-stakes sites in South Dakota (maximum bet: $100) and Colorado (maximum bet: $5), to riverboat casinos in Indiana, Illinois, Missouri, Kansas, Mississippi, and Louisiana.

Gambling in Nevada

Nevada is the home of the nation's gambling capital, Las Vegas, and has more casinos statewide than any other—more than half the commercial casinos in the United States (256). Gambling was legalized in Nevada in 1931, giving the state a huge head start over relative upstarts New Jersey (1976), Louisiana (1991), and Michigan (1996) in allowing full-scale land-based commercial casinos. In 2003 the state's casinos employed 192,812 people and took in $9.6 billion in gross revenues from 48.6 million visitors. Casinos are located throughout the state, with many found on the border of California.

FIGURE 6.1

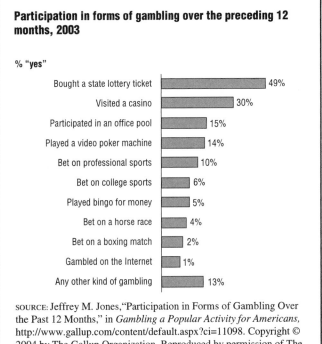

Participation in forms of gambling over the preceding 12 months, 2003

% "yes"

Bought a state lottery ticket	49%
Visited a casino	30%
Participated in an office pool	15%
Played a video poker machine	14%
Bet on professional sports	10%
Bet on college sports	6%
Played bingo for money	5%
Bet on a horse race	4%
Bet on a boxing match	2%
Gambled on the Internet	1%
Any other kind of gambling	13%

SOURCE: Jeffrey M. Jones, "Participation in Forms of Gambling Over the Past 12 Months," in *Gambling a Popular Activity for Americans*, http://www.gallup.com/content/default.aspx?ci=11098. Copyright © 2004 by The Gallup Organization. Reproduced by permission of The Gallup Organization.

Although its clientele does include a few wealthy "high rollers," as well as many avid small-stakes gamblers, visitors to Las Vegas are increasingly families drawn by the wide range of entertainment options, reasonably priced buffet dinners, and over-the-top architecture featuring the likes of an imitation Statue of Liberty and Eiffel Tower. Though the city was once America's primary gambling destination, with the growing legalization of various forms of gambling around the country, as well as the proliferation of Native American casinos, Las Vegas has been forced to seek new ways to entice customers.

In addition to attracting visitors with gambling, in 2004 the city offered seventeen performance halls with 1,700 seats or more and featured live performances by such celebrity performers as Céline Dion and Elton John. According to a 2004 press release from Enhanced Air Technologies, a firm based in British Columbia, at least one major Las Vegas casino also pumps synthetic human pheromones into the air to increase business. The company claims its "Commercaire" pheromone instills a sense of comfort and security in humans, which makes them feel more at ease and increases the likelihood of repeat visits.

Riverboat and Cruise Gambling

Some people gamble on riverboats (either excursion boats or stationary barges) or on cruises. First introduced in Iowa in 1991, the modern riverboat is little more than a floating casino. By 2002 revenues from riverboat gambling totaled more than $6 billion.

TABLE 6.1

Indian tribal gaming revenues, 1998–2002

Gaming revenue range	Number of operations	Revenues (in thousands)	Percentage of operations	Percentage of revenues	Mean (in thousands)	Median (in thousands)
Gaming operations with fiscal years ending in 2003						
$100 million and over	43	10,714,581	13%	64%	249,176	184,332
$50 million to $100 million	35	2,459,698	11%	15%	70,277	65,416
$25 million to $50 million	55	1,984,673	17%	12%	36,085	37,029
$10 million to $25 million	67	1,144,779	20%	7%	17,086	16,894
$3 million to $10 million	57	350,398	17%	2%	6,147	5,819
Under $3 million	73	76,019	22%	0%	1,041	833
Total	**330**	**16,730,148**				
Gaming operations with fiscal years ending in 2002						
$100 million and over	41	9,510,660	12%	65%	231,967	179,101
$50 million to $100 million	24	1,694,606	7%	12%	70,609	65,577
$25 million to $50 million	55	1,978,519	16%	13%	35,976	38,984
$10 million to $25 million	65	1,067,513	19%	7%	16,423	16,570
$3 million to $10 million	63	386,399	18%	3%	6,133	5,373
Under $3 million	100	78,359	29%	1%	784	461
Total	**348**	**14,716,056**				
Gaming operations with fiscal years ending in 2001						
$100 million and over	39	8,398,523	12%	65%	215,347	158,836
$50 million to $100 million	19	1,415,755	6%	11%	74,513	79,083
$25 million to $50 million	43	1,528,611	13%	12%	35,549	34,264
$10 million to $25 million	58	997,546	18%	8%	17,199	16,328
$3 million to $10 million	57	385,654	17%	3%	6,766	7,292
Under $3 million	114	96,257	35%	1%	844	575
Total	**330**	**12,822,346**				
Gaming operations with fiscal years ending in 2000						
$100 million and over	31	6,606,284	10%	60%	213,106	141,684
$50 million to $100 million	24	1,693,510	8%	15%	70,563	73,314
$25 million to $50 million	41	1,360,777	13%	12%	33,190	29,944
$10 million to $25 million	50	856,464	16%	8%	17,129	17,335
$3 million to $10 million	55	350,110	18%	3%	6,366	6,250
Under $3 million	110	91,545	35%	1%	832	541
Total	**311**	**10,958,690**				
Gaming operations with fiscal years ending in 1999						
$100 million and over	28	5,845,787	9%	60%	208,778	136,897
$50 million to $100 million	19	1,323,995	6%	14%	69,684	70,412
$25 million to $50 million	33	1,193,049	11%	12%	36,153	35,990
$10 million to $25 million	59	1,028,834	19%	10%	17,438	17,562
$3 million to $10 million	54	322,268	17%	3%	5,968	5,764
Under $3 million	117	86,907	38%	1%	537	395
Total	**310**	**9,800,840**				

Compiled from gaming operation audit reports received and entered by the National Indian Gaming Commission through June 30, 2004.

SOURCE: *National Indian Gaming Commision Tribal Gaming Revenues,* National Indian Gaming Commission, http://www.nigc.gov/nigc/nigcControl?option=TRIBAL_REVENUE (accessed July 15, 2004)

Although cruise lines emphasize that gambling is just one of many attractions to be enjoyed on their excursions, virtually all major cruise lines provide gambling. Many cruises, however, have a limit of $100 to $200 to control losses. "Cruises to nowhere," or day trips, are gambling opportunities available at coastal ports in Florida, Texas, New York, and Georgia. These ships travel three to twelve miles into international waters, where neither state nor federal gambling laws apply. Between 1985 and 2002 the day-cruise gambling industry more than doubled, growing from ten to twenty-five vessels.

Casino Gambling on Native American Reservations

The Indian Gaming Act of 1988 (PL 100-497) permitted Native American tribes to introduce gambling on their reservations. By 2003, 377 Native American gambling facilities were operating in twenty-eight states, ranging in size from bingo halls to full-scale casinos. Approximately 65% of the 341 federally recognized Indian tribes in the lower forty-eight states had revenues from gaming. Data from the National Indian Gaming Commission showed that total tribal gaming revenue grew from $9.8 billion in 1999 to $16.7 billion in 2003. (See Table 6.1.)

Gambling revenue helped provide employment for an estimated 205,000 Native Americans and non-Indians in gaming facilities, ancillary restaurants, and hotels, and brought in funds for housing, education, health care, and other reservation needs. Some tribes also distributed per capita payments to each member of the tribe from their gaming earnings. In 2003 this was

TABLE 6.2

Number of adults who gambled in a casino in the last 12 months, 2002

U.S. adult population (age 21+)	197.1 million
Casino gamblers	51.2 million
Casino participation rate*	26%
Average trip frequency	5.8 trips/year
Casino trips	297.2 million

*The percentage of adults who gambled at least once in a casino in the last 12 months

SOURCE: "Adults Who Gambled in a Casino in the Last 12 Months," in *Profile of the American Casino Gambler,* Harrah's Entertainment, 2003, http://www.harrahs.com/about_us/survey/index.html (accessed September 10, 2004). Data from Harrah's Entertainment, Inc., NFO WorldGroup, and U.S. Census Bureau.

TABLE 6.3

Age, income, and gender of casino gamblers vs. national average, 2002

Demographics	U.S. population	U.S. casino gamblers
Median age–age 21+	45	47
Median household income	$42,228	$50,716
Male/female ratio	48/52%	46/54%

SOURCE: "Age, Income and Gender of Casino Gamblers vs. National Average," in *Profile of the American Casino Gambler,* Harrah's Entertainment, 2003, http://www.harrahs.com/about_us/survey/index.html (accessed September 10, 2004). Data from Harrah's Entertainment, Inc., NFO WorldGroup, and U.S. Census Bureau.

done by seventy-three of the 224 tribal governments involved in gaming.

In 2000, according to the U.S. Census Bureau, the average per capita income of Native Americans on gaming reservations was nearly double that of those living on nongaming reservations, $14,737 to $7,781. Income on gaming reservations was also growing faster—it had gone up by 50.7% when compared with 1990, versus an increase of 16.4% for those on nongaming reservations. Unemployment rates on gaming reservations dropped by 17% during the decade, while the rate on nongaming reservations fell by only half this amount.

WHO IS GAMBLING?

Harrah's Entertainment, Inc., operates twenty-six casinos in the United States and publishes an annual survey to identify characteristics and preferences of casino gamblers. The survey results in *Profile of the American Casino Gambler: Harrah's Survey 2003* were based on three nationwide studies: "The Roper Reports," conducted by Roper ASW; and "The U.S. Gaming Panel" and "A Night in the Life of a Casino Gambler," conducted by the NFO World Group, Inc.

Harrah's reported that 26% of the U.S. population ages twenty-one and older gambled at a casino in 2002. This amounted to 51.2 million American adults, who took an average of almost six trips each to casinos per year. (See Table 6.2.) Gamblers were characterized as sharing many of the same leisure-time preferences as other Americans, but they tended to be more active during their leisure time—traveling, attending sports events, eating out, and using the Internet more than most American adults.

The Harrah's survey further showed that compared to the average American, the typical casino gambler was middle-aged, more likely to be female, and slightly better educated with a higher average household income. (See Table 6.3 and Figure 6.2.) The median household income for casino gamblers was a full 20% higher than that of the

average American; and 5% more casino gamblers held white-collar jobs than held white-collar jobs in the general population. (See Figure 6.3.)

Profile of the American Casino Gambler reported that casino gambling was most popular among adults ages fifty-one to sixty-five, and this group accounted for more than 30% of persons who had gambled during the twelve months prior to the survey. The second most frequent casino gamblers were persons over age sixty-six. (See Table 6.4.) One reason casino gambling was more popular among older adults may be that many have more free time and discretionary income (funds they could choose to use for recreation as opposed to life's necessities) than younger adults.

Casino participation rates rose with higher levels of income. Slightly more than one-fifth of adults with annual household incomes of less than $35,000 gambled in casinos, while more than a third of those earning more than $95,000 per year said they were casino players. (See Figure 6.4.)

There were also geographic variations in casino participation: the rates were highest in the western and north-central regions and lowest in the South. (See Figure 6.5.) The higher participation in the West was due in part to the proximity of Las Vegas with its many casinos, as well as the availability of Indian gaming in most other states in the region. The north-central region similarly offered commercial or Indian gaming in every state but Ohio. In 2002 one-third of all trips to casinos were made by residents of five states, with California at the top of the list (17% of total trips). (See Figure 6.6.) The top states in total commercial casino revenues that year were Nevada ($9.4 billion), New Jersey ($4.4 billion), Mississippi ($2.7 billion), Indiana ($2.1 billion), and Louisiana ($2 billion), according to the American Gaming Association.

Favorite Casino Games

According to the 2003 Harrah's survey, Americans greatly preferred slot machines and other electronic gaming

FIGURE 6.2

Education level of casino gamblers vs. national average, 2002

Legend:
- Post graduate
- College graduate
- Some college
- No college

Education: U.S. population
- 25%
- 48%
- 18%
- 9%

Education: U.S. casino gamblers
- 28%
- 45%
- 17%
- 8%

SOURCE: "Education Level of Casino Gamblers vs. National Average," in *Profile of the American Casino Gambler,* Harrah's Entertainment, 2003, http://www.harrahs.com/about_us/survey/index.html (accessed September 10, 2004). Data from Harrah's Entertainment, Inc., NFO WorldGroup, and U.S. Census Bureau.

TABLE 6.4

Casino participation rate by age, 2002

21–35 years old	25%
36–50	25%
51–65 years old	30%
66 and above	27%

SOURCE: "Age Differences in Casino Participation," in *Profile of the American Casino Gambler,* Harrah's Entertainment, 2003, http://www.harrahs.com/about_us/survey/index.html (accessed September 10, 2004). Data from Harrah's Entertainment, Inc., NFO WorldGroup, and U.S. Census Bureau.

FIGURE 6.3

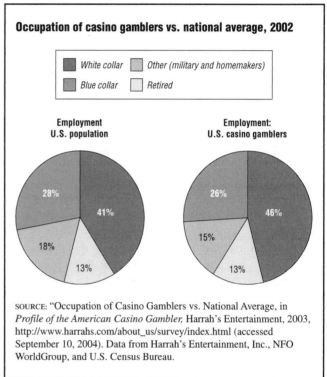

Occupation of casino gamblers vs. national average, 2002

Legend:
- White collar
- Blue collar
- Other (military and homemakers)
- Retired

Employment U.S. population
- 28%
- 41%
- 18%
- 13%

Employment: U.S. casino gamblers
- 26%
- 46%
- 15%
- 13%

SOURCE: "Occupation of Casino Gamblers vs. National Average, in *Profile of the American Casino Gambler,* Harrah's Entertainment, 2003, http://www.harrahs.com/about_us/survey/index.html (accessed September 10, 2004). Data from Harrah's Entertainment, Inc., NFO WorldGroup, and U.S. Census Bureau.

devices to table games such as blackjack, roulette, and craps. Nearly three-quarters of the games played were slots or video poker, with quarter slots the most popular denomination. The preference for slots and electronic gaming machines increased with age: more than three-quarters (78%) of casino players older than sixty-six favored machines over table games. Surprisingly, younger players who grew up playing video games were not the biggest fans of slots and electronic gambling devices, as they were more likely than older adults to prefer table games.

The Harrah's study also indicated that in 2003 women were far more likely than men to play slot machines and other electronic games: 81% of women favored slots and electronic gaming and just 8% played table games. Although more men played slots and machines than played table games (67% versus 20%), men were more than twice as likely as women to play blackjack, roulette, or craps.

BINGO AND OTHER CHARITY-SPONSORED GAMES

Charitable gambling is permitted in all states except Arkansas, Hawaii, Tennessee, and Utah. In 2002 it constituted almost 4% of the total amount wagered on legalized gambling in the United States, according to Christiansen Capital Advisors LLC. Of this total, bingo accounted for close to half. Charity games included bingo, raffles, casino nights, and jar tickets, among others. Bingo sessions were a common form of fund-raising by charitable organizations, such as churches, synagogues, and service clubs. It was a relatively inexpensive social and recreational pur-

suit; however, industry observers believed that bingo was declining in terms of both popularity and revenues.

PARI-MUTUEL WAGERING

Pari-mutuel wagering combines wagers into a common pool. Sports in which pari-mutuel wagering takes place are horse racing, greyhound racing, and jai alai. Winners are paid according to odds calculated with reference to the amounts bet on each contestant. In 2002 pari-mutuel wagering represented about 6% of the gaming industry. From 1974 to 2000 the overall trends in pari-mutuel wagering included an increase in horse racing and decreases in greyhound racing and jai alai.

Horse Racing

The largest sector in pari-mutuel wagering is horse racing. Horse racing has a long history in America. The

FIGURE 6.4

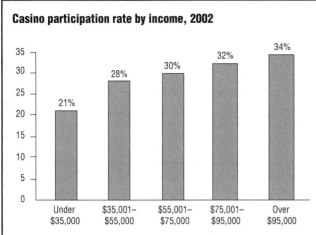

Casino participation rate by income, 2002

SOURCE: "Income Differences in Casino Participation," in *Profile of the American Casino Gambler,* Harrah's Entertainment, 2003, http://www.harrahs.com/about_us/survey/index.html (accessed September 10, 2004). Data from Harrah's Entertainment, Inc., NFO WorldGroup, and U.S. Census Bureau.

first American horse race took place in New York in the late 1660s. Several larger tracks, such as Churchill Downs, in Louisville, Kentucky, have been in operation since the 1800s.

Many Americans enjoy going to the racetrack for entertainment, some to enjoy the beautiful animals, and many more to gamble. Horse racing is a popular spectator sport, although it has declined significantly in popularity relative to other forms of gambling.

Even though the amount wagered on racing grew between 1974 and 2000, when the figures were adjusted for inflation, there was a noticeable decline. Although there are approximately 150 racetracks in America, most betting takes place off-site. Satellite broadcasting makes it possible to simultaneously broadcast races between racetracks or at off-track betting sites where there are no races. In addition, at-home pari-mutuel betting is now possible via the Internet, and several companies provide twenty-four-hour racing channels. There are also Internet simulcasts. Whereas in 1991 more than half of horse-racing wagers were made at the track, by 2003 just 15% of the $15.1 billion in bets handled were placed live, and less than 20% of the one thousand wagering sites nationwide were racetracks themselves, according to the National Thoroughbred Racing Association (NTRA).

The types of wagers placed have changed over time. Before the 1970s the "straight" wager (betting on a horse to either win, place, or show—finish first, second, or third) dominated, but in 2003 only a third of the pari-mutuel "handle" (the total amount wagered) came from this type of bet. So-called "exotic" bets made up the other two-thirds of wagers. These consisted of either intrarace exotics (Trifecta, Superfecta, Exacta—in which the exact

order of winning horses must be selected), which made up 58%, or inter-race exotics (Daily Double, Pick Three, Pick Six, and the like—in which winners of multiple races must be chosen), which made up 9%.

Account wagering was also possible in nine states. Patrons were permitted to set up accounts at racetracks and, in eight of those states, could phone in their bets from anywhere. Pari-mutuel wagering on horse races was legal in forty-three states and generated about $4 billion in gross revenue in 2002, according to Christiansen Capital Advisors LLC.

There are three major forms of horse racing: Thoroughbred, harness, and quarter-horse. In the United States, Thoroughbred was, by far, the most popular, followed by harness and then quarter-horse racing. For example, in 2000 nearly half (4,032) of the 8,475 live races run in California were Thoroughbred, while in Florida, more than half the races were Thoroughbred.

According to the NTRA, interest among Americans in the sport has been growing, with the horse-racing fan base rising from 31.2% in 1999 to 35.6% in 2003. This was attributed in part to the success of the film *Seabiscuit,* which told the story of a legendary racehorse. In the month after the film's release, betting at American racetracks increased by 5.5%.

Greyhound Racing—the Sport of Queens

Once a favorite pastime of Queen Elizabeth I of England, dog racing became known as the "Sport of Queens." Originally, a hare would be released and a pair of greyhounds set in pursuit. In the early 1900s a mechanical lure replaced the hare, eliminating the killing of the rabbit.

The first American greyhound racetrack with a mechanical hare opened in Emeryville, California, in 1919. In 2004 fewer than fifty tracks were operating in fifteen states, more than a third of which were located in Florida. Most other states had between one and three each.

A typical greyhound racing program featured thirteen races, each with eight dogs. Races were run on 5/16, 3/8, 7/16, and 9/16 mile courses. A typical race on a 5/16-mile course lasted thirty-one seconds, and the dogs reached speeds of up to forty-five miles per hour. Like horse tracks, dog tracks have turned to simulcasting and off-track betting.

The animal rights movement has protested the sport, claiming the dogs are mistreated and that many are killed by breeders who keep only the fastest ones from a litter. Although the claims have led many track owners to improve conditions, animal rights activists have persuaded some legislators to ban racing or rescind existing permits. The declining financial condition of many tracks is, however, the primary reason that so many have closed.

FIGURE 6.5

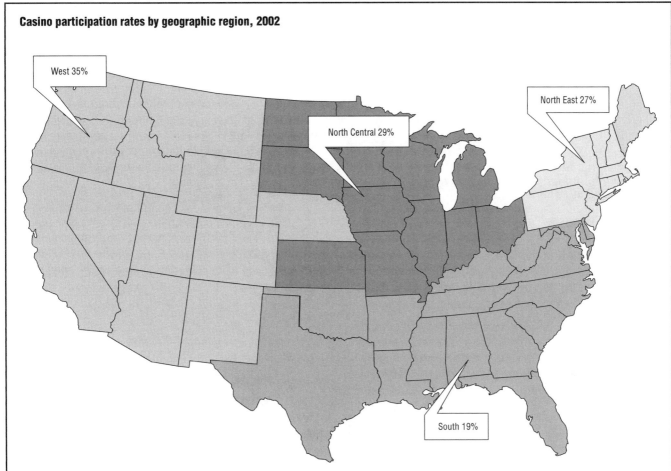

Casino participation rates by geographic region, 2002

West 35%

North Central 29%

North East 27%

South 19%

SOURCE: "Geographic Differences in Casino Participation," in *Profile of the American Casino Gambler,* Harrah's Entertainment, 2003, http://www.harrahs.com/about_us/survey/index.html (accessed September 10, 2004). Data from Harrah's Entertainment, Inc., NFO WorldGroup, and U.S. Census Bureau.

Jai Alai

Jai alai is a fast-paced game in which the players, using a large curved basket strapped to their arms, whip a small ball made of goatskin against the three walls and floor of a huge playing court (fronton). Jai alai was invented in the seventeenth century in the Basque regions of Spain and France. Although the game is popular in Latin America, its popularity has been declining in the United States. In 2004 it was legal in only three states: Florida, Rhode Island, and Connecticut.

By 2004 Connecticut and Rhode Island no longer had any jai alai frontons. Florida once had ten, but by 2004 only five remained. The future of the sport in the United States was uncertain. Lotteries and cruises (many of which offered casino gambling) had taken considerable business away from the frontons. Most jai alai frontons offered simulcasting of horse races, which gave gamblers an additional wagering opportunity. Because of their deteriorating financial condition, in 2004 legislation was introduced in Florida that would allow frontons to reduce their playing schedules from a hundred days to forty while continuing to keep their intertrack wagering licenses.

Problems for Pari-Mutuels

Because of the increased availability of other forms of gambling, pari-mutuels were facing hard times. Off-track betting and simulcasting had helped, but many owners of racetracks and frontons said more was needed for them to stay competitive. Track owners wanted to install video poker machines and other electronic gambling devices (EGDs) as an additional source of revenue. As of 2004 Delaware, Rhode Island, Iowa, Louisiana, New Mexico, and West Virginia permitted EGDs at racetracks. This was a highly controversial issue: According to the National Coalition against Legalized Gambling, attempts to legalize EGDs at racetracks were defeated in twelve states between 1995 and 2003.

LOTTERIES

A lottery is a game in which people purchase numbered tickets in hopes of winning a prize. A person wins if the number on his or her ticket is the one drawn from a pool of all the tickets purchased for that event. In the case of instant lotteries, a bettor wins if the ticket contains a predetermined winning number. Raffles are a form of lottery in which the prize is usually goods rather than cash.

FIGURE 6.6

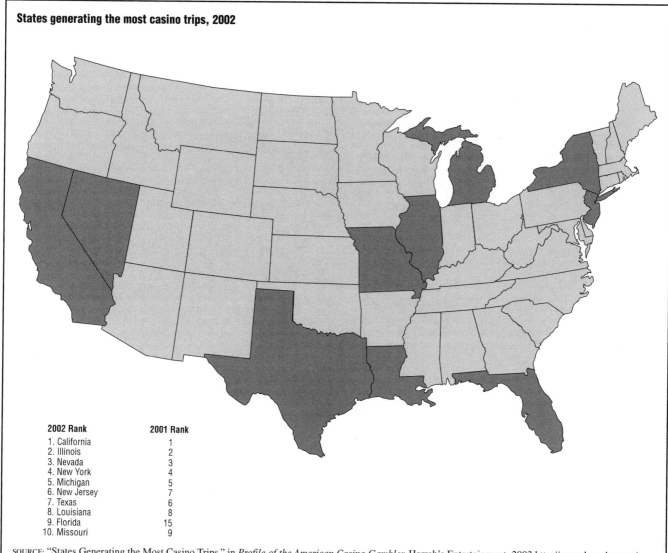

States generating the most casino trips, 2002

2002 Rank	2001 Rank
1. California	1
2. Illinois	2
3. Nevada	3
4. New York	4
5. Michigan	5
6. New Jersey	7
7. Texas	6
8. Louisiana	8
9. Florida	15
10. Missouri	9

SOURCE: "States Generating the Most Casino Trips," in *Profile of the American Casino Gambler*, Harrah's Entertainment, 2003 http://www.harrahs.com/about_us/survey/index.html (accessed September 10, 2004). Data from Harrah's Entertainment, Inc., NFO WorldGroup, and U.S. Census Bureau.

Lotteries are created and run by government bodies. In 2004 thirty-eight states, Washington, D.C., Puerto Rico, and the Virgin Islands had operating lotteries. Lottery revenues may go into the general fund of the state or may be earmarked for particular purposes, such as education, parks, or police pension funds. Developments in technology and communications have created many possible ways to conduct lotteries. There are five principal types of lottery games:

- Instant games, in which the player scratches a coating off the ticket to find out whether and what he or she has won

- Daily numbers games, in which the player picks a combination of numbers

- Lotto, or a variation of it, in which numbers are chosen from a large set of possibilities with winners selected periodically—Powerball is a popular lottery of this type

- Video keno, in which the player chooses numbers with drawings held very frequently—sometimes as often as several times an hour

- EGDs, which allow bettors to play a game, such as video poker, and receive an immediate payout

As more and more states have introduced lotteries to raise money for government, people have had the opportunity to do more gambling. State lottery tickets are sold in grocery stores, convenience stores, gas stations, and many other places. When the winnings become unusually large or when two or three states get together for a big lottery jackpot, the lines to buy lottery tickets can be long.

Some states were also looking at the possibility of online lottery ticket sales. In 2004 the Georgia House of Representatives passed a bill allowing online lottery ticket sales of up to $5 per day per person, though it was uncertain whether this law would be upheld if challenged in court.

According to the North American Association of State and Provincial Lotteries, in 2003 Americans bet $45.3 billion on lotteries, up from $38.9 billion in 2001. Per capita sales grew from $150 in 1997 to $175 in 2003. Although lottery sales were increasing each year, the number of Americans who played lotteries was declining, according to a 2003 Gallup poll. In 1999 57% said they had bought a ticket during the preceding year, but in 2003 just 49% said they had.

In general, poor people play lottery games less frequently than middle- and high-income groups. The lottery appeals to young people more than to older people. Most people who play the game report playing it regularly.

A number of studies have shown that while the poor tend to spend a higher percentage of their income on lotteries than do middle- or high-income persons, the lotteries tend to benefit high-income persons because they make greater use of the sporting and cultural organizations that receive lottery funds. Critics of lotteries have observed that if lotteries were considered a tax they would be seen as unfair, taxing the poor disproportionately for the benefit of the better-off.

Furthermore, detractors have also contended that lotteries are generally inefficient. Less than 40% of the funds they generated were returned to the causes they were meant to support, and about 47% was distributed as prize money. The remainder was used up for administration and promotion. Despite their inefficiency and relatively modest returns, governments have favored lotteries because those who buy the tickets do so voluntarily.

ELECTRONIC GAMBLING DEVICES

Electronic gambling devices (EGDs) include stand-alone slot machines, video poker, video keno, and other types of gambling games. Because EGDs are portable, they make gambling possible at locations that, unlike racetracks or casinos, are not dedicated to the business of gambling. Bars, truck stops, convenience stores, and other locations that did not formerly offer gambling have begun to feature EGDs. Some states, such as Louisiana, Montana, and South Carolina, have permitted private businesses to operate EGDs. In other states, such as Oregon and California, EGDs have been operated by the state lottery.

In addition to legal EGDs, in other states there are many illegal EGDs, or "gray machines," so called because they exist in a gray area of the law. Basically, if such a machine is used for amusement and no proceeds are paid out, then gambling laws have not been broken. Nevertheless, according to the 1999 *National Gambling Impact Study Commission Report,* many establishments with these machines have surreptitiously paid winners. Gray machines are reportedly common in bars and fraternal organizations in many states. The report estimated that there were fifteen

thousand to thirty thousand gray machines in West Virginia, ten thousand each in New Jersey and Alabama, and as many as sixty-five thousand in Illinois.

EGDs are highly regulated and are constructed to higher standards than electronic voting machines, according to a 2004 *New York Times* report. In Nevada, for example, the state must be provided with copies of all gambling software, and inspectors frequently spot-check machines to be sure they contain the version of the software on file. Machines must be able to withstand a twenty-thousand-volt shock, among other hazards, and manufacturers have to be certified by the state Gaming Control Board and all of their employees subjected to background checks. Gamblers who have a problem with a machine are entitled to an immediate investigation, and the state board keeps investigators on duty around the clock to respond to reports of problems.

Opponents of EGDs have expressed concerns that the easily accessible devices may encourage the unhealthy gambling practices that can result in addiction. They have also cautioned that EGDs provide immediate, intense, and potentially prolonged gambling experiences and that consumers unfamiliar with gambling may be encouraged to wager recklessly.

SPORTS GAMBLING

The only states where legal betting on sports took place as of 2004 were Nevada and Oregon. In Nevada in 2003 there were 142 legal sports books that permitted wagering on professional and amateur sports. Bettors had to be over twenty-one years of age and physically present to wager. It was also possible to bet on sports via the Oregon lottery, which offered a game called "Sports Action" in which players could win money based on the number of correct winners they picked from a weekend's National Football League games.

Championship games, such as the Super Bowl or the World Series, were some of the most popular sporting events on which people bet, though one-third of bets were placed on college sporting events. Nevada did not allow betting on high school or Olympic events.

In addition to this legalized sports gambling, an unknown number of people participated in illegal gambling in 2004, such as office pools. Estimates of illegal sport betting have ranged from $80 billion to $380 billion annually. Furthermore, some Americans crossed the Mexican border to gamble or traveled to the Caribbean or Central America, where sports gambling was legal.

Does Gambling Threaten College Athletics?

Wagering on college sports is a hotly contested issue. A poll conducted by the Gallup Organization in March 2002 found that Americans were divided about whether gambling on college athletics should be made illegal throughout the country. Nearly half the surveyed respondents (49%) thought betting on college sports should be illegal and 47% felt it should be allowed.

The National Collegiate Athletic Association (NCAA) has been staunchly opposed to sports wagering because the organization contends that it attracts organized crime and has the potential to undermine the integrity of college sports contests. In its position paper, the NCAA stated that "sports wagering demeans the competition and competitors alike by a message that is contrary to the purposes and meaning of sport. Sports competition should be appreciated for the inherent benefits related to participation of student-athletes, coaches and institutions in fair contests, not the amount of money wagered on the outcome of the competition."

INTERNET GAMBLING

Internet gambling first appeared on the World Wide Web in the summer of 1995. By May 1998, according to the 1999 *National Gambling Impact Study Commission Report,* there were ninety online casinos, thirty-nine lotteries, eight bingos, and fifty-three sports books. In 2003 the River City Group, a research organization specializing in online gaming, estimated that there were over 810 casino-style gambling Web sites and more than 440 sports betting sites. Christiansen Capital Advisors LLC (CCA) projected that global Internet betting would increase from an estimated $5.7 billion in 2003 to nearly $10 billion in 2005. CCA estimated that 45% of the approximately twelve million 2003 online casino customers were from the United States. A survey by Inland Entertainment Corp. of five hundred online gamblers found that 86% were male, 20% were aged eighteen to twenty-five, 31% were twenty-six to thirty-four, 29% were thirty-five to forty-four, and 20% were over forty-five.

The primary legal obstacle to Internet gambling has been the 1961 Interstate Wireline Act (18 U.S.C. section 1084), which makes it illegal to offer or take bets from gamblers over phone lines or through other wired devices unless otherwise authorized by a particular state. Other federal legislation has become stalled in Congress. The Internet Gambling Prohibition Act, introduced in 1997, was passed by the Senate in 1998 but was held up in the House during 1999 because some legislators felt it might adversely affect other forms of e-commerce. Despite many revisions and amendments, the House rejected the act on July 18, 2000, leaving operators of online gambling businesses elated by the outcome. In 2003 the House of Representatives passed a bill to ban the use of financial instruments for the purpose of online gambling, but the necessary Senate passage of a similar measure was not immediately forthcoming.

While more than fifty global jurisdictions have allowed some form of Internet wagering, by 2004 the states of Illinois, Louisiana, Michigan, Oregon, and South Dakota had all passed laws prohibiting it, and attorneys general in other states had brought lawsuits against Internet gambling businesses using existing legislation. The Department of Justice has arrested or caused arrest warrants to be issued for dozens of Internet gambling operators, and several have been indicted.

Many countries, as well as the U.S. Department of Justice, have expressed concerns about the enforceability of any kind of Internet gambling prohibition. Most Internet gambling businesses were operating offshore and were licensed by foreign governments. In 2004, in response to a complaint filed by the Caribbean island nation of Antigua and Barbuda, the World Trade Organization (WTO) issued an interim ruling that found the U.S. government's efforts to curb Internet gambling were in violation of WTO commercial services agreements.

WHEN RECREATION BECOMES ADDICTION

Although gambling is simply one form of recreation and fun for many people, studies have shown that for 4% to 6% of gamblers it can become a compulsion or addiction. This behavior may cause them to gamble away their paychecks and go deeply into debt. It may harm marriages and relationships with children, other relatives, and friends.

The overwhelming majority of problem gamblers are male, and most are bright, scoring well above average or high on intelligence quotient tests. For many, gambling had begun during the early teen years. They usually excelled at trading stocks, commodities, futures, options, and bonds and at games requiring skill, such as blackjack and poker. Problem gamblers have been described as controlling, risk-taking, self-involved, sociable, and in need of approval, affirmation, and confirmation.

A review of fourteen U.S. and six Canadian gambling studies on adolescents found that from 1990 to 2000 the number of teens aged twelve to seventeen reporting serious gambling problems increased from 10% to 15%. Teens' involvement in gambling was believed to be greater than their use of tobacco, hard liquor, and marijuana. Furthermore, gambling affected children as well as teens. In 2000 a majority of twelve-year-olds had had at least one experience with gambling.

Problem gambling is not new—the first Gamblers Anonymous group was started in 1949. In 1972 the National Council on Problem Gambling (NCPG) was founded, and in 1975 the first nationwide study was conducted to determine the scope of the problem. Maryland opened the first state-funded treatment program in 1979.

In 1980 the American Psychiatric Association accepted pathological gambling as a "disorder of impulse control," describing it as an illness that is chronic and progressive but one that can be diagnosed and treated. There are three phases in the progression of gambling addiction:

• The winning phase—Gamblers experience a big win or a series of wins that give them unreasonable confidence and optimism that their winning streak will continue. During this phase they often increase the amounts of their wagers.

• The losing phase—When they are losing, gamblers often start to gamble alone, borrow money, and become irritable and withdrawn, especially when they are unable to pay off debts. Many accelerate their gambling in an effort to win back their losses.

• The desperation phase—During this phase, more time is spent gambling. The gamblers often blame others for their problems and alienate family and friends. Some may even engage in illegal activities to finance their gambling. They may feel hopeless, attempt suicide, abuse alcohol and/or other drugs, or suffer an emotional breakdown.

A national survey conducted by the NCPG found that during 1998 about $20 million in public and private funds was spent on problem gambling programs. The programs included prevention, employee education and training, research, and treatment. In 2000 the NCPG established the National Problem Gambling Helpline (1-800-522-4700), which received almost 116,000 calls during its first year.

Does Internet Gambling Encourage Addiction?

Some researchers and industry observers have stated the belief that the Internet may attract problem gamblers, especially those who are trying to hide their gambling addiction. Others have been concerned because the anonymity offered by the Internet creates the potential for children and teens, posing as adults, to gamble.

George T. Ladd and Nancy M. Petry, in "Disordered Gambling among University-Based Medical and Dental Patients: A Focus on Internet Gambling" (*Psychology of Addictive Behaviors,* March 2002), determined that while Internet gambling was the least common activity reported by problem gamblers (about 8%), persons with Internet gambling experience had the most severe problems with gambling addiction.

Only 22% of the participants without any Internet gambling experience had problems, compared to 74% of those who used the Web. Internet gamblers were younger, more likely to be unmarried, and tended to have less education and income than persons who did not use the Internet to gamble.

Ladd and Petry cautioned that "the availability of Internet gambling may draw individuals who seek out isolated and anonymous contexts for their gambling behaviors. Accessibility and use of Internet gambling opportunities are likely to increase with the explosive growth of the Internet."

CHAPTER 7
VACATIONS AND TRAVEL

Americans love to take vacations. Their destinations may vary from a trip to a national park for camping, fishing, boating, or hiking, to a visit to a theme park such as Disneyland. A vacation can also be a flight to Egypt, a cruise to the Virgin Islands, a romantic three-day weekend in New York, or staying home to read a book. The way Americans vacation and travel and their expectations of vacation time have been changing as U.S. society has evolved. Unchanged, however, is Americans' conviction that travel and vacationing improve the quality of their lives.

The perception that Americans work more and have less vacation time than people in other countries around the world has its basis in fact. Data gathered on twenty countries by Catherine Valenti in the ABCNEWS.com report "Vacation Deprivation—Americans Get Short-Changed When It Comes to Holiday Time" (June 25, 2003) showed that Americans, who averaged just 10.2 vacation days per year, took the least vacation time of workers in the countries surveyed. Many European countries, such as Italy, Germany, Spain, and Norway, had an average of thirty days per year, while residents of the United Kingdom averaged twenty-five, and even the hard-working Japanese had 17.5.

Perhaps because of this reduced amount of vacation time, Americans often try to pack as much activity as possible into their trips. This desire to make the most of a vacation can sometimes backfire, however, as a 2002 Gallup poll found. Rather than returning rested and relaxed, 54% of Americans who had taken a vacation trip during the previous twelve months reported they had gotten back feeling tired, while 19% said they were "very tired" or "exhausted."

In part, this was because many had started their trip with too little sleep—32% reported that the night before their vacation, they got to bed at least two hours later than normal because of a lack of advance planning, while 54% said they got up earlier than normal the next day to get an early start. Although some may have been awake because they were excited about going away, 46% said they were up late packing things the night before they left, while 10% packed the day they left. Once on vacation, the majority of travelers said they had stayed up too late on at least one night of their trip, and 22% of vacationers on ten- to fourteen-day trips said they went to bed later than normal nearly every night.

DOMESTIC TRAVEL

Where Do Americans Travel?

According to a poll of travel agents conducted by Fodor's and the American Society of Travel Agents, published online by TravelSense.org, the top ten domestic vacation destinations for Americans in 2004 were Orlando, Las Vegas, New York City, San Francisco, Honolulu, Los Angeles, the Hawaiian Islands, Miami, New Orleans, and San Diego. A poll of visitors to the TravelSense Web site revealed a similar list, with their top responses consisting of Las Vegas, Hawaii, Orlando, New York, San Francisco, Alaska, Miami, Maui, Florida, and Disney World.

The top states to visit in 2003, according to the Travel Industry Association of America (TIA), were California, Florida, and Texas. Pennsylvania, New York, North Carolina, Georgia, Virginia, Ohio, and Illinois made up the rest of the TIA's list of top ten destination states.

The U.S. Department of Transportation periodically conducts surveys of the travel habits of Americans. The most recent such effort, the 2001 *National Household Travel Survey,* (NHTS; 2003), reported that Americans took nearly 2.6 billion trips of fifty miles or more during that year. Almost 98% of these trips were to destinations in the United States, with only 2.2% to destinations outside the United States. More than 62% of trips were to locations within the traveler's home state. (See Table 7.1 and Figure 7.1.)

TABLE 7.1

Long-distance trips and miles by destination, 2001

	Trips (percent)	Miles (percent)
International	2.2	16.4
Different region	10.9	33.3
Different state, different division, same region	7.5	9.9
Different state, same division	17.0	13.8
Same state	62.4	26.7
Total	**100.0**	**100.0**

SOURCE: "Table A-25. Long-Distance Trips and Miles by Destination, in Percent," in *National Household Travel Survey Highlights Report,* U.S. Department of Transportation, Bureau of Transportation Statistics, 2003, http://www.bts.gov/publications/national_household_travel_survey/highlights _of_the_2001_national_household_travel_survey/pdf/entire.pdf (accessed September 10, 2004)

TABLE 7.2

Long-distance trips and trip miles by mode, 2001

	Total trips (millions)	Median miles	Total miles (millions)
Personal vehicle	2,336.1	194	760,324.7
Air	193.3	2,068	557,609.3
Bus	55.4	287	27,081.3
Train	21.1	192	10,546.0
Other	5.8	188	5,117.9
Total	**2,611.7**	**210**	**1,360,679.1**

SOURCE: "Table A-22. Long-Distance Trips and Trip Miles by Mode, in Millions," in *National Household Travel Survey Highlights Report,* U.S. Department of Transportation, Bureau of Transportation Statistics, 2003, http://www.bts.gov/publications/national_household_travel_survey/highlights _of_the_2001_national_household_travel_survey/pdf/entire.pdf (accessed September 10, 2004)

Means of Travel

The NHTS reported that the total of domestic miles traveled by U.S. citizens taking long-distance trips in 2001 was 1,360 trillion. Of this total, more than half were taken by personal vehicle (760.3 billion), with air travel accounting for most of the remainder (557.6 billion). Bus travel (27.1 billion) and trains (10.5 billion) were used far less. (See Table 7.2.)

The mode of travel varied with distance. For trips of 100–299 miles, 97.2% of trips were taken by personal vehicle, with just 1.6% by bus and 0.9% by train. These proportions were similar for trips of between 300–499 miles and 500–999 miles, with 10.3% of the latter trips taken by air, but for trips of between 1,000 and 1,999 miles, vehicle (53.9%) and air (42.4%) were in closer competition. Almost three-quarters of trips over two thousand miles were taken by air. (See Table 7.3.)

AIR TRAVEL DECLINES. The entire travel industry, including hospitality and other tourism-dependent businesses, was hit hard following the September 11, 2001, terrorist attacks. After four airplanes were hijacked and used as missiles to attack New York's World Trade Center, the Pentagon, and (unsuccessfully) one other target in Washington, D.C., numerous gaps in airplane security were discovered, and the number of Americans willing to travel by air dropped sharply.

On November 19, 2001, President George W. Bush signed the Aviation and Transportation Security Act (PL 107-71), which established the new Transportation Security Administration (TSA) within the Department of Transportation (later shifted to the Department of Homeland Security). The agency soon began implementing a number of new maritime, ground transportation, and aviation security programs, which included replacing private airport security screeners with TSA employees and requiring strengthened cockpit doors on planes. The organization was later charged with training airline pilots who

wished to carry weapons in the air, and the first group of forty-four such pilots was deputized on April 19, 2003, after a week's training.

While these and other new security measures had been implemented, many Americans remained nervous about flying. A Gallup poll taken in November 2003 showed that nearly two-thirds of Americans felt it was likely that terrorists would either blow up a plane or hijack one within the next five years. Slightly more than half believed terrorists would shoot one down with a shoulder-fired missile. (See Figure 7.2.)

In 2003, according to the Federal Aviation Administration (FAA), 587.3 million passengers boarded (or "enplaned") large commercial and regional commuter airplanes, an increase of 2.2% over the 2002 figure of 574.5 million, but equal to the level of 1998. Large carrier enplanements declined by 0.8%, while regional/commuter enplanements rose by 18.7%. International enplanements increased by 5.7% in 2003, to 54.1 million, but this number was slightly below the 1998 level.

The FAA found that landings and takeoffs dropped 3.3% in 2003 and were at the lowest level since 1996. The airline industry remained in a state of financial depression during the year, with total losses of $5.3 billion reported, although this was less than the $10.5 billion lost in 2002. No major air carrier had reported an annual profit since 2000, with just Continental Airlines posting a quarterly profit during that time. Philip Baggaley, the managing director for airlines and aerospace companies at credit-rating agency Standard & Poor's, estimated in 2004 that only three or four of the six major air carriers (American Airlines, United Airlines, Delta Air Lines, Northwest Airlines, Continental Airlines, and U.S. Airways) would still be solvent by 2010. Both U.S. Airways and United had sought bankruptcy protection from the courts in the aftermath of September 11, and American and Delta had officially given notice that they were in danger of going under.

FIGURE 7.1

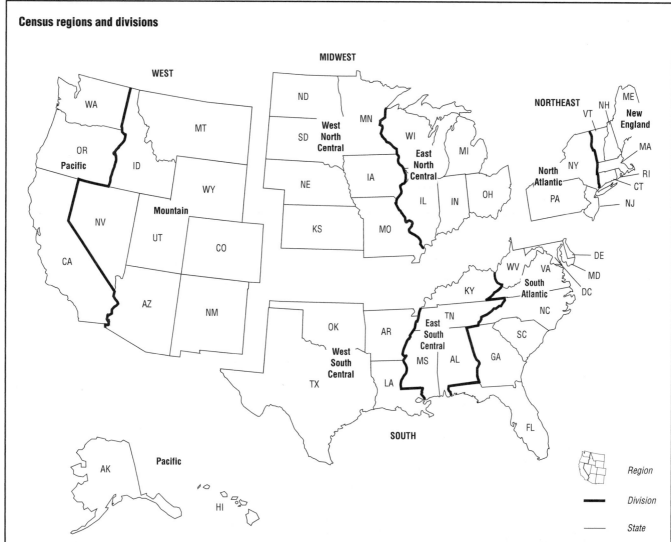

Census regions and divisions

SOURCE: "Census Regions and Divisions of the United States," in *National Household Travel Survey Highlights Report,* U.S. Department of Transportation, Bureau of Transportation Statistics, 2003, http://www.bts.gov/publications/national_household_travel_survey/highlights_of_the_2001_national_household _travel_survey/pdf/entire.pdf (accessed September 10, 2004)

Looking to the future, the FAA forecast an average annual growth rate of 4.2% between 2003 and 2015, with boarding expected to return to pre–September 11 levels by 2005. By 2014 the total number of passengers boarding commercial planes in the United States was expected to reach one billion.

In 2003 the U.S. large air carrier passenger fleet consisted of 4,090 aircraft, and this number was projected to grow to 5,732 by 2015. More planes were expected to be operated by low-cost carriers in the future, however, with older airlines projected to decline in size over time.

Reasons for Travel

Research done by the TIA found that of the 1.1 billion "person trips" Americans took during 2003 (defined as one person traveling on a trip of fifty miles or more, one-way, away from home), 82% were for pleasure. Of the

remaining trips, 12% were for business, and 6% combined business and pleasure.

In 2003, the TIA reported, 30% of travelers shopped while on a trip. Other popular activities included attending a social or family event (27%), outdoor activities (11%), city or urban sightseeing (10%), rural sightseeing (10%), and going to the beach (10%). Activities engaged in by fewer than 10% of travelers included visiting historic places/sites or museums (8%), gambling (7%), visiting a theme/amusement park (7%), visiting a national or state park (7%), attending seminars or courses (6%), nightlife/dancing (6%), and attending a sports event (6%).

Weekend Travel

The growing number of two-career families has made it increasingly difficult for families to schedule

TABLE 7.3

Long-distance trips by mode and distance, 2001

	100–299 miles	300–499 miles	500–999 miles	1,000–1,999 miles	2,000+ miles
	Percent	Percent	Percent	Percent	Percent
Personal vehicle	97.2	94.3	85.9	53.9	22.2
Air	0.2	1.5	10.3	42.4	74.8
Bus	1.6	3.4	3.2	2.6	1.4
Train	0.9	0.7	0.6	0.9	0.8
Other	0.2	0.1	0.0	0.1	0.8
Total	**100.0**	**100.0**	**100.0**	**100.0**	**100.0**

SOURCE: "Table A-23. Long-Distance Trips by Mode and Distance, in Percent," in *National Household Travel Survey Highlights Report*, U.S. Department of Transportation, Bureau of Transportation Statistics, 2003, http://www.bts.gov/publications/national_household_travel_survey/highlights_of_the_2001_national_household_travel_survey/pdf/entire.pdf (accessed September 12, 2004)

FIGURE 7.2

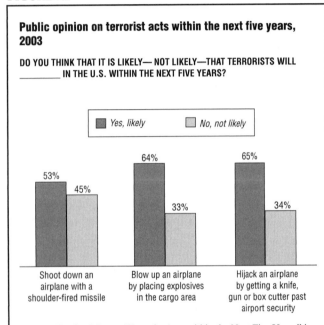

Public opinion on terrorist acts within the next five years, 2003

DO YOU THINK THAT IT IS LIKELY— NOT LIKELY—THAT TERRORISTS WILL _____ IN THE U.S. WITHIN THE NEXT FIVE YEARS?

- Yes, likely
- No, not likely

53% / 45% — Shoot down an airplane with a shoulder-fired missile

64% / 33% — Blow up an airplane by placing explosives in the cargo area

65% / 34% — Hijack an airplane by getting a knife, gun or box cutter past airport security

SOURCE: Heather Mason, "Terrorist Acts within the Next Five Years," in *Enhanced Security Hasn't Calmed All Travel Fears*, http://www.gallup.com/content/default.aspx?ci=10237&pg=1 (accessed September 12, 2004). Copyright © 2003 by The Gallup Organization. Reproduced by permission of The Gallup Organization.

or more per year. Destinations for weekend trips included cities (33%), small towns (26%), beaches (16%), mountain areas (10%), and lake areas (4%).

Not all travel is planned in advance. According to the TIA, in 2001 more than eighty-three million American adults took last-minute trips. Most last-minute travelers (70%) used their own cars, 15% used air transportation, and 8% took recreational vehicles (RVs). About one-third of these trips involved overnight stays of three to four days, just 12% were longer than eight days, and 9% of last-minute travelers made day trips.

Type of Lodging

Of travelers who spent one or more nights away from home in 2003, the TIA reported that 39% stayed with friends or family, while more than half (55%) stayed in a hotel, motel, or bed and breakfast. Five percent stayed in RVs or tents, 4% found lodging in condos or time-shares, and the remaining 7% found other accommodations.

Who Travels?

The TIA reported that baby boomers (categorized for the study as those aged thirty-five to fifty-four) generated the highest volume of domestic travel in 2003, with the average head of a traveling household forty-seven years of age. Slightly less than two-thirds of domestic travelers were married, while 22% were single or never married, and 16% were divorced, widowed, or separated.

Of the travelers who headed their households, 58% held college degrees. Eighty-one percent were employed full- or part-time, while 14% were retired. The average annual household income of travelers increased from $68,800 in 2001 to $69,500 in 2003.

TAKING THE KIDS ALONG. According to the TIA, more adults traveled with children during 2003 than they had during 2002—more than 167 million household trips included a child or children. Not surprisingly, children accompanied adults on more pleasure trips than business

long trips. Weekend trips, especially three-day weekends, have become the practical, if not ideal, solution for such couples.

According to the TIA, the most common type of travel in 2003 was short trips involving either no overnight stay at a destination (reported by 24% of travelers) or short stays of one to two nights (34%). Just 29% of domestic travelers took three- to six-night trips, while 14% were away for seven or more nights.

Americans began taking increasing numbers of weekend trips in the late 1990s, according to the TIA. Nearly half of U.S. adults (103 million) took at least one weekend trip per year, and close to 30% of Americans took five

TABLE 7.4

Information sources that influenced last vacation choice, 2003

	(Representative sample)	Cruisers	Vacationers	Cruiser Destination	Cruiser Luxury	Cruiser Premium	Cruiser Contemporary
Word of mouth	45%	41%	46%	30%	38%	35%	41%
Always wanted to go	36	40	34	32	47	43	40
Good price	27	31	26	25	31	32	31
Spouse or travel companion	25	27	25	27	20	26	27
Destination website	16	15	17	12	17	12	17
Magazine advertisement	11	16	8	12	19	16	16
Internet advertisement	10	9	10	7	7	6	9
Travel magazine	9	16	6	21	22	18	14
Travel agent recommendation	8	17	4	15	21	24	16
Travel guide	8	11	7	10	10	12	11
Direct mail	7	13	5	15	22	18	12
Television/radio commercial	6	7	6	3	9	6	7
Cruise website	3	10	—	4	15	12	12
Other	23	21	24	22	17	21	21

Base: Cruises/vacationers

SOURCE: "Information Sources That Influenced Last Vacation Choice," in *The Cruise Industry—An Overview*, Cruise Lines International Association, Spring 2004, http://www.cruising.org/press/overview/SPRING040V1.pdf (accessed July 7, 2004)

---

trips, although the percentage of adults who brought children along on business trips was 10% in 2003.

PLANNING AND ENJOYING FAMILY TRAVEL. A family travel survey commissioned in 2002 by the car rental company Avis looked at how American families prepared for car trips and summer road vacations. Along with travel planning, the one thousand American parents who participated in the survey were asked about passenger concerns, automobile maintenance, and entertaining children while on the road.

The survey found that many families (46%) planned summer vacations that would enable them to spend quality time with one another. Other motivations for planning family trips included visiting family and friends (25%) and exploring new parts of the country (14%).

Nearly half of parents surveyed said they would prefer to take several short trips during the summer, as opposed to one long trip. When families took to the road, fathers typically handled more of the driving (62%), while mothers drove just 33% of the time.

Rather than relying on digital videodisc (DVD) and videocassette recorder (VCR) players to amuse children, as they might when they were at home, respondents said they preferred to entertain children during car trips by engaging them in traditional pastimes, such as sing-alongs, reading, and made-up games. Only 14% of parents used DVD and VCR players to entertain children in the car.

CHOOSING WHERE TO GO—WHO DECIDES? According to research performed in 2003 by the Cruise Lines International Association (CLIA), many sources influence a family's decision on where to vacation. For all respondents, as well as the subsets of cruisers and "vacationers"

(defined by CLIA as those who took leisure trips away from home of at least three days' duration), the most influential source of information was word of mouth, which had an impact on almost half of respondents in each category of travelers. Almost as many respondents, more than a third in each case, said they chose a vacation destination where they had "always wanted to go." A quarter or more were influenced by a spouse or travel companion, while close to one-sixth chose their destination based on information they saw on a Web site. (See Table 7.4.)

THE NATURE TRAIL

National parks are one of America's biggest tourist attractions. The United States has set aside more than eighty-three million acres of land for national parks. The National Park System includes parks, monuments, historical and military areas, parkways, recreation areas, nature preserves, rivers, seashores, and lakes. For additional information on the U.S. National Parks system, see Chapter Three.

According to the TIA study *The National Parks Traveler* (2004 edition), in 2002 U.S. households generated eighty-seven million person trips (that is, individuals who traveled more than fifty miles) to state or national parks. Twenty percent of international travelers also visited U.S. national or state parks. Forty percent of U.S. adults had visited a national park at least once during the preceding five years.

Reasons for visiting the parks included experiencing nature, cited by 92% of visitors, educational benefits (90%), experiencing culture and history (89%), and spending time with family (89%). Activities visitors engaged in included outdoor sports (44%), outdoor recreation (39%), tourism and sightseeing (39%), water recreation (17%), and National Park Service programs (11%).

Planning for National Park visits in 2002 was done via the Internet by 38% of visitors, with 47% planning their trip one month or more in advance. One-quarter of visitors did not decide where they would stay before making their visit. Three-fourths of visitors stayed overnight in the parks, or within ten miles, on their most recent trip.

The TIA reported that 7% of U.S. domestic travelers visited a national or state park in 2003, down from 10% in 2001. Participating in outdoor activities, including visits to national or state parks, was the third most popular activity cited by American travelers.

THE LURE OF SAND, SURF, AND OCEAN BREEZES

Americans flock to the beach in the summer. The TIA reported that in 2003 one in ten person trips, or nearly 110 million, were made to beaches. Slightly more than two-fifths of trips to beaches were made with children, and 36% of beach trips lasted a week or longer.

According to the TIA, beach travelers did more than swim, sunbathe, and stroll along the shores. Nearly half of beach trips involved shopping, almost one-quarter of beachgoers visited historical sites or museums, about a fifth enjoyed national or state parks, and a sixth went to an amusement or theme park while on their beach trip.

AMUSEMENT AND THEME PARKS

The TIA reported on its Web site (www.tia.org) that seventy-nine million trips of fifty miles or more were taken by domestic travelers to visit theme and amusement parks in 2003. Overall, about 7% of domestic travelers visited a theme or amusement park while away from home. This is about the same percentage as those who participated in gambling or visited a national park. However, among households with children, 12% traveled to an amusement or theme park while on vacation. Amusement and theme park vacations were typically more expensive than other types of trips, costing an average of $810 compared to the U.S. average for all trips, $398. This was in part due to the fact that vacationers who visited amusement and theme parks tended to stay longer (5.7 nights) versus the average U.S. trip (4.1 nights). About 60% of households vacationing at an amusement or theme park included children, compared to about one quarter of vacationing households overall.

GOING ON CRUISES—PORTS AND OPTIONS

A New Generation of Cruisers

For many travelers, few experiences compare to sailing to exotic destinations on a cruise ship. According to the Cruise Lines International Association, an organization of

TABLE 7.5

Annual cruise ship passengers, 1980–2003

	Actual (in thousands)
1980	1,431
1981	1,453
1982	1,471
1983	1,755
1984	1,859
1985	2,152
1986	2,624
1987	2,898
1988	3,175
1989	3,286
1990	3,640
1991	3,979
1992	4,136
1993	4,480
1994	4,448
1995	4,378
1996	4,656
1997	5,051
1998	5,428
1999	5,894
2000	6,882
2001	6,906
2002	7,640
2003	8,195
Average growth rate 1980–2003	+8.1%

SOURCE: "Annual Passenger Growth," in *The Cruise Industry—An Overview*, Cruise Lines International Association, Spring 2004, http://www.cruising.org/press/overview/SPRING040V1.pdf (accessed July 7,2004)

nineteen member cruise lines, the cruise industry grew by an average of more than 8% each year from 1980 to 2003. In 1980 1.4 million Americans took cruises. In 2003 about 8.2 million people went on a cruise. (See Table 7.5.)

Although the North American cruise industry suffered in the aftermath of the events of September 11, 2001, according to the CLIA the industry had already rebounded by February 2002. Several of the CLIA's member cruise lines reported record numbers of reservations made in the first three weeks of January 2002, the period known in the cruise industry as the "wave period" because it usually provided a good indication of booking activity for the balance of the year.

CLIA research has found that cruising appeals to Americans seeking to be pampered and to enjoy fine dining, as well as to those who wished to visit several destinations. Cruising was also considered better than other vacations in terms of ease of planning, being a good value, and offering quality entertainment. Historically, most cruise passengers were over the age of sixty. Modern cruise vacationers were generally younger, more active, and adventurous. The CLIA looked at the demographic characteristics of its target market—Americans age twenty-five and older, who had household incomes of more than $20,000 per year. (See Table 7.6.) They found that typical cruisers within this sample of the population were:

TABLE 7.6

Demographic profile of cruise passengers, 2003

	(Representative sample)	Cruisers	Vacationers	Non-cruise/ non-vacationer
Age				
25–29	6%	4%	7%	3%
30–39	22	16	25	19
40–49	26	18	30	21
50–59	19	21	19	20
60–74	19	26	14	24
75+	8	15	5	13
Total	**100%**	**100%**	**100%**	**100%**
Average	50	55	47	53
Median	46	52	43	51
Income				
$20,000 to less than $40,000	27%	18%	29%	49%
$40,000 to less than $60,000	27	26	27	30
$60,000 to less than $80,000	19	21	19	9
$80,000 to less than $100,000	11	14	10	4
$100,000 to less than $150,000	8	10	8	3
$150,000+	3	3	3	—
Refused	5	8	4	5
Total	**100%**	**100%**	**100%**	**100%**
Average (in 1,000s)	$64	$71	$63	$45
Median (in 1,000s)	$50	$57	$49	$34
Gender				
Male	49%	50%	49%	51%
Female	51	50	51	49
Marital status				
Married	74%	78%	76%	67%
Single/divorced/separated	26	22	24	33
Employment status				
Full-time	56%	46%	61%	48%
Retired	23	37	17	27
Educational attainment				
College grad or higher	49%	56%	49%	27%
Post graduate	18	24	17	5
Race				
White	92%	93%	93%	89%
Black	3	2	2	3
Other	5	5	5	8

SOURCE: "Table 4. Demographics Summary," in *The Cruise Industry—An Overview*, Cruise Lines International Association, Spring 2004, http://www.cruising .org/press/overview/SPRING040V1.pdf (accessed July 7, 2004)

- Nearly evenly distributed among all age ranges. One-fifth were under forty, nearly two-fifths were forty to fifty-nine, and the remaining two-fifths were over the age of sixty. The average age was fifty-two years

- Almost equally male (50%) and female (50%)

- Predominantly married (78%)

- Spread among all income ranges, but with an average income of $71,000

- More than twice as likely to be retired (37%) as other vacationers (17%)

According to the CLIA, from 1997 to 2003 cruises sailed, in general, at about 90% of capacity. In 2003 the average length of cruises was 6.9 days. (See Table 7.7.) Cruises ranged in cost from approximately $75 to more than $500 per day per adult, depending on cabin choices, upgrades, and other features, but nearly all included meals and entertainment. Children often traveled free or at reduced cost. Growth was predicted in all types of cruises, especially short cruises (one to five days).

Unprecedented Cruise Options

According to the organization's Web site (www.cruis-ing.org), CLIA-member lines visited 1,800 ports of call around the world during 2004. From Antarctica to the Caribbean, and Africa to the Mississippi River, cruises reached virtually all waters of the world. Cruise ship passengers could visit ancient Buddhist temples in Indonesia, sip cappuccino in Venice, watch whales on the Pacific Coast, scuba dive in the Caribbean, or shop in Turkey. Cruises were sometimes organized around a particular theme, which could include big band or jazz music; arts and crafts; wine and food; or film. For passengers who preferred relaxing, as opposed to stimulating vacations, the opportunity to simply lounge in a deck chair or read was enjoyable. Cruise ship cuisine is legendary, as is the pampering most cruisers experienced.

TABLE 7.7

Average length of cruises, 1981–2003

	Average length of cruise (days)	Percent of total passengers in 2–5 day category
1981	6.7	29.6%
1982	6.9	25.3
1983	6.9	21.6
1984	6.9	22.3
1985	6.8	26.3
1986	6.4	35.1
1987	6.4	32.8
1988	6.4	32.9
1989	6.4	33.8
1990	6.2	38.3
1991	6.1	37.4
1992	6.2	35.2
1993	6.4	36.7
1994	6.3	38.0
1995	6.5	33.7
1996	6.4	35.9
1997	6.5	33.6
1998	6.7	34.7
1999	6.6	35.8
2000	6.5	36.9
2001	6.4	37.2
2002	6.9	35.5
2003	6.9	32.9

SOURCE: "Average Length of Cruise," in *The Cruise Industry—An Overview,* Cruise Lines International Association, Spring 2004, http://www.cruising.org/press/overview/SPRING040V1.pdf (accessed July 7, 2004)

The most popular cruise locations in 2004 were the Caribbean, the Mediterranean, Alaska, the Bahamas, the Panama Canal, western Mexico, Europe, and Bermuda. (See Table 7.8.) Short cruises were popular, with 32.9% of those who cruised in 2003 going on two- to five-day excursions. (See Table 7.9.) Many people also enjoyed day trips, also known as "cruises to nowhere," which typically included gambling.

In an effort to attract families, many ships offered extensive youth facilities and programs that included kids-only shore excursions. The CLIA reported that about 18% of people going on cruises in 2003 traveled with children, up from 15% two years earlier. Cruise lines such as Disney's Big Red Boat were designed and outfitted to appeal to families.

CULTURAL AND HERITAGE TOURISM

Heritage tourism seeks to draw visitors to historic and cultural sites. Although historic and cultural destinations were not as popular with leisure travelers as cities, visits to friends and family, beaches, and lakes, a significant number of travelers choose educational experiences.

According to the TIA/*Smithsonian* magazine report *The Historic/Cultural Traveler* (2003 edition), nearly 118 million American adults attended at least one cultural, arts, heritage, or historic activity or event while traveling in 2002. Many travelers prolonged their trips solely to participate in cultural or historic events and activities. Four in ten historic/cultural travelers said they added extra time to their trips to enable them to attend a historic activity or cultural event.

The TIA/*Smithsonian* report found that these travelers spent more—an average of $623 per trip, compared to $457 for all U.S. travelers, excluding transportation to their destinations. The report also distinguished historic/cultural travelers from other travelers, describing them as more inclined to take longer trips (seven nights or more), and more likely to utilize air travel, a rental car, and a hotel.

The TIA/*Smithsonian* survey found that 39% of historic/cultural travelers said that trips that included cultural, arts, historic, or heritage activities or events were more enjoyable to them. Visits to destinations with historical significance were preferred by 38% of travelers, while 29% felt that it was important that the trips they took for vacation or leisure provide cultural experiences. Slightly more than a quarter felt that a vacation or leisure trip away from home was not complete without visiting a museum, historic site, or landmark, while 17% felt a trip was not complete without attending a cultural event or arts performance.

The list of most-visited destinations for historic/cultural travelers was topped by Washington, D.C., New York City, Chicago, and Boston. Other cities in the top ten included Las Vegas; Norfolk, Virginia; Atlanta; Orlando, Florida; San Francisco; and Los Angeles.

Consumer interest has led many corporate sponsors to invest in programs promoting heritage tourism. Travel services companies have invested in projects by the National Trust for Historic Preservation to help communities develop and maintain their historic and cultural sites. Some hotels and car rental agencies have contributed to school programs to educate children about historic sites across the United States.

Mock Combat—Civil War Reenactments

A growing number of people enjoy participating in reenactments of historical events, often involving military battles. A group of Massachusetts residents have reenacted the events of April 19, 1775 (which marked the beginning of the Revolutionary War) for more than seventy years, and other groups dress as English knights, Spanish conquistadors, Roman gladiators, or Vikings.

One of the most popular eras to reenact is the U.S. Civil War (1861–65). Estimates of the number of these hobbyists have varied. In 1996 a reenactment of the Battle of Antietam drew thirteen thousand costumed people to Maryland. In 1997 almost twenty thousand costumed soldiers and civilians went to Gettysburg for the 134th anniversary of that battle. In 2003 an article in the Minneapolis *Star Tribune* estimated that there were as many as

TABLE 7.8

Cruise destinations, 1987–2003

Destination	1987 Total bed days	1989 Total bed days	1995 Total bed days	1999 Total bed days	2000 Total bed days	2001 Total bed days	2002 Total bed days	2003 Total bed days	2003 Percent	2004 Total bed days	2004 Percent	2004 vs. 2003 change
Caribbean	8,828,791	10,982,227	15,254,551	16,666,238	21,510,142	21,833,347	26,741,052	28,999,049	41.03%	31,210,605	40.38%	7.63%
Mediterranean	841,051	1,879,561	3,477,729	5,898,948	6,277,064	7,546,816	6,497,444	8,153,251	11.53%	9,704,398	12.55%	19.02%
Alaska	1,715,197	1,598,268	3,008,146	4,086,620	4,197,332	4,698,538	5,052,907	5,265,159	7.45%	5,913,967	7.65%	12.32%
Bahamas	1,922,386	2,483,732	2,761,224	3,060,866	3,200,346	4,698,724	2,876,295	3,305,636	4.68%	3,656,705	4.73%	10.62%
Trans Canal	970,191	979,691	2,277,201	3,036,208	2,573,444	2,396,424	2,092,723	3.94%	3.94%	2,930,528	3.79%	5.26%
Mexico West	1,131,462	1,628,824	1,754,312	2,529,106	2,680,934	1,166,756	3,386,475	3,390,768	4.80%	4,827,262	6.24%	42.36%
Europe	357,516	774,149	1,582,589	3,475,922	3,744,693	4,837,375	6,922,608	7,721,741	10.92%	7,560,171	9.78%	−2.09%
Bermuda	1,141,121	868,655	1,094,707	1,482,573	988,391	1,269,952	1,226,806	1,476,443	2.09%	1,324,690	1.71%	−10.28%
Transatlantic	339,388	407,218	658,928	961,213	1,015,625	1,129,669	1,005,665	1,145,651	1.62%	1,425,596	1.84%	24.44%
Hawaii	602,728	835,638	601,542	885,268	857,390	1,557,438	1,903,302	1,953,200	2.76%	2,629,458	3.40%	34.62%
South Pacific	352,983	383,210	574,218	947,382	1,155,217	1,158,044	835,464	1,099,056	1.55%	683,506	0.88%	−37.81%
South East Asia	272,592	207,405	430,123	150,107	244,620	429,550	346,196	123,350	0.17%	20,372	0.03%	−83.48%
Africa	0	0	347,432	184,373	502,773	401,011	259,962	188,964	0.27%	17,640	0.02%	−90.66%
Canada/New England	283,714	219,992	334,735	681,689	1,107,689	1,138,975	1,150,950	1,105,274	1.56%	1,488,585	1.93%	34.68%
Far East (Orient)	465,608	238,630	327,009	188,038	201,582	215,022	360,022	219,358	0.31%	403,538	0.52%	83.96%
Mississippi	231,392	181,446	286,228	353,088	347,140	403,956	0	0	0.00%	0	0.00%	0.00%
World	0	175,028	272,425	565,824	414,342	613,046	582,314	375,384	0.53%	462,934	0.60%	23.32%
South America	620,396	458,246	255,834	657,992	825,670	1,422,755	1,394,808	1,653,535	2.34%	1,088,569	1.41%	−34.17%
U.S. Coastal West	22,185	64,444	108,092	65,108	217,518	1,944,752	216,338	376,709	0.53%	643,792	0.83%	70.90%
Indian Ocean	0	0	84,009	40,572	120,698	227,483	93,708	23,148	0.03%	10,544	0.01%	−54.45%
Unclassified	0	19,325	69,560	86,890	108,676	239,774	233,258	290,163	0.41%	989,750	1.28%	241.10%
Trans Pacific	17,904	113,684	42,610	86,150	52,400	67,120	143,020	78,930	0.11%	11,600	0.02%	−85.30%
U.S. Coastal East	132,794	84,920	42,480	113,387	1,402,429	80,312	147,422	837,540	1.18%	60,072	0.08%	−92.83%
Antarctica	0	17,240	12,240	53,179	48,499	48,517	73,176	108,598	0.15%	219,296	0.28%	101.93%
Party cruises	85,336	140,658	3,602	59,846	68,203	56,010	43,296	10,635	0.02%	14,888	0.02%	39.99%
	20,376,994	**24,699,932**	**35,661,526**	**46,316,587**	**53,862,817**	**59,581,366**	**63,585,211**	**70,685,517**	**100.00%**	**77,298,466**	**100.00%**	**9.36%**

Note: Current destination classifications were established in 1994. Prior to 1994, Bermuda was included in Bahamas/Caribbean; Mississippi and Coastal East were included in Bahamas/Caribbean. Prior to 1985, Bermuda was included in Bahamas/Caribbean. Prior to 1992, Indian Ocean and Africa were part of unclassified. In 1993 Mexico East was changed to Western Caribbean.

SOURCE: "Geographical Destination/Application," in *The Cruise Industry—An Overview*, Cruise Lines International Association, Spring 2004, http://www.cruising.org/press/overview/SPRING040V1.pdf (accessed July 7, 2004)

TABLE 7.9

Category shares of cruise passengers, by length of cruise, 1980–2003

(In percent)

	1980	2003	% Point change
2–5 days	24.3%	32.9	8.6
6–8 days	59.1	56.3	−2.8
9–17 days	15.4	10.4	−5.0
18+ days	1.2	0.4	−0.8
Total	**100.0%**	**100.0%**	**0.0**

SOURCE: "Growth by Length of Cruise—North American Market-Share," in *The Cruise Industry—An Overview*, Cruise Lines International Association, Spring 2004, http://www.cruising.org/press/overview/SPRING040V1.pdf (accessed July 7, 2004)

forty-five thousand military and civilian Civil War reenactors in the United States. When they attended a reenactment, they were often accompanied by their families.

Reenactors may visit school classrooms, march in parades, teach seminars, hold public demonstrations, or participate in weekend battle games. Groups also meet in a number of overseas countries, including England, Germany, Taiwan, France, Belgium, Spain, Japan, Sweden, and Norway. Dozens of reenactment groups have Internet sites.

Civil War reenactments began during the 1960s at the time of the Civil War's centennial. A love of history and a desire to educate are the primary motivations mentioned by reenactors. Interest in reenactments has tended to increase after mass-market films about the war are shown on television or in movie theaters.

Civil War reenactments are not for everyone, however. Just getting started requires buying period clothes, boots, a tent, mess equipment, and a gun, at a cost of $1,000 to $1,500. The investment can reach $2,000 for members of groups that strive for high levels of authenticity. These groups can be so exacting that they do not allow members to use modern speech or eyeglasses. An estimated two hundred businesses have grown to satisfy the need for authenticity in costumes, including "great coats" and brogans (heavy, ankle-high shoes) and equipment. Participating in reenactments requires physical strength, vigor, and endurance. Young men typically serve as soldiers because the average age of soldiers fell from twenty-five in 1862 to eighteen in 1864. Some older adult enthusiasts may remain involved in the activity as spectators when marching long distances in inclement weather becomes too physically demanding.

ROMANTIC VACATIONS

Many Americans dream about romantic getaways with a spouse or other love interest to ignite or rekindle romantic feelings in the relationship. According to the 2002 *TIA Travel Poll,* more than forty-two million American adults said they had taken a romantic vacation in the prior year. Many of these romantic vacations consisted of honeymoons or anniversary celebrations.

Not surprisingly, the TIA survey found that Americans without children in their households took more romantic vacations than parents with children. The poll revealed that romance-related travel was most popular among baby boomers—four out of ten (41%) romance travelers were aged thirty-five to fifty-four. One-third (33%) of these travelers were aged eighteen to thirty-four. The majority (67%) of romance-related travelers were married. Many of these travelers (38%) had above-average annual household incomes of $50,000 or more.

A 2002 poll by America Online (AOL) and *Travel + Leisure* magazine asked AOL members to rank their "favorite way to spend a dream honeymoon or special anniversary." The top responses were a luxury cruise in the Caribbean (34%) and a visit to an island in the South Pacific (32%). Other popular choices were spending time in a country inn (16%), in the heart of a European city (14%), skiing in the Rocky Mountains (3%) or on an African safari (2%). When asked what, in their "wildest dreams," would be their most romantic trip, 53% said they wished they could rent out an entire private-island resort. Another 18% said they dreamed of chartering a yacht to sail to all seven continents, while 12% said they'd like to lease a castle with a full staff.

SHOPPING AS RECREATION

Americans love to shop, and for many, shopping means "heading to the mall." According to the International Council of Shopping Centers (ICSC), in 2003 there were 46,990 shopping centers in the United States, which contained a total of 5.9 billion square feet of leasable retail space. California had the most shopping centers, with 6,243, and Wyoming the fewest—fifty-five.

An estimated 203.1 million adults visited shopping centers each month in 2003, up from 201.1 million in 2002. The average customer spent $68.20 per mall visit. The ICSC estimated that 76% of all nonautomotive retail sales (nearly $2 trillion worth) were generated by shopping centers, and that 17.6 million Americans were employed by them, or 14% of all nonagricultural workers in the United States.

According to the ICSC, the five largest shopping centers in the United States in 2003 were the Mall of America (Bloomington, Minnesota), King of Prussia Plaza (King of Prussia, Pennsylvania), South Coast Plaza (Costa Mesa, California), The Galleria (Houston, Texas), and Woodfield Mall (Schaumburg, Illinois). Although many of the largest ones were enclosed, 95% of shopping centers were open-air—according to the ICSC, there were just 1,130 enclosed malls in the United States.

Outlet Malls

Outlet shopping malls have become major attractions for American travelers. Outlet stores typically offer bargains on overstocked, discontinued, or slightly imperfect merchandise from major brand names. In 2003, according to the ICSC, there were 230 outlet malls, which had generated an estimated $16.5 billion in retail sales during 2002. The 2000 *TIA Travel Poll* reported that out of all travelers on trips of one hundred or more miles away from home, almost 40% visited an outlet mall. Of the visitors, 46% were men and 54% were women. One out of ten respondents cited outlet shopping as the primary reason for the trip. Most said it was the secondary reason, and about 10% said it was not an original reason for the trip, although they did visit an outlet mall.

The Mall of America

Opened in 1992, the Mall of America in Bloomington, Minnesota, was America's largest shopping mall in 2004, and the second largest in the world. More than 4.2 million square feet in size, it had more than 520 shops, sixty restaurants, eight nightclubs, a walk-through aquarium, and Camp Snoopy, the world's largest indoor family theme park. Built at a cost of $650 million, the mall employed more than eleven thousand people year round and was visited by approximately forty million people per year. Many were tourists who visited for a weekend of shopping. Tourists, 73% of whom drove there by car or bus, spent an average of $129 per visit in 2002, according to Mall of America officials.

FAMILY REUNIONS

Family reunions provided incentive for about one-third of Americans to travel, according to the 2002 *TIA Travel Poll*. Thirty-four percent of U.S. adults (seventy-two million) had traveled to a family reunion during the three-year period preceding the poll, and one in five had traveled to a family reunion in the year before the poll.

Married people were more likely to take a trip to attend a family reunion than unmarried people (38% versus 30%). Similarly, adults with children under eighteen were more inclined than those without children to take a family reunion trip (39% versus 32%). There was a widespread willingness to travel great distances to reconnect with far-flung family members: 34% of surveyed respondents reported traveling five hundred or more miles one way away from home. Another 34% traveled between 150 and 499 miles, while 32% traveled less than 150 miles to attend reunions.

Family reunions were most often held in a private home (52%). The TIA poll found that other popular locations for reunions were city or town parks (12%) and national or state parks or forests (6%).

TRENDS: ECOTOURISM AND SERVICE-ORIENTED TRAVEL

"Green" (advantageous to the environment) travel is important to many travelers. The 2002 TIA/*National Geographic Traveler* report *Geotourism: The New Trend in Travel* classified more than fifty-five million Americans as geotourists. This term was defined as people whose travel was intended to sustain or enhance the geographical character of the place being visited (including its environment, culture, aesthetics, and heritage) and the well-being of its residents.

According to the report, although most travelers were concerned with price and value, 58.5 million Americans said they would pay more to use a travel company that strove to protect and preserve the environment. Of these, 61% said they would be willing to pay 5% to 10% more. Almost a third of respondents said they believed it was important for travel companies they used to employ local residents and to support the local communities of their destinations, while 30% said they were "very" or "extremely" likely to buy products and services from companies that donated part of their proceeds to charitable organizations.

The TIA/*National Geographic Traveler* report also found that 71% of the traveling public felt it was important that their visit to a destination not damage its environment. Nearly two-thirds (61%) believed that their travel experience was better when a destination preserved its natural, historic, and cultural sites and attractions. Seeing and doing something "authentic" was also important, with 41% of travelers saying it made their experience better.

More than half of travelers were aware of at least one practice that travel companies employed to preserve and protect the environment of destinations. These included reusing towels and sheets, reducing energy use, and recycling, or using local vegetation on property grounds.

A late 1990s study by the Vermont-based Ecotourism Society reported that nearly half (48.1%) of the more than 3,340 surveyed participants indicated a degree of enthusiasm for activities such as biking, hiking, canoeing, and visiting parks, as well as observing animals and other wildlife when they vacationed. Of these nature enthusiasts, more than 30% were termed either "heavy users" (those who planned trips that involved nature-based recreation the majority of the time) or "moderate users" (those who planned trips that entailed some time spent pursuing nature-based activities).

The Ecotourism Society characterized the typical ecotourist as between the ages of thirty-five and fifty-four, a college graduate, and as likely to be male as female. Experienced ecotourists preferred trips of longer duration, from eight to fourteen days, and were willing to spend more on travel than general tourists. The activities ecotourists favored included visiting parks, hiking, exploring preserved areas, and wildlife viewing.

A further trend in travel includes those foregoing traditional tourist excursions in favor of service trips that combine work and leisure, often in a foreign country. For example, Habitat for Humanity International offers a Global Village program that combines volunteer home-building activities with the opportunity to live with a host family abroad. Trips planned for July 2005 include building cement block homes near Lusaka at Tiyende Pamodzi in Zambia and building timber homes in Papua New Guinea.

COMBINING BUSINESS AND PLEASURE TRIPS

According to the TIA, business travel volume in 2003 was 210.5 million person trips, a drop of 2% from 2002. Business travel comprised 18% of total U.S. domestic person trips. The most common purposes for business trips were general business (meetings/consultations/presentations/sales), which accounted for 44% of trips, and conventions/conferences/seminars (22%). One-third (34%) of business trips were made for combined business and pleasure purposes. One in ten business/convention/ seminar trips included multiple adults from the same household, and 5% included children.

According to the 2001 TIA report *Business and Convention Travelers,* half of trips that combined business and pleasure were taken by solo travelers, one-third were taken by multiple adults from a household, and one in five included a child. Baby boomers were the most likely to take combined business and pleasure trips, and households with at least one college degree took two-thirds of combined trips. About half of these travelers were professionals or employed in managerial capacities. One-third of combined business and pleasure trips were taken by households with children who lived at home.

ARRANGED TRIPS FOR OLDER ADULTS

Elderhostel, a nonprofit organization that arranges trips that combine learning and recreation for people fifty-five and older, grew from 220 participants and six programs in its founding year of 1975 to 170,000 participants and ten thousand programs in 2003. In 2004 Elderhostel offered 8,300 programs in the United States and Canada and 2,000 in over ninety countries overseas.

Along with exotic travel adventures around the world, Elderhostel has developed a popular group of intergenerational programs that pair grandparents with their grandchildren in a range of learning adventures. It has turned ships and barges into floating classrooms and created service programs that offer participants the chance to volunteer for worthy causes around the world.

TECHNOLOGY AND TRAVEL

The TIA's 2004 *Travelers' Use of the Internet* survey reported that sixty-four million travelers used the Internet in 2003, about the same number as in 2002. Use of the Internet for travel planning had risen dramatically since 1997, when just twelve million Americans planned and researched travel online. The rate of growth in the online travel planning market slowed in response to the slower rate of growth of "wired" (Internet-connected) households.

Although the overall number of people doing travel planning online did not increase from 2002 to 2003, consumers were doing more travel research and planning online than ever before. Twenty-nine percent of surveyed respondents said they did all of their trip research and planning online, up from 23% in the previous year. During 2003 more than forty-two million people booked travel using the Internet, an increase of 8% from 2002. The Internet was also used more frequently to make reservations—more than two-thirds of respondents (70%) did at least half of their travel booking online, up from 56% in 2001.

The TIA report speculated that the Internet was responsible for changing booking patterns—more consumers booked later to take advantage of low prices on last-minute travel and specials available exclusively online. Airline tickets were the most frequently purchased travel products online, reported by 75% of all online travel bookers, followed by accommodations (71%) and rental cars (43%). The average amount spent online increased in 2003 to $2,600 from $2,300 in 2002. Travel companies found e-mail to be a useful promotional tool, with thirty-five million travelers signing up with supplier Web sites or online travel services to receive special offers, and ten million acting on an offer to take a trip they might not have otherwise taken, according to the TIA.

The study highlighted problems facing travel agents, who had seen a substantial portion of their business taken by online services. According to the TIA, in 2002, 26% of Americans, or fifty-four million adults, said they had used a travel agent to book at least one business, pleasure, or personal trip, flight, hotel room, rental car, or tour in the preceding three years. This figure was down from the reported 32% in 1999. One bright spot for travel agents was the continuing growth of the cruise industry, according to the 2004 CLIA report. The CLIA found that 88% of cruisers booked some or all of their trip with an agent, compared to more than half of all vacationers who said they never used a travel agent.

INTERNATIONAL TRAVEL

Americans like to travel abroad, though many are not able to or can only do so occasionally because of the expense involved. A 2003 Harris poll of countries Americans would choose to visit if cost were not a factor found that the number one choice was Australia, followed by Italy, Great Britain, France, and Ireland. Australia had topped the poll for seven years running, although Italy moved up from fifth place in 1997 to second in 2003. Lower down in the poll were Germany (sixth), New Zealand (seventh), Japan (eighth), Spain (ninth), and Greece (tenth). Interest in Japan had grown since 2002, when it did not place in the top fifteen, while New Zealand had risen from thirteenth place, possibly because of interest in the *Lord of the Rings* films, which were shot there. Between 2002 and 2003 Canada fell from third to twelfth, while Jamaica and Barbados dropped off the list entirely, after sharing ninth place in 2002.

According to a poll of travel agents conducted by the American Society of Travel Agents and Fodor's and published online in 2004 by TravelSense.org, the top international destinations were London; Rome; Cancun, Mexico; Paris; Punta Cana, Dominican Republic; Aruba; Dublin, Ireland; Frankfurt; Montego Bay, Jamaica; and the Caribbean. Visitors to TravelSense.org's Web site were polled as well, and their top ten choices were Cancun, Paris, London, Jamaica, the Caribbean, Aruba, Europe, Mexico, the Bahamas, and Puerto Vallarta.

CHAPTER 8
THE ROLE OF RECREATION IN AMERICAN SOCIETY

A CHANGING ROLE

The expectations of free time have shifted and expanded over time. Eric Miller, in *At Our Leisure* (New York: EPM Communications, Inc., 1997), depicted recreation and leisure in the United States in the 1950s as an expression of comfort; it rounded out lives and reaffirmed the importance of home and family. During the 1960s it acquired an identity of its own apart from "traditional values." In the 1970s free time became an expression of an individual's identity; it pushed work into secondary importance. During the 1980s many Americans began to work at having fun—they were intent on working hard and "playing hard."

Americans of the 1980s spent wildly on material necessities, pleasures, and extravagances. Shopping was elevated to a form of recreation; American leisure included unabashed consumerism. At the turn of the twenty-first century, Americans started to demand even more of their free time—recreation had to provide personal satisfaction. Aging baby boomers, poised to become the largest group of older Americans in the country's history, exerted tremendous influence over societal views and values about work, life, and leisure. As the members of this generation began to recognize a limit to the length of life, they turned their attention to improving the quality of life.

American culture's structuring of leisure changed significantly in the mid twentieth century. The five-day workweek was institutionalized as a part of President Franklin D. Roosevelt's New Deal (1938), and Americans settled into "nine-to-five" workdays (or slight variations) after World War II. When free time became a national institution, no corresponding leisure industry existed. Since then, leisure has developed into a huge industry. According to the U.S. Department of Labor in its survey *Consumer Expenditures in 2002,* about 5.1% of Americans' annual expenditures were on entertainment, just slightly less than the 5.8% they spent on health care.

WHAT AMERICANS SEEK THROUGH RECREATION

The nature of modern work has a significant impact on the types of activities people pursue in their free time. For instance, workers whose jobs keep them in front of a computer monitor for many hours a day often seek physical activities to offset the many hours they are required to sit. Conversely, people whose jobs require many hours on their feet welcome an opportunity to relax at the end of the day. The types of activities Americans pursue in their leisure time are as various as the people themselves, and for some who derive little satisfaction from their work, recreational activities can provide an important opportunity for personal fulfillment. Stress-relief, physical well-being, artistic satisfaction, deepening spirituality, and intellectual development can all be motivating factors in Americans' recreational choices.

Many of Americans' favorite forms of recreation are popular for three reasons: They are convenient, possible to do alone or with others, and able to be performed for pleasure rather than for competition. For example, walking for exercise is popular because it can be performed almost anywhere, at any time, and alone or with others.

Americans Want More Time

The perception of Americans as hardworking, stressed, and lacking leisure time is often supported by the observation that they routinely work more hours per day and more days per year than residents of other countries. According to *Key Indicators of the Labor Market* (Geneva: U.N. International Labor Organization, 2003), U.S. workers put in an average of 1,815 hours at their jobs in 2002. While this was less than the 2,447 hours workers in South Korea averaged, or the 1,848 hours of the Japanese, it was more than in many other countries, including Canada (1,778 hours), Sweden (1,625 hours), and Germany (1,444 hours).

While Americans rely on the generosity of their employers, or their union's bargaining skills, to receive paid vacation time, in many other countries vacation time is

TABLE 8.1

Public opinion on amount of time available for recreational activities, December 2003

Amount of time available for each activity

	Right amount	Too little	Too much
Relaxing or doing nothing	45%	44%	11%
Hobbies	40%	51%	5%
Reading	38%	54%	7%
Personal exercise and recreation	37%	59%	3%
Watching television	50%	16%	32%

SOURCE: Lydia Saad, "Have Enough Time to Do What You Want These Days?" in *No Time for R&R,* http://www.gallup.com/content/default.aspx?ci =11656&pg=1 (accessed September 12, 2004). Copyright © 2004 by The Gallup Organization. Reproduced by permission of The Gallup Organization.

FIGURE 8.1

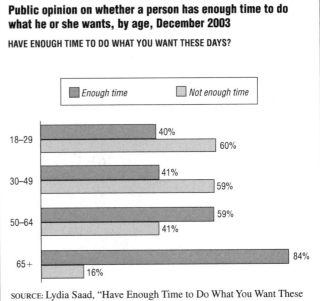

Public opinion on whether a person has enough time to do what he or she wants, by age, December 2003

HAVE ENOUGH TIME TO DO WHAT YOU WANT THESE DAYS?

SOURCE: Lydia Saad, "Have Enough Time to Do What You Want These Days?" in *No Time for R&R,* http://www.gallup.com/content/default .aspx?ci=11656&pg=1 (accessed September 12, 2004). Copyright © 2004 by The Gallup Organization. Reproduced by permission of The Gallup Organization.

mandated by law. In such European countries as Sweden, Austria, Denmark, France, and Spain, workers in 2002 were guaranteed twenty-five days of paid vacation per year, while those in Germany and Finland received twenty-four, and those in Italy, Switzerland, Ireland, Belgium, Greece, and the United Kingdom got twenty. Communist China gave all workers fifteen vacation days per year, and Japan ten, but the United States had no national law requiring that workers be given a paid vacation from work.

While the time off that workers were guaranteed in these countries might seem generous to Americans, the actual amount they took was even more, averaging five or more additional days, according to information compiled by Catherine Valenti in the ABCNEWS.com report "Vacation Deprivation—Americans Get Short-Changed When It Comes to Holiday Time" (June 25, 2003). By contrast, Americans took an average of 10.2 days per year of vacation.

This lack of time off from work may be one reason why a December 2003 Gallup poll found that 44% of Americans felt they had too little time to relax or do nothing, while 51% said they had too little time to pursue hobbies, 54% had too little time to read, and 59% had too little time for personal exercise and recreation. (See Table 8.1.) Forty years earlier, a similar Gallup poll had found that 74% of Americans reported they had enough leisure time.

The 2003 Gallup poll also found that the amount of time Americans had for leisure varied according to age. For those eighteen to twenty-nine, 40% said they had enough time to do whatever they wanted, while 60% said they did not. The data for those between thirty and forty-nine was almost identical, but older Americans had more free time—from age fifty to sixty-four, 59% said they had enough time to do what they wanted, and 84% of those over sixty-five reported having enough time to do what they wanted. (See Figure 8.1.)

How Leisure Time Is Spent

The National Endowment for the Arts (NEA) *2002 Survey of Public Participation in the Arts* (2004) looked at how American adults spent their leisure time. The most popular leisure activity in 2002 was going to movies, which 60% of respondents said they had done at least once. Exercise came in second, at 55.1%, followed by gardening (47.3%), doing home improvements (42.4%), and visiting amusement parks (41.7%). Thirty-nine percent of Americans also partook of at least one "Benchmark Arts Activity," which consisted of attending jazz, classical music, or opera performances; musical plays; plays; ballet; or art museums. (See Table 8.2.)

The NEA survey uncovered several trends in leisure activities when the 2002 results were compared with those of earlier years. From 1982 to 2002, while participation in movie and television viewing held relatively steady, the number of Americans who enjoyed outdoor activities declined dramatically. Participation in gardening by American adults dropped from 60% in 1982 to 47.3% in 2002, while the number playing active sports fell from 39% to 30.4%, although the amount doing exercise increased from 51% to 55.1%. Attendance at sporting events once or more during the year fell from 48% to 35%, while the number making improvements to their homes in their leisure time dropped from 60% to 42.4%. (See Table 8.2.)

Participation in each activity varied by gender, age, ethnicity, income, and educational status. For example, participation in gardening was much more common among women (62.4% of all gardeners) than men (37.6%), while more men played sports (61%) than women (39%). Whites tended to participate in more outdoor activities than African-Americans or Hispanics, while visiting

TABLE 8.2

Participation in leisure activities other than the arts, 1982, 1992, 2002

Type of activity	Percent of adults participating		
	1982	1992	2002
Movies	63.0%	59.0%	60.0%
Exercise	51.0	60.0	55.1
Gardening	60.0	55.0	47.3
Home improvements	60.0	48.0	42.4
Amusement parks	49.0	50.0	41.7
Benchmark arts events*	39.0	41.0	39.0
Sporting events	48.0	37.0	35.0
Outdoor activities	36.0	34.0	30.9
Active sports	39.0	39.0	30.4
Volunteer/Charity	28.0	33.0	29.0
TV hours per day	3.0	3.0	2.9

*Benchmark arts events include going to at least one jazz, classical music, or opera performance; musical play; play; ballet; or art museum

SOURCE: "Table 26. Participation in Other Leisure Activities, 1982, 1992, 2002," in *2002 Survey of Public Participation in the Arts,* National Endowment for the Arts, 2004, http://www.arts.gov/pub/NEASurvey2004.pdf (accessed September 9, 2004)

amusement parks was almost equally popular among all ethnic groups. Younger adults had more interest in playing and watching sports; attending arts events, performing charity work, and gardening had more older participants. Those with a college education or a higher income level tended to participate in all types of leisure activities more than people with less education or income. (See Table 8.3.)

The Value of the Performing Arts

Public support for the arts and appreciation of their importance was confirmed by the results of a three-year public opinion survey conducted by the Performing Arts Research Coalition, *The Value of the Performing Arts in Ten Communities* (2004). The survey was designed to assess participation rates, characteristics of attendees, the perceived value of the performing arts to individuals and their communities, and barriers to attendance. It was conducted in Alaska; Austin, Texas; Boston; Cincinnati; Denver; Minneapolis–St. Paul; Pittsburgh; Sarasota, Florida; Seattle; and Washington, D.C. The survey found that three-quarters of the respondents in each community agreed or strongly agreed with the statement, "Attending live performing arts is enjoyable to me." More than 90% agreed or strongly agreed that the performing arts contributed to the education and development of children, while over 80% agreed or strongly agreed that the performing arts improved the quality of life in their community. More than two-thirds of respondents in each community surveyed also agreed or strongly agreed that performing arts helped them understand other cultures better.

Recreation as Socialization

Many forms of recreation are popular because they offer opportunities to socialize and interact with others.

Many young people enjoy sports as an inexpensive dating practice, believing they can get to know another person better while spending time skating or bicycling together. Billiards in modern, upscale parlors has become a "hip" couples' activity, and bowling has regained popularity. Gyms, health clubs, and sporting activities have been touted as great ways to simultaneously improve health and fitness, engage in recreation, and meet people.

There is mounting evidence that socialization and recreation hold important health benefits. Family, friends, active interests, and community involvement may do more than simply help people enjoy their lives. Social activities and relationships may actually enable people to live longer by preventing or delaying development of many diseases, including dementia (impaired mental function). Furthermore, social activities seem to protect against disease and increase longevity even when the activities do not involve physical exercise. In "Social Engagement and Disability in a Community Population of Older Adults" (*American Journal of Epidemiology,* April 1, 2003), C. F. Mendes de Leon and colleagues tracked the health and longevity of 2,812 older adults living in New Haven, Connecticut. After nine years, the researchers reported that "higher levels of social engagement are associated with reduced disability and that this effect was consistent across three different measures of disability as well as across gender and racial subgroups."

TRENDS IN THE LEISURE MARKET

The Influence of the Baby Boom Generation

According to Jeffrey Ziegler in the article "Recreating Retirement: How Will Baby Boomers Reshape Leisure in Their 60s" (*Parks & Recreation,* October 2002), the leisure interests of "baby boomers" (those born between 1946 and 1964, when the U.S. birth rate peaked) were different from those of the generations that preceded them. Writing about how baby boomers would fare as they began to reach retirement age, he observed that:

- Boomers tended to be better educated than preceding generations, and worked and played hard.

- Boomers viewed themselves as younger than their chronological age.

- Boomers purchased more upscale goods and services than other age groups.

- Boomers tended to overschedule themselves, seeking to pack activity into every hour of the day.

- Boomers were less likely to volunteer their time than other age groups.

- Boomers wanted to separate themselves from things that made them feel old.

TABLE 8.3

Demographic distribution of adults participating in leisure activities other than the arts at least once in the 12-month period ending August 2002

	U.S. adult population		Movies	Sports events	Amusement park	Exercise program	Playing sports	Outdoor activities	Charity work	Home improve-ment/repair	Gardening	Benchmark arts activities[1]
	Millions	Percent										
Gender												
Male	98.7	47.9%	47.4%	56.5%	46.4%	47.8%	61.0%	53.2%	42.2%	52.2%	37.6%	44.2%
Female	107.2	52.1	52.6	43.5	53.6	52.2	39.0	46.8	57.8	47.8	62.4	55.8
Total	**205.9**	**100.0**	**100.0**	**100.0**	**100.0**	**100.0**	**100.0**	**100.0**	**100.0**	**100.0**	**100.0**	**100.0%**
Race and ethnicity												
Hispanic	22.7	11.0	9.6	8.3	10.3	8.0	8.1	5.3	5.8	7.3	8.1	6.5
White [1]	150.1	72.9	76.5	79.9	74.8	78.2	79.1	88.1	81.6	82.0	80.5	80.5
African-American[2]	23.7	11.5	9.4	8.9	10.1	9.6	8.7	3.1	9.0	7.1	7.4	8.1
Other [2]	9.5	4.6	4.5	2.9	4.8	4.2	4.1	3.5	3.5	3.7	4.0	4.9
Total	**205.9**	**100.0**	**100.0**	**100.0**	**100.0**	**100.0**	**100.0**	**100.0**	**100.0**	**100.0**	**100.0**	**100.0**
Age												
18–24	26.8	13.0	17.9	17.1	17.9	14.5	21.1	15.8	11.3	6.5	5.7	11.8
25–34	36.9	17.9	22.0	21.4	24.2	19.6	23.4	22.5	16.1	17.4	15.7	18.0
35–44	44.2	21.5	24.2	25.7	27.3	23.1	25.7	27.0	24.5	26.7	23.4	23.0
45–54	39.0	18.9	19.0	19.4	16.8	20.1	17.8	20.2	21.8	24.5	22.1	22.1
55–64	25.9	12.6	9.8	9.2	8.2	11.1	6.6	8.9	12.2	13.3	15.1	13.0
65–74	17.6	8.5	4.6	4.8	3.8	7.3	3.9	4.2	8.5	7.8	10.4	7.7
75 and over	1 5.5	7.5	2.4	2.4	1.7	4.3	1.5	1.4	5.5	3.9	7.6	4.4
Total	**205.9**	**100.0**	**100.0**	**100.0**	**100.0**	**100.0**	**100.0**	**100.0**	**100.0**	**100.0**	**100.0**	**100.0**
Education												
Grade school	11.6	5.6	1.8	1.5	2.3	2.2	1.3	1.1	1.6	2.6	3.9	1.1
Some high school	20.1	9.8	6.4	4.9	7.2	5.8	5.5	4.9	4.2	5.7	6.4	3.4
High school graduate	63.8	31.0	26.7	25.0	28.2	25.7	23.1	25.0	21.6	26.0	28.7	19.5
Some college	56.9	27.6	31.7	31.5	32.4	31.2	32.0	32.3	31.4	30.3	29.0	31.4
College graduate	36.1	17.5	22.5	25.5	21.0	23.2	26.0	24.4	25.7	23.1	20.7	28.5
Graduate school	1 7.4	8.5	10.9	11.6	8.9	11.9	12.1	12.4	15.5	12.3	11.3	16.2
Total	**205.9**	**100.0**	**100.0**	**100.0**	**100.0**	**100.0**	**100.0**	**100.0**	**100.0**	**100.0**	**100.0**	**100.0**
Income												
Less than $10K	14.4	7.0	4.9	3.6	5.5	5.1	3.7	3.7	4.3	3.5	5.2	4.1
$10K to $20K	22.7	11.0	8.5	6.9	8.8	9.2	7.3	6.8	7.8	6.7	10.0	6.8
$20K to $30K	25.0	12.1	10.7	8.8	11.0	10.9	9.3	9.1	9.5	8.9	11.6	8.7
$30K to $40K	24.2	11.8	12.3	10.9	12.0	12.4	11.1	12.3	12.0	12.6	12.7	11.5
$40K to $50K	17.6	8.5	9.9	9.3	9.5	9.4	9.0	10.2	9.4	10.2	9.8	9.4
$50K to $75K	34.7	16.9	21.4	23.6	22.1	21.1	21.7	22.7	22.4	23.2	21.4	21.3
$75K and over	45.8	22.2	32.2	36.9	31.1	31.9	37.9	35.2	34.5	34.9	29.1	38.2
Total	**205.9**	**100.0**	**100.0**	**100.0**	**100.0**	**100.0**	**100.0**	**100.0**	**100.0**	**100.0**	**100.0**	**100.0**

[1]Benchmark arts activities include going to at least one jazz, classical music, or opera performance; musical play; play; ballet; or art museum
[2]Not including Hispanics.
Note: Totals may not equal 100% due to rounding

SOURCE: Adapted from "Table 8. Demographic Distribution of U.S. Adults Who Attend/Visit/Read at Least Once in the 12-Month Period Ending August, 2002" and "Table 27. Demographic Distribution of Adults Participating in Other Leisure Activities at Least Once in the 12-Month Period Ending August, 2002," in *2002 Survey of Public Participation in the Arts,* National Endowment for the Arts, 2004, http://www.arts.gov/pub/NEASurvey2004.pdf (accessed September 9, 2004)

- Boomers tended to prefer more individualized activities than group events, and preferred to socialize in small circles.

- Boomers viewed retirement as only a "mid-life" event, and planned to work part-time, change careers, or start new businesses.

Given these characteristics, as well as other societal trends, Ziegler noted that retirement centers for members of this generation would have to include high-end fitness centers, opportunities for adult education, and up-to-date computer facilities, and offer such amenities for extended hours.

Productivity vs. Fun

A May 2003 survey conducted by Harris Interactive for the Hilton Family of Hotels, the *Hilton Family Leisure Time Advocacy Study* (LTA), found that 32% of those polled postponed fun because they felt guilty when not doing something they believed was productive. At the same time, more than two-thirds said they needed to have more fun in their lives. Seventy-four percent said they thought Americans placed a higher value on success in the workplace than success at home, and 34% said they felt these priorities were wrong. Americans were unsure about whether the national ethic of hard work and long hours was good or bad—a third said it had a positive effect on the culture, while 31% said it had a negative one.

As for the rejuvenating effect of leisure time, the LTA study reported that just 23% of Americans said they felt energized and ready for the workweek at the end of a weekend, while the remaining 77% were in a negative state—tired, stressed, apprehensive, or simply on "autopilot." When asked what they would do if they could "do it all over again," 15% said they would work harder in life, while 40% said they would spend more time enjoying leisure activities.

While the LTA did find that nine out of ten Americans reported being happy, and 53% said they were "very" or "extremely" happy, 46% also said that their lives were more stressful than five years earlier. Ultimately, most Americans said they wished they had one more day of leisure time per week. The number one choice for spending it was to be with friends and family, followed by pursuing hobbies.

VACATIONING. The LTA also found that while 69% of Americans said they felt as though they needed a vacation "right now," more than half (55%) said they did not take all the vacation days they were entitled to at work each year. The main reasons cited for not vacationing were guilt, time, and money.

When Americans did find time to get away, they found a range of options available. A survey conducted in 2001 by the Cruise Lines International Association (CLIA) and published in *Cruise Industry Overview* (spring 2004), found that among persons who had taken cruises, more than two-fifths (43%) said they were "extremely satisfied" with their vacations. This response was nine percentage points higher than the number who reported being extremely satisfied with a visit to friends or relatives. Packaged land-based vacations were ranked extremely satisfying by 30%, as were camping trips. Vacation house rentals (29%) and nonpackaged trips (28%) were slightly lower on the list. (See Table 8.4.)

SPORTS: AN EXPRESSION OF NATIONAL VALUES

A Brief History of American Sports

From ancient times, sports have played a role in defining manhood. Powerful men displayed their status and wealth by building horseracing tracks or sponsoring sporting events, while humbler ones gained a sense of power, prowess, masculinity, and sometimes wealth as participants or spectators in games. Despite differences in social rank, sports united men in a shared patriarchal culture. Athletics encouraged men to display their competitiveness and physical abilities and motivated them to think in terms of winning and losing. Sports generally helped to support a vision of masculinity that emphasized aggression and physicality.

TABLE 8.4

Percentage reporting themselves to be "extremely satisfied" with their vacation, by type of vacation, 2001–2002

	2000 Total	2001 Total	2001 Cruisers	2001 Vacationers
Cruise vacation or ocean/sea voyage	34%	43%	44%	—
Visit to friends/relatives	29	34	36	32%
Land-based package	24	30	31	31
Camping trip	33	30	31	30
Vacation house rental	30	29	31	29
Trip (non-package)	23	28	27	29
Resort vacation (own arrangements)	24	27	30	24
Resort vacation (package)	N/A	27	33	27
Land-based escorted tour	24	26	29	26
Vacation as part of business trip	19	25	26	26

Note: Data was based on a 5-point scale where "5" is "Extremely satisfied" and "1" is "Not at all satisfied"

SOURCE: "Satisfaction Levels with Various Vacation Alternatives," in *The Cruise Industry—An Overview*, Cruise Lines International Association, Spring 2004, http://www.cruising.org/press/overview/SPRING040V1.pdf (accessed July 7, 2004)

In the late 1800s the advent of daily sports newspaper pages and telegraph lines to transmit baseball scores contributed to a growing sporting culture. The expansion of cities spurred the growth of sports, which developed most rapidly in urban areas, where a burgeoning manufacturing economy was producing huge amounts of wealth. As cities grew, recreation was increasingly transformed into entertainment, an amusement to be purchased with earnings.

Despite events that drew many thousands of fans and hundreds of newspaper reporters, professionalism in sports was still unusual, profits were secondary to pleasure, organizations were informal, and scheduling was irregular. Sports continued to be voluntary associations based on class, ethnic, or occupational background. Sports, like religion, politics, and business, became threads binding the tapestry of American culture.

Not only were sports changing and growing during the nineteenth century, but many Americans were also beginning to view sports as a moral force. Taking charge of one's physical condition became a prerequisite for a virtuous, self-reliant, spiritually elevated life. Moral improvement, self-mastery, and godliness were invoked in the name of sports. By the mid-1800s, even clergymen, intellectuals, and reformers took up the cause. As Henry David Thoreau declared, "The body existed for the highest development of the soul."

THE PROFIT MOTIVE EMERGES—PROFESSIONALIZATION AND COMMERCIALIZATION. In an era of urban overcrowding and strict labor discipline, leisure activities had the potential to blunt workers' rebelliousness. Reformers argued that sports refreshed workers' spirits, improved their productivity, and alleviated class tensions. If these benefits were insufficient motivation to participate, sports advocates claimed a moral high ground, contending that sports built character. Other people found they could earn money by teaching a game or hustling other players.

Sports became part of a new consumerism during the twentieth century. New technologies led to better sports gear and equipment, and as a result, improved performance. A sports team became an employer with a "bottom line." Unlike athletes who earlier participated because they believed it would improve their body or their character, players now threw a ball to earn a living. At the beginning of the twenty-first century, professional sports were generally recognized as commercial endeavors. Sports were big business, and those who did not compete in sports could pay to see other people compete or wager on the outcomes of competitions.

Amateur Sports

Following the lead of professional sports, amateur sports have also become big business. Some critics believe that the status of amateur sports, even at the middle school and high school levels, is threatened by an increasing emphasis on commercialization. They cite scandals involving recruiting, redshirting (holding a player back a year until he or she grows bigger, gets better, or a player in his or her position graduates; although the player attends school, he or she does not use up a year of athletic eligibility), phony courses, and inflated or bogus grades. There is even fear that the scandals plaguing professional and Olympic sports, such as steroid and drug use, sexual misconduct, and corruption, could derail the careers of promising high school and college athletes.

Looking Good

When Americans participate in a sports activity, they often buy the best equipment and gear. Beginning in the 1980s and continuing through the turn of the century, many Americans possessed a considerable amount of discretionary income, and many used it to support their varied sports and fitness interests. Sporting goods continued to be a thriving market, with new technologies and products arriving on the shelves weekly.

Many Americans not only participate in a sport or fitness activity but also increasingly compete against others. While many people still jog or run for health, growing numbers do so competitively—in marathons. A biker may not necessarily ride his or her bike to the grocery store, but he or she may enter (with a racing bike costing thousands of dollars) bike races or weekend group rides. Some cyclists take biking holidays or biking day trips.

National Values

Labor and play once overlapped more freely than in recent years because leisure time and work time were not so rigidly delineated. For example, sports were not necessarily played according to standardized rules—they were often a part of local culture, passed on by word of mouth, with rules varying from place to place. Today's sports include multiple layers of communication, transportation, professionalism, regulating bodies, records, statistics, and media coverage.

Sports respond to, and reflect, American values. It would be very easy to confuse a Super Bowl presentation with a Fourth of July celebration, with its veneration of nationalism, racial and ethnic integration, "rugged individualism," and hard work. Yet, some see the Super Bowl as more than just a big game celebrating athletic skill; they see it as an enormous commercial undertaking intended to sell advertisements and generate huge profits for owners, players, and television networks.

Violence in the Sports Arena

Although physical prowess continues to find a place in American society, it competes with an appreciation of, and need for, other qualities, such as intellect and cooperation. Furthermore, valuing and rewarding physical aggression in a civil society has sometimes presented serious challenges. When athletes and others are trained and encouraged to excel at physically aggressive pursuits, they are sometimes unable to harness those tendencies outside the sports arena. Hitting an opponent so hard that he has trouble getting up is a positive act loudly applauded in the boxing ring, while the same action in the parking lot after a bout could send an athlete—or spectator—to jail.

The Deification of Sports Figures: Who Are the Heroes?

The sudden flowering of a mass culture during the twentieth century brought about by the growth in media and communications produced a wealth of new sports heroes. Increasingly, the public world became populated by sports celebrities with national reputations and appeal—heroes such as Babe Ruth, Jim Thorpe, Joe Louis, Jackie Robinson, Babe Didrikson Zaharias, Muhammad Ali, Joe DiMaggio, Sandy Koufax, and Chris Evert.

The Gallup Organization conducted a poll, reported in January 2000, that basketball player Michael Jordan, by an enormous margin, was considered to be the top athlete of the twentieth century. A sampling of adults, aged eighteen and older, were asked "what man or woman living any time this century do you think was the greatest athlete of the century, in terms of their athletic performance?" Jordan was chosen by 23%.

In 2004 ESPN.com asked its visitors to rank the top twenty-five athletes of the previous twenty-five years; Jordan was again ranked first, followed by hockey player Wayne Gretzky, bicyclist Lance Armstrong, golfer Tiger Woods, and football wide receiver Jerry Rice.

ARE THEY WHAT THEY SEEM? Celebrity athletes serve as role models for young people and aspiring athletes, and they can exert powerful marketing effectiveness. Advertising and public relations professionals quickly understood the benefit of linking these icons to products. The public's fascination with fame and glamour enabled heroes to mold the taste of their fans. Sports heroes gained widespread recognition and became known as marketing images rather than real human beings.

As a result, many people have come to revere sports figures, to regard them as heroes, and to credit them with attributes they may not possess. The American public holds its sports figures in high esteem, puts them on pedestals, and appears shocked when heroes demonstrate they are mortals who share the weaknesses of others. Although sports have always had their share of misbehavior, in recent years the media has been able to publicize the indiscretions, such as allegations of substance abuse and domestic violence, of a number of sports figures. Famous athletes who earned reputations as models of athletic prowess and success have sometimes disappointed and disenchanted admiring fans.

RECREATION FOR HEALTH

Americans are living longer and are generally healthier. More people are able physically and, increasingly, financially to participate in recreational activities. Older adults are a growing market in the sales of many consumer items, including recreational vehicles, sporting goods, books, and computers.

Active Recreation Prevents Disease

Lack of physical exercise not only contributes to the risk of heart disease but also increases the risk of colon cancer, diabetes, high blood pressure, osteoporosis, and arthritis. Regular physical activity is also linked to improved mental health by reducing mild anxiety and depression. Health professionals agree that even moderate amounts of exercise, such as walking thirty minutes a day, five times a week, as opposed to strenuous physical activity, such as running, provides substantial health benefits. Despite unassailable evidence demonstrating its potent disease prevention and health promotion benefits, the Centers for Disease Control and Prevention has found that more than 50% of American adults do not exercise enough to reap health benefits and 25% do not exercise at all during their leisure time.

Physical activity was the first leading health indicator of *Healthy People, 2010,* the source document that served as a blueprint for improving the health status of Americans. Administered by the U.S. Department of Health and Human Services through its Office of Disease Prevention and Health Promotion, *Healthy People, 2010* defined regular leisure-time physical activity as performing light to

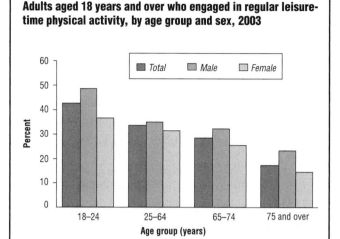

FIGURE 8.2

Adults aged 18 years and over who engaged in regular leisure-time physical activity, by age group and sex, 2003

Notes: Regular leisure-time physical activity is defined as engaging in light-moderate leisure-time physical activity for greater than or equal to 30 minutes at a frequency greater than or equal to five times per week, or engaging in vigorous leisure-time physical activity for greater than or equal to 20 minutes at a frequency greater than or equal to three times per week. The analyses excluded 903 persons (3.0%) with unknown physical activity participation.

SOURCE: "Figure 7.2. Percent of Adults Aged 18 Years and Over Who Engaged in Regular Leisure-Time Physical Activity, by Age Group and Sex: United States, 2003," in *2003 National Health Interview Survey,* U.S. Department of Health and Human Services, Centers for Disease Control and Prevention, National Center for Health Statistics, 2004, http://www.cdc.gov/nchs/data/nhis/earlyrelease/200406_07.pdf (accessed September 12, 2004)

moderate physical activity for thirty or more minutes, five or more times per week, or vigorous physical activity for twenty or more minutes, three or more times per week. The National Health Interview Survey, conducted by the U.S. Centers for Disease Control and Prevention's National Center for Health Statistics, used this definition to track Americans' leisure-time physical activity. The survey data showed a slow, steady increase in the percentage of adults ages eighteen and older who engaged in regular leisure-time physical activity, from 29.9% in 1998 to 33% in 2003. The number of adults who engaged in regular leisure-time physical activity declined with advancing age, however, and women in every age group reported less physical activity. (See Figure 8.2.) Regular leisure-time physical activity was highest among whites (35.9%), followed by African-Americans (25.9%) and Hispanics (24.6%).

THE PRESIDENT MAKES PHYSICAL FITNESS A TOP PRIORITY. Concern about Americans' lack of physical activity prompted President George W. Bush to announce a federal effort to improve fitness levels among adults and children on June 20, 2002. In a campaign that recalled the one launched by President John F. Kennedy four decades earlier, President Bush appointed a presidential council and issued an executive order along with twelve pages of recommendations about how Americans could improve their health and fitness. The president urged Americans to follow his example of running three miles a day and lifting weights to stay fit. A Web site (www.presidentschallenge.org) was also set up to offer fitness tips and help Americans track their progress online. President Bush subsequently declared May 2004 to be National Physical Fitness and Sports Month.

RECREATION FOR HEALING

Ancient teachings are replete with claims of the benefits of recreational experiences: "A merry heart doeth good like a medicine" (Proverbs) and "You can learn more about a man in an hour of play than in a lifetime of conversation" (Plato). But starting in the nineteenth century, such principles began to be applied in health care settings in a purposeful, organized manner.

Increasingly, medical professionals have begun applying recreation to healing. Therapists have researched the effects of aquatic therapy on the treatment of multiple sclerosis. Others have found that horseback riding, for as yet unknown reasons, produces a remission in some patients suffering from multiple sclerosis. Mental health facilities have recognized the importance of bright, healthy surroundings and pleasant diversions for sufferers of mental and emotional conditions, unlike the harsh penal atmosphere generally accorded to patients in early mental facilities.

Many people have found that the presence of animals helps the recovery of the ill and improves the health and well being of residents in nursing homes. Some studies have documented the relaxation response and resulting reduction in blood pressure from simply observing an aquarium. Almost everyone understands that engaging in satisfying forms of recreation and pleasurable leisure-time pursuits is vital for maintaining overall health.

IMPORTANT NAMES AND ADDRESSES

American Gaming Association
555 13th St. NW, Suite 1010 East
Washington, DC 20004
(202) 637-6500
URL: http://www.americangaming.org

Association of American Publishers
71 Fifth Ave.
New York, NY 10003-3004
(212) 255-0200
FAX: (212) 255-7007
URL: http://www.publishers.org

Association of Racing Commissioners International
2343 Alexandria Dr., Suite 200
Lexington, KY 40504
(859) 224-7070
FAX: (859) 224-7071
E-mail: support@arci.com
URL: http://www.arci.com

Book Industry Study Group, Inc.
19 West 21st St., Suite 905
New York, NY 10010
(646) 336-7141
FAX: (646) 336-6214
E-mail: info@bisg.org
URL: http://www.bisg.org

Consumer Electronics Association
2500 Wilson Blvd.
Arlington, VA 22201-3834
(703) 907-7600
FAX: (703) 907-7675
E-mail: cea@ce.org
URL: http://www.ce.org

Craft & Hobby Association
319 East 54th St.
Elmwood Park, NJ 07407
(201) 794-1133
FAX: (201) 797-0657
E-mail: info@craftandhobby.org
URL: http://www.craftandhobby.org

Cruise Lines International Association
80 Broad St.
New York, NY 10004
(212) 921-0066
FAX: (212) 921-0549
E-mail: clia@cruising.org
URL: http://www.cruising.org

The League of American Theatres and Producers, Inc.
226 West 47th St.
New York, NY 10036
(212) 764-1122
FAX: (212) 719-4389
URL: http://www.livebroadway.com

Motion Picture Association of America
15503 Ventura Blvd.
Encino, CA 91436
(818) 995-6600
URL: http://www.mpaa.org

Motorcycle Industry Council
2 Jenner St., Suite 150
Irvine, CA 92618
(949) 727-4211
FAX: (949) 727-3313
E-mail: aftmgr@mic.org
URL: http://www.mic.org

Museum of Television and Radio
25 West 52nd St.
New York, NY 10019
(212) 621-6600
URL: http://www.mtr.org

National Association of Theatre Owners
750 First St. NE, Suite 1130
Washington, DC 20002
(202) 962-0054
FAX: (202) 962-0370
E-mail: nato@mindspring.com
URL: http://www.natoonline.org

National Collegiate Athletic Association
700 West Washington St.
P.O. Box 6222
Indianapolis, IN 46206-6222
(317) 917-6222
FAX: (317) 917-6888
URL: http://www.ncaa.org

National Endowment for the Arts
1100 Pennsylvania Ave., NW
Washington, DC 20506
(202) 682-5400
URL: http://arts.endow.gov

National Indian Gaming Commission
1441 L St. NW, Suite 9100
Washington, DC 20005
(202) 632-7003
FAX: (202) 632-7066
E-mail: info@nigc.gov
URL: http://www.nigc.gov

National Marine Manufacturers Association
200 East Randolph Dr., Suite 5100
Chicago, IL 60601
(312) 946-6200
URL: http://www.nmma.org

National Park Service
1849 C St., NW
Washington, DC 20240
(202) 208-6843
FAX: (202) 219-0910
URL: http://www.nps.gov

National Sporting Goods Association
1601 Feehanville Dr., Suite 300
Mt. Prospect, IL 60056
(847) 296-6742
FAX: (847) 391-9827
E-mail: info@nsga.org
URL: http://www.nsga.org

National Trust for Historic Preservation
1785 Massachusetts Ave., NW
Washington, DC 20036-2117
(202) 588-6000
URL: http://www.nthp.org

Newspaper Association of America
1921 Gallows Rd., Suite 600
Vienna, VA 22182-3900
(703) 902-1600
FAX: (703) 917-0636
URL: http://www.naa.org

Office of Travel and Tourism Industries
International Trade Administration
U.S. Department of Commerce
1401 Constitution Ave., NW, Rm. 7025
Washington, DC 20230
(202) 482-0140
FAX: (202) 482-2887
E-mail: webmaster@tinet.ita.doc.gov
URL: http://www.tinet.ita.doc.gov

Performing Arts Research Coalition
c/o Opera America
1156 15th St. NW, Suite 810
Washington, DC 20005
(202) 293-4466
E-mail: parc@operaamerica.org
URL: http://www.operaamerica.org/parc

Photo Marketing Association International
300 Picture Place
Jackson, MI 49201
(517) 788-8100
FAX: (517) 788-8371
E-mail: webmaster@tinet.ita.doc.gov
URL: http://www.pmai.org

Recording Industry Association of America
1330 Connecticut Ave., NW, Suite 300

Washington, DC 20036-1704
(202) 775-0101
URL: http://www.riaa.com

Recreation Roundtable
American Recreation Coalition
1225 New York Ave., NW, Suite 450
Washington, DC 20005-6405
(202) 682-9530
FAX: (202) 682-9529
E-mail: arc@funoutdoors.com
URL: http://www.funoutdoors.com

Recreational Vehicle Industry Association
1896 Preston White Dr.
P.O. Box 2999
Reston, VA 20195-0999
(703) 620-6003
FAX: (703) 620-5071
URL: http://www.rvia.org

Sporting Goods Manufacturers Association
200 Castlewood Dr.
North Palm Beach, FL 33408-5696
(561) 842-4100
FAX: (561) 863-8984
E-mail: info@sgma.com
URL: http://www.sgma.com

Theatre Communications Group
520 Eighth Ave., 24th Fl.
New York, NY 10018-4156
(212) 609-5900
FAX: (212) 609-5901
E-mail: tcg@tcg.org
URL: http://www.tcg.org

Toy Industry Association, Inc.
1115 Broadway, Suite 400
New York, NY 10010
(212) 675-1141
FAX: (212) 633-1429

E-mail: info@toy-tia.org
URL: http://www.toy-tia.org

Travel Industry Association of America
1100 New York Ave., NW, Suite 450
Washington, DC 20005-3934
(202) 408-8422
FAX: (202) 408-1255
E-mail: feedback@tia.org
URL: http://www.tia.org

U.S. Department of Labor
Frances Perkins Bldg.
200 Constitution Ave., NW
Washington, DC 20210
(202) 693-5000
Toll-free: 1-866-4-USA-DOL
URL: http://www.dol.gov

U.S. Fish and Wildlife Service
U.S. Department of the Interior
1849 C St., NW
Washington, DC 20240-0001
(202) 208-4717
Toll-free: 1-800-344-WILD
E-mail: contact@fws.gov
URL: http://www.fws.gov

U.S.D.A. Forest Service
1400 Independence Ave., SW
Washington, DC 20250-0003
(202) 205-8333
E-mail: webmaster@fs.fed.us
URL: http://www.fs.fed.us

World Trade Organization
Centre William Rappard
rue de Lausanne 154, CH-1211
Geneva 21, Switzerland
(41-22) 739.51.11
FAX: (41-22) 731.42.06
E-mail: enquiries@wto.org
URL: http://www.wto.org

RESOURCES

The Gallup Organization provided much valuable information on public opinion for this book in a variety of subject areas. Other information about public opinion came from Harris Interactive, the Leisure Trends Group, and Roper Starch Worldwide.

The U.S. Department of Transportation Bureau of Transportation Statistics *National Household Travel Survey* (2001) provided extensive information on the travel patterns of Americans. The Travel Industry Association of America, the American Society of Travel Agents, and the World Tourism Organization also provided information about travel, including the number of trips, people's activities during trips, favorite destinations, and demographic data about American travelers. The Cruise Lines International Association provided much information about cruise lengths, destinations, consumers, and industry trends.

The National Park Service of the U.S. Department of the Interior published the *National Park Service Statistical Abstract 2003*, with information about the national parks, their facilities, services, accommodations, hours of operation, costs, and utilization. The U.S. Fish and Wildlife Service of the U.S. Department of the Interior published the *2001 National Survey of Fishing, Hunting, and Wildlife-Associated Recreation*. Additional information about outdoor recreation came from the Recreation Roundtable, in a report conducted by Roper Starch Worldwide, *Outdoor Recreation in America, 2003*. Information about nature-based recreation and ecotourism was gleaned from the Ecotourism Society and a joint Travel Industry Association of America/*National Geographic Traveler* report, *Geotourism: The New Trend in Travel* (2002).

The U.S. Bureau of Labor Statistics 2002 *Consumer Expenditure Survey* and the U.S. Department of Commerce Bureau of Economic Analysis contributed information about consumer spending. The Consumer Electronics Association was a valuable source of information about sales of electronics products and computers, while the Photo Marketing Association International supplied information about film and camera sales. Information on boat sales and boating participation came from the National Marine Manufacturer's Association.

The National Endowment for the Arts *2002 Survey of Public Participation in the Arts* (2004) provided important information about trends in attendance of performing arts events, personal participation in the arts, and Americans' preferred leisure activities. The Association of Art Museum Directors' *State of the Nation's Art Museums* (2004) was a source of information on museum attendance and funding. Information about rock and pop concert tours came from *Billboard* magazine.

The Centers for Disease Control and Prevention provided information about Americans' leisure-time physical activity, while the United States Department of Labor Bureau of Labor Statistics report *Volunteering in the United States, 2003* was a valuable source of information on volunteers.

Ipsos-Insight and the Association of American Publishers provided book sales data, and the Book Industry Study Group and the American Booksellers Association shared the results of their research on reading and purchasing behavior in the United States. The International Association of Amusement Parks and Attractions provided helpful statistics about amusement parks and other attractions, as did *Amusement Business* magazine.

The Motion Picture Association of America offered economic data about U.S. theatrical box office receipts and revenues, along with information about average ticket prices and the number of movie screens. The Toy Industry Association, Inc. and the NPD Group reported on toy sales, while the Craft & Hobby Association and Unity Marketing provided information on the craft and collectibles markets, respectively.

The Sporting Goods Manufacturers Association supplied many data tables and much useful information about the sporting goods market and participation in sports from its *Sports Participation Topline Report* (2004) and *Recreation Market Report* (2004) publications. The National Sporting Goods Association provided additional information on the sporting goods market and participation in sports, while the National Collegiate Athletic Association collected information on student athletes. The National Golf Foundation, U.S. Soccer, and the American Bowling Congress were also sources of valuable sports information.

Harrah's Entertainment's *Profile of the American Casino Gambler* (2003) described American gambling preferences and habits, while the National Indian Gaming Commission and the Indian Gaming Association provided a wealth of information about tribal gambling. The National Thoroughbred Racing Association was a source of information about horse racing, as was the Association of Racing Commissioners International, which also provided information about greyhound racing and other pari-mutuel gambling activities. Wagering data compiled by Christiansen Capital Advisors LLC proved highly useful in profiling the gambling industry in America, as did information from the American Gaming Association. Data on gambling addiction came from the National Council on Problem Gambling.

The Pew Internet & American Life Project was an invaluable resource for information about Americans' use of the Internet. The Recording Industry Association of America's *2003 Consumer Profile* contained data about music industry sales and demographics. Other sources of data for this book included the Recreational Vehicle Industry Association and the Motorcycle Industry Council.

INDEX

Page references in italics refer to photographs. References with the letter t *following them indicate the presence of a table. The letter* f *indicates a figure. If more than one table or figure appears on a particular page, the exact item number for the table or figure being referenced is provided.*